FUNCTION KEYS AND THEIR US

	Key	Shift–Key	Alt–Key	Description (Key; *Shift–Key;* Alt–Key)
F1	Help			Provides help screen relating to where you are in Quattro Pro (press Escape to exit)
F2	Edit	Debug	Macro Menu	Enters Edit mode so you can change cell entries; *enters Debug mode so you can execute a macro step by step;* displays the Macro menu
F3	Choices	Macros	Functions	Displays a list of block names on the current spreadsheet (press + on keypad to show coordinates and – to remove them); *displays a list of macro commands;* displays a list of functions (use in Edit mode or when entering a formula)
F4	Abs(olute)			Makes cell addresses to left of cursor absolute (press repeatedly to cycle through combinations)
F5	Go To	Pick Window	Undo	Moves cell selector to specified address; *shows list of open spreadsheets;* undoes deletions, edits, etc.
F6	Pane	Next Window	Zoom	Moves cell selector to inactive window when screen is split into two windowpanes; *displays next open window;* zooms window either to fill screen or shrink to previous size
F7	Query	Select	All Select	Repeats previous Query command; *highlights block of cells to use in a menu command you select next;* selects/deselects all files in active File Manager file list
F8	Table	Move		Repeats last What-If command; *removes files marked in File Manager file list for insertion somewhere else*
F9	Calc(ulate)	Copy		Calculates entered formulas in Ready mode, rereads current directory in File Manager window, repaints screen in Graphics Display mode; *copies files marked in File Manager file list for insertion somewhere else*
F10	Graph	Paste		Displays current graph (press Escape to cancel), redraws current graph in Graph Annotator; *inserts moved/copied files into directory shown in File Manager file list*
0			Pick Window	Shows list of open spreadsheets (same as Shift–F5)

The ABC's of

QUATTRO PRO 3

The ABC's of

QUATTRO® PRO 3

Second Edition

Alan Simpson

Douglas J. Wolf

SYBEX®

San Francisco • Paris • Düsseldorf • Soest

Acquisitions Editor: David Clark
Editors: Kathleen Lattinville, Stefan Grünwedel
Technical Editor: Glenn Saika
Word Processors: Ann Dunn, Susan Trybull
Book Designer: Suzanne Albertson
Chapter Art: Helen Bruno
Page Layout and Paste-up: Eleanor Ramos
Screen Graphics: Cuong Le
Typesetter: Elizabeth Newman
Proofreader/Production Assistant: Bill Cassel
Indexer: Julie Kawabata
Cover Designer: Thomas Ingalls + Associates
Cover Photographer: Mark Johann
Screen reproductions produced by XenoFont.

Library of Congress Card Number: 91-65564
ISBN: 0-89588-838-6
Manufactured in the United States of America
10 9 8 7 6 5 4 3

To Robert G. Kelly, my first partner in the computer software business, who remains an analeptic friend and confidant

D.J.W.

To Susan and Ashley

A.C.S.

ACKNOWLEDGMENTS

The authors would like to thank Nan Borreson at Borland International, William Gladstone and Matthew Wagner at Waterside Productions, and Kathleen Lattinville at SYBEX for their help in the creation of this book.

CONTENTS AT A GLANCE

CONTENTS

INTRODUCTION

This book is about Quattro Pro version 3.0, the electronic spreadsheet package from Borland International, Inc. It is a sophisticated tool with three components that can help you greatly in your work. Quattro Pro's spreadsheet replaces the ledger book, pencil, and hand-held calculator as a means of analyzing and calculating data. With the help of many sophisticated built-in functions, you can develop budgets, annual reports, portfolio analyses, invoices, tax statements, etc., with ease.

Quattro Pro also features a startlingly powerful and flexible, full-color graphing capability that gives you many quick, creative ways to present data visually, either on paper or on-screen—even *sequentially* on-screen, like a slide show.

This software is also a database, which allows you to store large volumes of information, sort them any way you wish, and extract specific entries as the need arises—such as invoices that are past due or addresses in the 92112 zip-code area.

If you are using Quattro Pro version 2.0, you will discover several differences in version 3.0, most of which are enhancements of 2.0, not wholesale changes. So, this book is of value to you whether you have version 2.0 or 3.0. The 3.0 enhancements are as follows:

- What You See Is What You Get (WYSIWYG) display option. The Quattro Pro screen can now be displayed in high-resolution graphics mode. You must have an EGA or VGA monitor with at least 640x350 resolution to use this feature.
- Save All command. When selected, this new command on the File menu sequentially rolls through all open files and saves them. If a file has been modified, Quattro Pro checks with

you to determine if the modified file should replace the existing file.

- Progress Bars. As you load spreadsheet files, a progress bar appears at the bottom of the screen indicating what portion of the file has been retrieved from disk.
- Banner Printing. In addition to printing in landscape mode, version 3.0 includes Banner Printing, which directs Quattro Pro to ignore hard or soft page breaks and print spreadsheets as a continuous sheet. To use this option, you must print to a dot-matrix printer.
- Printer Name on Print menu. The name of the printer you have installed is now displayed on the Print menu.
- Print Multiple Copies. You can direct Quattro Pro to print more than a single copy of a spreadsheet.
- Graph Enhancements. You can add different sound and screen effects to slide shows.
- Right Margin. The right margin setting can be increased to 511 characters.
- Autosave Graph Edits. You can now tell Quattro Pro to automatically save all changes you make to an existing graph.

In the text, you will be alerted when there is a distinction between the capabilities of Quattro Pro 2.0 and 3.0.

Whom This Book Is For

This book is written for people who are not familiar with computer terminology, other spreadsheets, or even computers in general. Quattro Pro is sophisticated, but not difficult to learn. For that reason, we have designed this book so that you can start using Quattro Pro *now,* without first wading through a 700-page manual of details and technical information.

What This Book Covers

Before you can start running the software, you'll need to install it on your computer. The Appendix describes how to do that straightforward task.

Once you have installed Quattro Pro, start at the beginning. The first four chapters offer a step-by-step approach, in plain English, that introduces you to Quattro Pro's capabilities quickly and easily. Spreadsheets that you create in one chapter will be modified and built upon in the next. Later chapters discuss ways to edit entries, manipulate data, and handle blocks of data conveniently—as well as how to graph and print data and use them in a database.

Stylistic and Typographical Conventions

One key you will use very often is the Enter key (also labeled "Return" on some keyboards). When you read "enter such-and-such," it means to type the text on-screen and then hit the Enter key. When you read "type such-and-such," it means simply to type the word or number on-screen and *not* press Enter. Because some procedures require you to press Enter, while others do not, we have made it clear when it is necessary to do so.

There are also some keystroke-combination shortcuts that you will want to know how to use. One is the Ctrl-key shortcut, which involves holding the Ctrl (Control) key down while pressing another key, usually a letter. Thus "press Ctrl–M" means to first press the Ctrl key, and then hit the letter *M.*

Another shortcut is the Alt-key combination. If you read "press Alt–F3," that means to hold down the Alt key and then press the F3 function key.

A third convention is a shortcut for describing commands you access from the overhead spreadsheet menus. When we want you to select the Save option from the File menu, for instance, we'll write the instructions out in full and also include the shortcut **/FS**, which means to press the forward slash key (/) and *then* press the letters *F* and *S,* in that order.

Besides the stylistic conventions above, this book features two typefaces, aside from the regular text, that you should be aware of. Any data or keystrokes that we ask you to key in appear in **boldface**. For example, we might instruct you to "type in the label **TOTALS**" or "type /**OCM**."

Words, data, or instructions that you read *directly* from the screen, on the other hand, appear in **program font**. For instance, you might read, "displays the message **File already exists**" or "Quattro Pro will display the prompt

Enter label block: A1..A1

and wait for you to specify…"

These conventions will become clear as you read on. So read the Appendix if you haven't already installed Quattro Pro on your computer. Then start with Chapter 1 to get to know your spreadsheet!

1

GETTING TO KNOW YOUR SPREADSHEET

FEATURING

- *Starting Quattro Pro*
- *Special Quattro Pro Keys*
- *How to Get On-Line Help*
- *Navigating the Spreadsheet*

What Is a Spreadsheet?

If you've ever worked with invoices, budgets, loan analyses, tax statements, production schedules, and so forth, then you're familiar with a ledger, which is simply a sheet of paper with rows and columns. Figure 1.1 shows such a ledger with some calculations for a home mortgage worked out.

A spreadsheet program such as Quattro Pro is basically an electronic ledger sheet. It too contains rows and columns and allows you to place numbers, text, and formulas (for doing calculations) into individual *cells.* Figure 1.2 shows the information from the paper ledger as it would appear on the Quattro Pro spreadsheet.

Now you may be thinking, "Big deal, so I type on a TV screen rather than on paper." But there is a quite a bit more to it than that. For example, if you were to change the interest rate on the paper ledger sheet, you'd need to recalculate all the different results, such as the payment on the loan, total payback, and total interest paid. (On a ledger sheet with 1000 calculations this would indeed be a laborious task!)

On an electronic spreadsheet, by contrast, you can change any number, or group of numbers, and Quattro Pro will instantly recalculate all of the formulas affected by the change. You'll never need to use

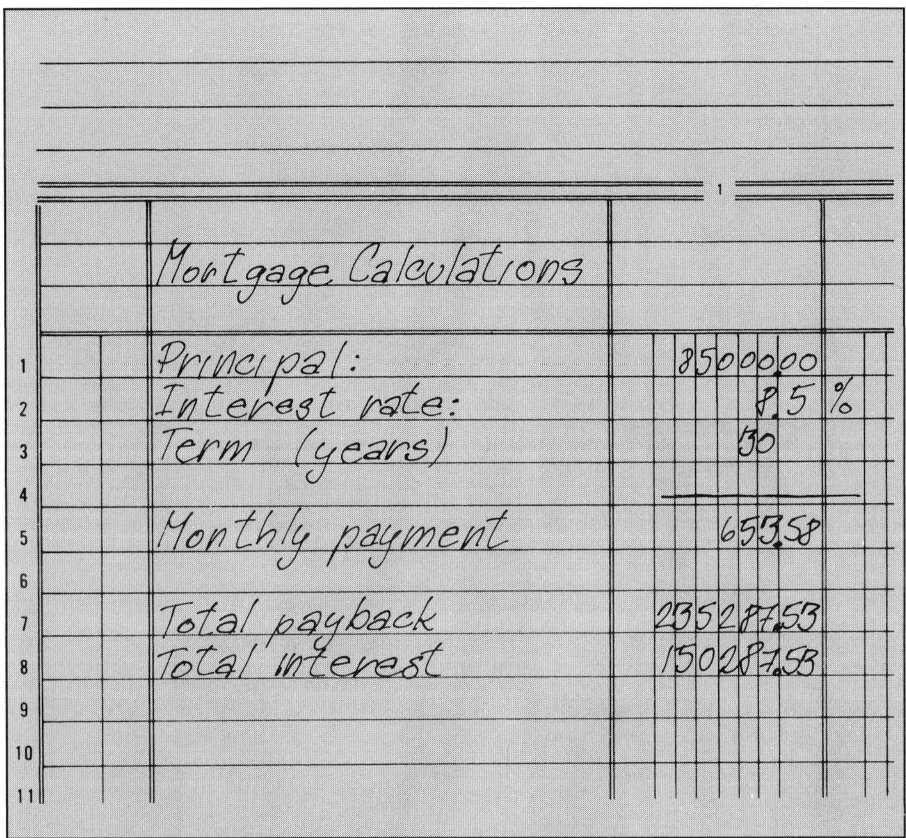

Figure 1.1: A sample paper ledger sheet

a calculator or eraser for this kind of work again. For example, Figure 1.3 shows the results of changing the interest rate of the loan from 8.5% to 10%. As soon as the new interest rate was entered, all the other calculations were updated immediately.

This "instant recalculation" feature alone makes Quattro Pro an invaluable tool, allowing you to experiment with options and create "what-if" scenarios. But Quattro Pro offers much more. You can display (and print) business graphs and replot them whenever you change your assumptions. You can also store and retrieve various types of information such as names and addresses, financial transactions, and inventory data.

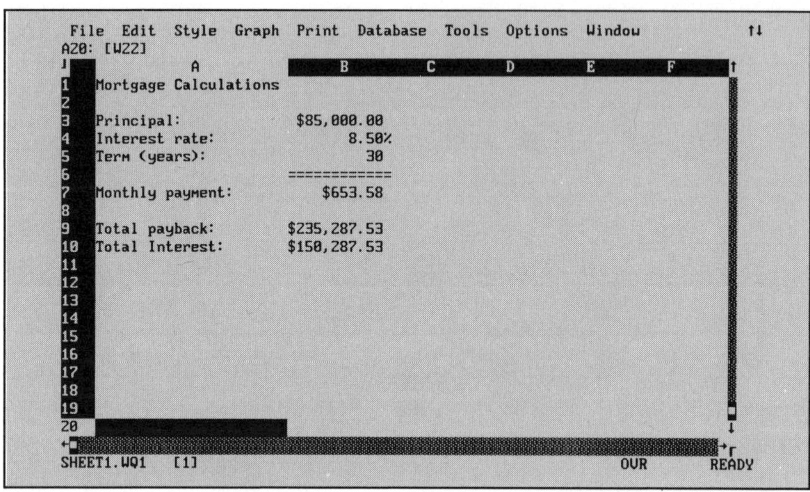

***Figure 1.2:** The spreadsheet version of a ledger sheet*

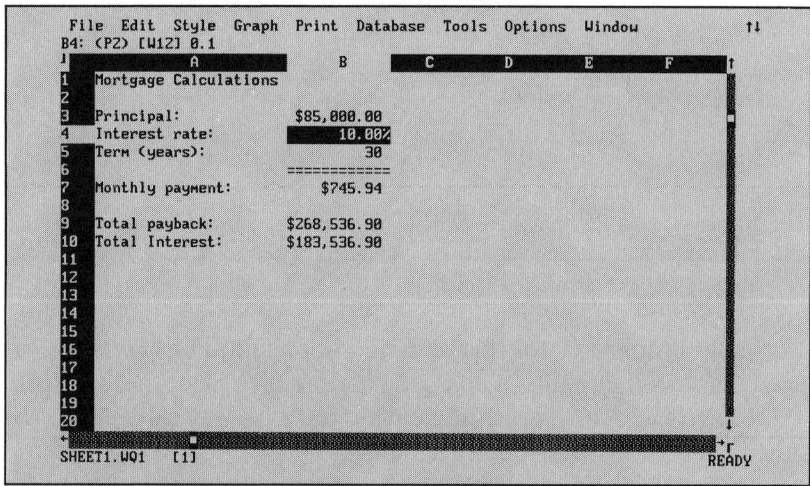

***Figure 1.3:** The results of changing the interest rate*

As you read through this book, you'll learn a great deal about the many capabilities of Quattro Pro. Of course, the first thing you need to learn is how to get Quattro Pro "up and running" on your computer, so let's start with that.

Starting Quattro Pro

First off, Quattro Pro comes with a couple of tools that can make learning and using the software a bit easier.

The Keyboard Templates

The booklet, "Getting Started with Quattro Pro," which comes with your spreadsheet, includes some cardboard *templates* that you can place over your keyboard to help identify the uses of various function keys (those labeled F1 through F10 or F12 on your keyboard). One template is for the IBM PCs, XTs, and their clones, on which the function keys are at the left side of the keyboard. The others are for IBM ATs and their clones, on which the function keys appear horizontally across the top.

You should remove the appropriate template from the booklet and place it on your keyboard whenever you use Quattro Pro.

The Menu Maps

The user's guide that comes with your Quattro Pro package includes a series of maps of the spreadsheet's menu structure. After you are a bit more familiar with Quattro Pro and its menus, you may wish to refer to the maps once in awhile to review the various menu options. The endpapers to this SYBEX book also include a menu map.

The README File

Last-minute changes and corrections to the program and manuals are stored on the Quattro Pro System Disk, which comes with your software package. To browse through the README file, turn on your computer in the usual manner. Insert the disk in drive A. Type **A:** and press the Enter key (sometimes labeled Return or ↵.) Then type the command **README** and press Enter.

While the README file is displayed, you can press the Page-Down and Page-Up keys to scroll through the document. To leave the

README file and return to the DOS prompt (in this case, something like **A:>**), press the Escape (Esc) key. If you have a word-processing program or the DOS PRINT program, you can use either to print a hard copy of this file.

Now you're ready to start up the program.

Installing the Software

Quattro Pro must be installed on your computer before you can use it. It will only work on an IBM PC or 100-percent compatible computer with a *hard-disk drive.* Quattro Pro version 2.0 needs 4 Mb and version 3.0 needs 5 Mb for best results. Remember, Quattro Pro need only be installed once. Installation instructions are provided in the Appendix. Read it first before proceeding.

After you have installed Quattro Pro, follow the instructions below to run it:

1. Enter or log onto the hard disk, if necessary, by typing the command **C:** and pressing the Enter (↵ or Return) key. (If the hard disk that contains Quattro Pro is not C, substitute the appropriate letter in the command.)
2. Log onto the Quattro Pro directory by typing the command **CD\QPRO** and pressing Enter. (To make sure that you are in the Quattro Pro directory called QPRO, type the command **CD** and press Enter to display the name of the currently logged directory.)
3. Type **Q** and press Enter. You should now see the Quattro Pro opening screen.

The Quattro Pro Screen

The various parts of Quattro Pro's opening screen are named in Figure 1.4. Each of them serves a purpose, as described in the following sections.

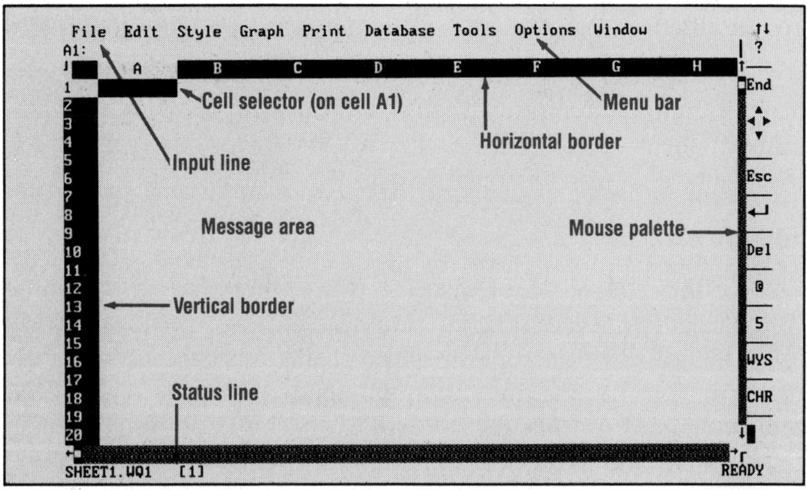

Figure 1.4: Components of Quattro Pro's opening screen

The Menu Bar

Across the top of the screen is a series of words beginning with *File* and ending with *Window*. These are the *menu* names; the menus themselves are "pulled down" over the Quattro Pro screen when activated. Each of them has a letter that is either displayed in a different color from the rest of the word (on a color monitor) or highlighted (on a monochrome screen). For example, in the menu called File, the letter *F* appears different from the rest of the letters. The letter *F* is the "access letter" for the File menu, the letter *E* for the Edit menu, and so forth.

The Horizontal Border

Across the top of the spreadsheet is the *horizontal border,* which initially contains the letters A through H. These letters are the names of the *columns* in the spreadsheet. Although you cannot see the additional columns now, they are lettered A to Z, then AA to AZ, BA to BZ, and so forth up to column IV, for a total of 256 columns.

The Vertical Border

The *vertical border* on the left side of the screen contains *row* numbers. Now you can only see rows 1 through 20, but there are many more of them—8,192 to be exact. WYSIWYG mode (version 3.0 only) will show rows 1 through 20.

The Cells

At the intersection of each row and column lies an individual spreadsheet *cell,* whose function is to store data and formulas. Every cell is identified by an address, which is simply its column and row position. For example, the cell in the upper-left corner (column A, row 1) is named A1. The cell to the right of A1 is B1, directly beneath cell B1 is B2, and so on to the bottom-most right corner, cell IV8192.

The Cell Selector

The *cell selector,* positioned on cell A1 in Figure 1.4, highlights the current cell on the spreadsheet. Any information you typed now would be placed in this cell. Later in the chapter you'll see how to move the selector to other cells on the spreadsheet.

The Input Line

The *input line* is directly underneath the menu bar and above the horizontal border. It's where the data first appear as you type them in. The input line displays the contents of any highlighted cell, as well as other information, such as the cell's format, address, or a special font you have assigned it.

The Status Line

At the very bottom of the screen is the *status line.* The left side displays the name of the current window, and the right side the spreadsheet mode, such as **READY**. When the spreadsheet is in the Edit mode, the contents of the current cell are displayed on the left side of this line. If the Caps Lock or Num Lock key is activated, **CAPS** or **NUM** may also appear.

The Mouse Palette

If your computer system includes a mouse, and the mouse software is loaded, the *mouse palette* will appear on the right edge of the screen, as shown in Figure 1.4. The mouse pointer will also appear on your screen.

This book does not assume that you have a mouse, so the screen images that appear here omit this palette; however, the icons that you can click on the palette are as follows:

- The ? icon activates the Help Screens.
- The triangle icons control cell selector movement. Click the triangle appropriate to the direction you wish to go. The cell selector jumps to the edge of the spreadsheet in the direction chosen. For example, if cell G10 is the furthest bottom-right cell containing data, that is where the cell selector moves to.
- The Esc icon activates Escape.
- The ↵ icon activates Enter.
- The Del icon activates Delete.
- The @ icon opens the @ function window.
- The 5 icon is a macro. The default is the BEEP macro. You may assign any macro you choose to the 5 icon.
- The WYS and CHR icons designate the screen display without using the Options menu. Clicking the WYS icon changes the screen display to WYSIWYG (What You See Is What You Get), which allows you to display the Quattro Pro screen in high-resolution graphics mode. Clicking the CHR icon changes the display to character display. These last two icons are unavailable in version 2.0 and are replaced by the numbers 6 and 7 respectively.

The Message Area

When you make a mistake, an error message will appear in a box on the left side of the screen. The message will try to convey to you the type of error you made. (Further information about error messages is available through the Help system, described later in this chapter.) Don't be too concerned about making mistakes. Quattro Pro will just beep and display the error message in response. If this occurs, you can simply press the Escape key and try again.

The Important Keys

In most cases, you will use many different cells on the spreadsheet to store and display information and perform calculations. Here we describe the special keys you can use to move the cell selector and work with your spreadsheet. Figure 1.5 shows three keyboards for the IBM PC and PS/2 families of computers. Refer to the appropriate keyboard to locate the keys described.

The Arrow Keys

You can move the cell selector to any cell on the spreadsheet by using the ↑, ↓, →, and ← keys on your keyboard. Hitting an arrow key moves the cell selector one cell in the appropriate direction; holding it down advances it continuously. On some computers, these are combined respectively with the numbers 8, 2, 6, and 4 on the numeric keypad; on other keyboards, there is a separate set of arrow keys.

Note that if your computer has the arrow keys on the numeric keypad, they will not work when Num Lock is on. As the name suggests, Num Lock locks the numeric keypad in the "numbers mode." You can always tell it is on when you see **NUM** on the status line. So to use the arrow keys, make sure Num Lock is off.

The Enter Key

The Enter key "sends" whatever you type from the input line to the current cell. You will use this key quite regularly in your work with Quattro Pro (and computers in general), so be sure to become familiar with its location now, if you have not done so already. Note that on some keyboards only the ↵ symbol appears on the Enter key. On other keyboards, the Enter key may be labeled Return.

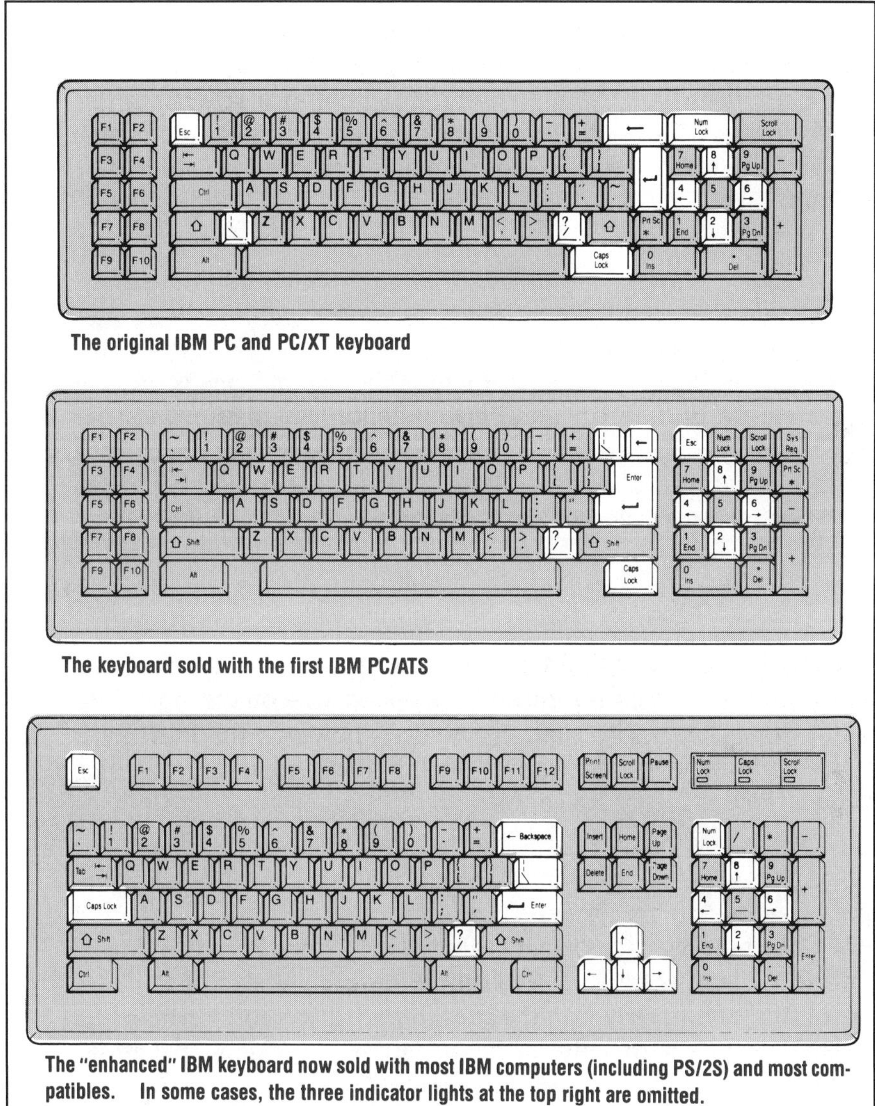

The original IBM PC and PC/XT keyboard

The keyboard sold with the first IBM PC/ATS

The "enhanced" IBM keyboard now sold with most IBM computers (including PS/2S) and most compatibles. In some cases, the three indicator lights at the top right are omitted.

Figure 1.5: *Where to find the important keys*

The Escape Key

When first learning Quattro Pro, you will occasionally make a mistake or feel a bit lost. When you find yourself in unfamiliar territory, you can usually press the Escape key (labeled Esc, Escape, or Cancel) to move backwards through the series of steps you've just taken.

In some situations, you may need to press the Escape key repeatedly to get back to familiar territory. For now, just remember this simple saying: "If in doubt, escape key out." Keep pressing the Escape key until you find yourself in more familiar territory (or until **READY** appears on the right side of the status line).

The Num Lock Key

As mentioned just a moment ago, the Num Lock key controls the numeric keypad on your keyboard. When Num Lock is off, the arrow, Home, End, PgUp, and PgDn functions are in effect, instead of the numbers, and **NUM** does not appear on the screen. (You can use the row of numbers above the letters Q through P, rather than those on the keypad, regardless of the Num Lock setting.)

The Backspace Key

The Backspace key is used in the same manner as on a typewriter. When you hit it, the cursor moves back one space—on the input line, in this case. Unlike with some typewriters, however, the Backspace key erases as it moves backward. Note that Backspace and ← are *not* the same key, as Figure 1.5 shows.

The Slash Key

One of the most important keys used in Quattro Pro is the / (forward slash) key, which is located on the lower-right side of the keyboard. (It shares the key with the question mark on most keyboards.) Press this key now to activate the menu bar and highlight the File menu. Your screen should look like Figure 1.6.

Take note of the mode indicator at the bottom-right corner of the screen: **MENU** means that you are in the Menu mode. The File-menu commands are not yet visible. (In this book, menu commands are also referred to as *options*.) To see the File-menu commands, type **F** or press Enter now. The screen should appear as in Figure 1.7. (Quattro Pro version 2.0 does not have the Save All command on the File menu.) We'll

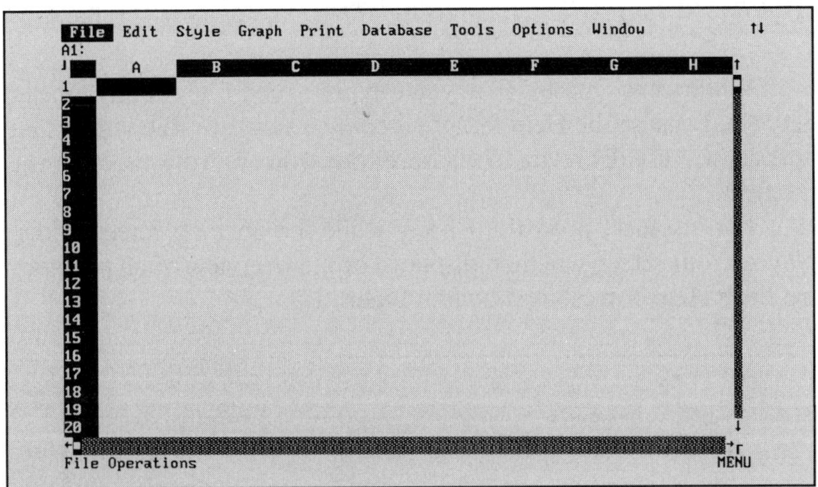

Figure 1.6: The menu bar activated

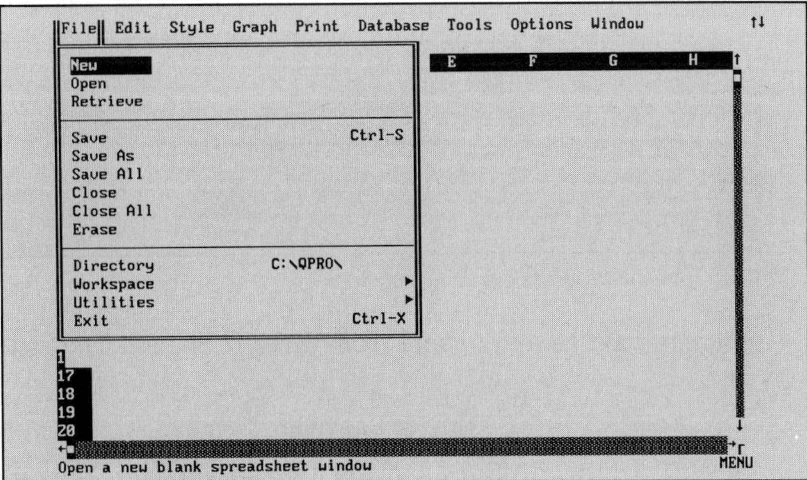

Figure 1.7: The File menu

discuss the menu commands in later chapters. For now, simply press the Escape key to "back up" and return to the spreadsheet Ready mode.

Also note that you *cannot* use the forward slash (/) and backslash (\) keys interchangeably—only / activates the menu bar. You should make a point of always distinguishing between the / and \ keys.

Getting Help from Quattro Pro

While using Quattro Pro, you can press the F1 key at any time to get help. Because the Help feature is *context sensitive,* the screen that appears will usually relate to whatever task you are working on at the moment.

For instance, press the F1 key while the opening screen is displayed. Your screen will then display a broad overview of all of Quattro Pro's Help Topics, as shown in Figure 1.8.

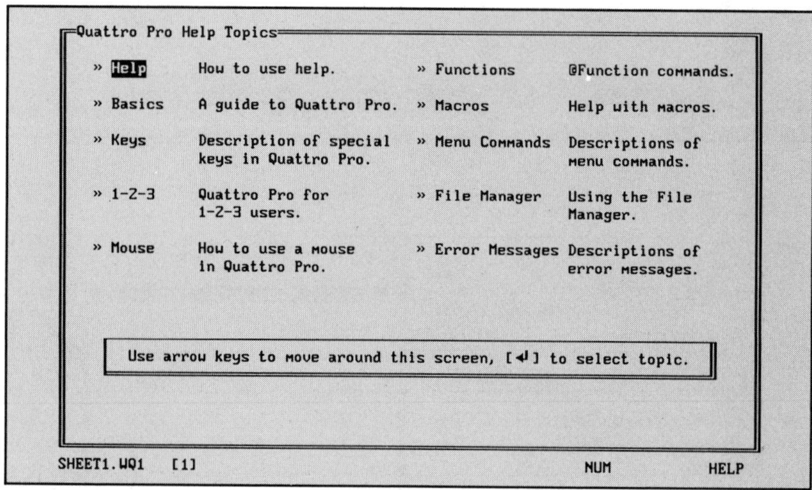

Figure 1.8: The Quattro Pro Help Topics screen

You now have various options from which to choose. The first topic line

» **Help** **How to use help.**

is already highlighted. Hit Enter and you'll see a Help screen appear with further instructions on how to use the Help system, as shown as Figure 1.9.

When you are through, press Enter again while the Help Topics option at bottom-left is still highlighted. You'll then return to the original Help Topics screen.

For additional information on any of the other topics listed, simply use the arrow keys to highlight that topic, then press Enter.

For example, suppose you wish to get help using the keyboard. Press ↓ four times to highlight the Keys option, then press Enter to select it. To obtain more information about the direction (or arrow) keys, press ↓ once to highlight the Cursor Keys option on the Keys Help screen and press Enter. You'll see a whole new Help screen that summarizes the functions of the basic arrow keys and other keys for moving the cell selector, as shown in Figure 1.10.

```
Using the Quattro Pro Help System (1/2)

  Help       Press the Help key (F1) at any time to get help about
  Key        the highlighted menu command, displayed error message,
  [F1]       or general topics.

  Keywords   Items shown in bold face and marked by "»" are keywords.
  »          You can select them to display additional information
             (use the arrow keys to highlight one, then press Enter)

  Control    Other selectable items are the words listed at the bottom
  Buttons    of each help screen.  Select them to display the next,
             previous, main, or related help screens.

  Backspace  Press the Backspace key to back up to the previously
             displayed help screen.

  Help Topics                                   Next (Help 2/2)
SHEET1.WQ1   [1]                                NUM          HELP
```

Figure 1.9: Instructions for using the Help screen

```
Cursor-Movement Keys

                 [↑]  Up Arrow              [Ctrl][→]  Control Right Arrow
 Left Arrow [←]      [→]  Right Arrow       [Ctrl][←]  Control Left Arrow
                 [↓]  Down Arrow                  [ ]  Tab
                                           [Shift][ ]  Shift Tab
                                                 [F5]  Go To
          [Home]      [PgUp]  Page Up
           [End]      [PgDn]  Page Down

  Cursor-movement keys have different effects, depending on the mode
  you use them in. You use them in:

 » Ready Mode         to move the selector around the spreadsheet.
 » Menu Mode          to highlight different menu commands.
 » Edit Mode          to position the edit cursor or enter data.
 » Value/Label Mode   to enter data or begin pointing.

 Help Topics                                Basics
 Keys                                       Next (Ready Mode)
SHEET1.WQ1   [1]                            NUM          HELP
```

Figure 1.10: The Help screen for the direction keys

You can continue to make selections from the Help Topics screen and see what information is provided. To return to the spreadsheet, press Escape. The Help screen will disappear and return you to the spreadsheet.

While exploring the various Help screens, you'll notice that each one leads to another. The next screen will provide either more in-depth information about the topic or other information related to the option you selected at the opening menu. Remember, pressing Escape will always return you to the spreadsheet when you are finished.

As you perform the exercises in this book, use the Help screens whenever you want to review information pertaining to the topic at hand.

Navigating the Spreadsheet

Now that you've had an overview of your keyboard and the Help system, it's time to start interacting directly with the Quattro Pro spreadsheet. In this section, we discuss techniques that allow you to position the cell selector on any cell in the spreadsheet.

Moving the Cell Selector

Let's try some simple exercises. Assuming that the cell selector is currently in cell A1, press ↓ twice. The cell selector will move down two rows to cell A3. (If you see **22** on the input line instead, you know the keypad is in the wrong mode. So hit Escape and Num Lock; then try ↓ twice again.) Next, press → once. The cell selector will move one column to the right to cell B3. Take a look at the input line in the upper-left corner of the screen. It now indicates that the cell selector is indeed on cell B3.

Experiment with the arrow keys for awhile and watch the cell selector move from cell to cell. To move quickly across the spreadsheet, keep the arrow keys depressed, rather than tap them repeatedly. If you try to move the cell selector beyond the boundaries of the spreadsheet, such as above row 1 or to the left of column A (or below row 8192 or to the right of column IV), Quattro Pro will beep to let you know that it cannot move the cell selector in the direction you've requested. If you hold down an arrow key when it comes to a border, it may beep at you several times. Not to worry, though—the noise will stop shortly after you release the key.

When you have finished experimenting, press the key labeled Home to move the cell selector quickly back to cell A1.

Moving to a Specific Cell

The F5 key lets you move the cell selector quickly to a specific cell on the spreadsheet. This key is named Go To on your Quattro Pro template that came with your software package. If you press F5 now, the input line at the top of the screen will display the following prompt:

Enter address to go to: A1

Because the cell selector is currently at cell A1, that cell's address appears with the prompt.

To move to a different cell, type in the cell's address, then press Enter. For example, if you type in **B6** and press Enter, the cell selector will jump to cell B6.

Moving the Spreadsheet Window

When you first look at the Quattro Pro spreadsheet, you see only a small portion of the worksheet. As mentioned earlier, the spreadsheet actually contains 256 columns and 8192 rows, totaling 2,097,152 cells!

Because it can't fit all the cells on your screen at once, Quattro Pro displays only a portion of the larger worksheet. Figure 1.11 shows how you can envision the screen as a fragment of the whole, a window into the huge electronic spreadsheet.

Let's move this window around to view the other parts of the spreadsheet.

1. Press the Home key to move the cell selector back to the upper-left corner of the spreadsheet—cell A1.
2. To jump to the extreme upper-right corner of the spreadsheet, press the End key, followed by the → key. The cell selector will

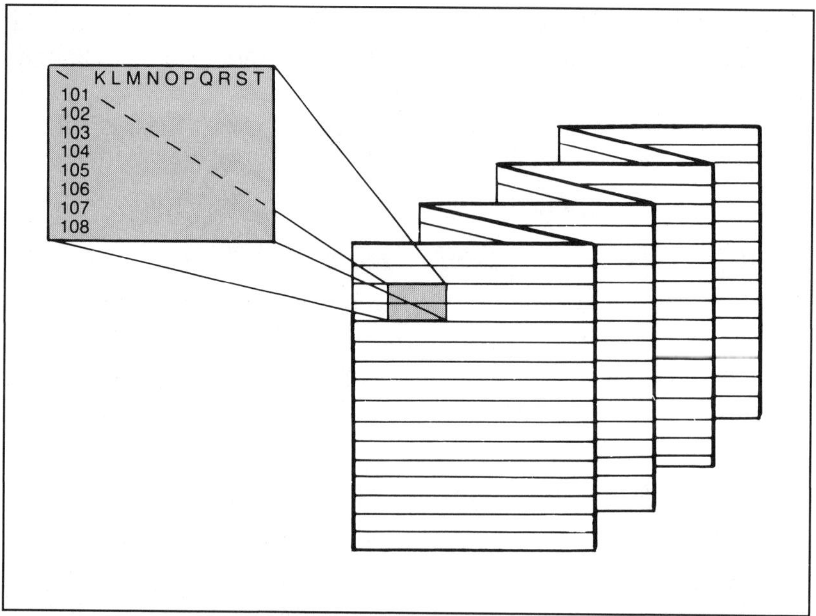

Figure 1.11: The screen as a window into the larger spreadsheet

move onto cell IV1 (column IV, row 1). Notice that the entire window has moved to the right as well, showing columns IO to IV.

3. To move to another corner of the spreadsheet, press the End key and the ↓ key. This time the cell selector moves to the extreme bottom-right corner of the spreadsheet, to cell IV8192. Now the bottom-most rows, numbered 8173 to 8192, are visible.

4. Pressing the End and ← keys will now move the cell selector to the extreme lower-left corner of the spreadsheet. The window now shows columns A through H and rows 8173 to 8192.

5. To return to cell A1, hit the Home key.

At this point, we've made a trip around the four extreme corners of the spreadsheet, as Figure 1.12 illustrates.

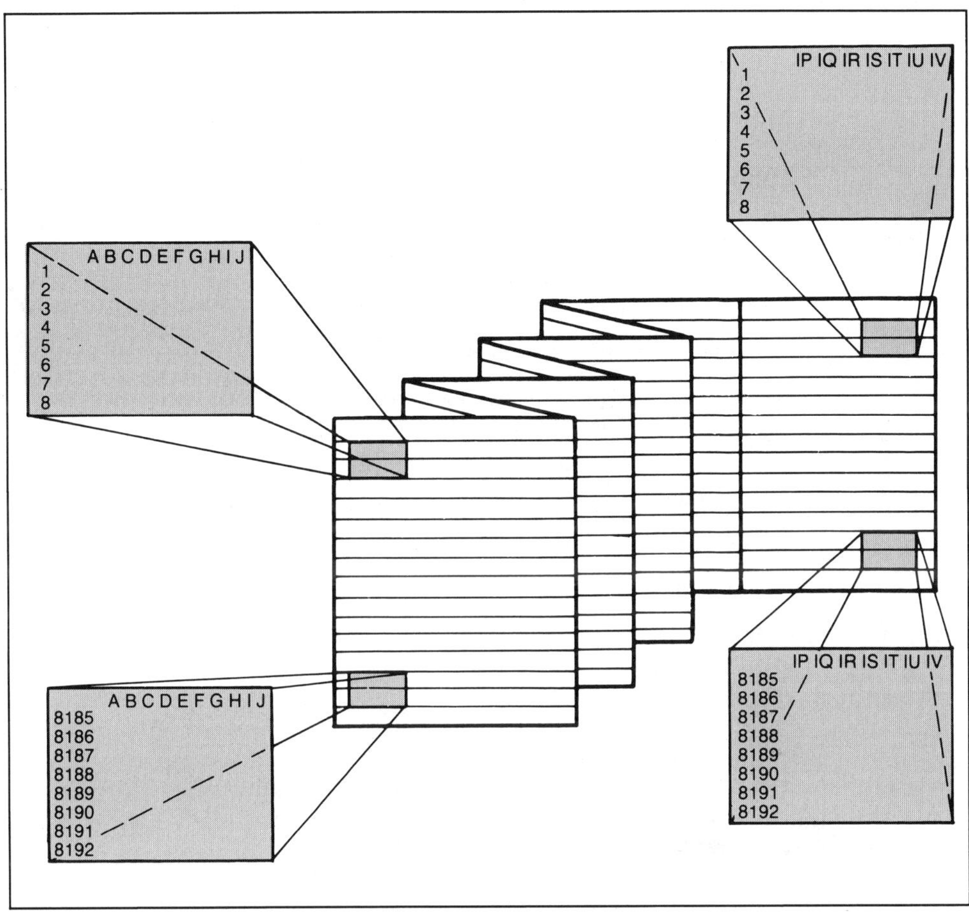

Figure 1.12: *The window moved to four corners of the spreadsheet*

Summary of Quattro Pro's Special Keys

Table 1.1 lists all the special keys you can use to move the cell selector around on the spreadsheet. In this table, a hyphen between two key names means that you should hold down the first key while pressing the second. For example, Ctrl-→ means hold down the Ctrl (Control) key while tapping the → key. Similarly, Shift-Tab means to hold down the Shift key while hitting the Tab key.

You may want to practice using the keys listed in Table 1.1 for awhile. When you have finished, press Home to move the cell selector back to cell A1.

***Table 1.1:** Keys for Moving the Cell Selector*

KEY	ACTION
→	Moves cell selector one cell to the right
←	Moves cell selector one cell to the left
↑	Moves cell selector up one cell
↓	Moves cell selector down one cell
Home	Moves cell selector "home" to cell A1
PgUp	Moves window up one screen
PgDn	Moves window down one screen
Tab	Moves cell selector one screen to the right
Ctrl–→	Same as Tab
Shift–Tab	Moves cell selector one screen to the left
Ctrl–←	Same as Shift-Tab
End, Arrow key	Relocates the cell selector to the beginning or end of a block in the arrow's direction, or else to the far end of the spreadsheet
F5	Moves cell selector to any cell you specify

Leaving Quattro Pro

To exit Quattro Pro, press the / key, which activates the menu bar and moves the highlight to the File menu. Open it by pressing either Enter or the letter *F*, which is the access letter for the File menu. The File menu is shown in Figure 1.7.

The last command on the menu is the Exit command. There are two ways to execute it. One is to type the letter *X*, as it is the access letter for the Exit command. Another is to use the ↓ key to move the highlight to the word Exit and then press Enter.

If at any time in your work you have entered or changed information on a spreadsheet and then selected Exit from the File menu without having previously saved your work, the screen will display the message

Lose your changes and Exit?
No
Yes
Save & Exit

If you select No, or press Escape, you will stay in Quattro Pro. If you select Yes, you'll be sent to the DOS prompt, from which you first entered Quattro Pro. Now you can turn off the computer or run another program. If you select the Save & Exit command, Quattro Pro will open a directory window and ask you to name the spreadsheet file if it has not already been named. After you name it, the computer will save the file and send you to the DOS prompt.

For now, you have not done any work worth saving, so if the above prompt appears in the middle of your screen, type the letter **Y** or move the highlight to the word Yes and press Enter. You'll be returned to the DOS prompt shortly.

In the next chapter, you'll learn valuable techniques for actually putting the spreadsheet to work, using the menus, and saving your work for future use.

2

BUILDING A SPREADSHEET

FEATURING

- *Entering Information*
- *Erasing Mistakes*
- *Building Formulas*
- *Saving Your Work*

In this chapter, we discuss the basic techniques for building your own spreadsheets. These include entering data, creating formulas to calculate results, and saving your work. We start with a fairly simple example—a family budget. But as you will see later in the book, you can use these same techniques to build business spreadsheets of any size and sophistication.

Types of Cell Entries

There are several types of information that you can enter into any cell on the spreadsheet:

- Labels (words, sentences, and any other nonnumeric data)
- Numbers (real numbers on which you perform calculations)
- Dates
- Times
- Formulas (entries that perform calculations)
- Functions (built-in, complex formulas that come with the software)

- Macros (shortcuts for oft-repeated keystrokes)
- Graphs (pictures placed inside blocks of cells)

The sample spreadsheet we develop will include each of these *data types.*

If you exited Quattro Pro at the end of the last chapter, you need to start it again. Refer to the beginning of Chapter 1 if you need a refresher on this.

Entering Your Text in a Cell

To enter a label into a cell, simply move the cell selector to where you want the label to appear, type the label, and press Enter. Suppose, for example, that you want to title your first sample spreadsheet, "Monthly Budget for the Dorf Family." Here are the steps to do just this:

1. Move the cell selector to cell A1 by pressing the Home key.
2. Type **Monthly Budget for the Dorf Family**. You'll notice that as you type, the letters appear on the input line.
3. If you make a mistake, you can erase it with the Backspace key (but not the ← key).
4. When you have finished typing, press Enter.

The label appears in cell A1 (though it overflows onto other cells), as shown in Figure 2.1.

That was easy, wasn't it? Notice that the label appears on the input line, just above the horizontal border. As you can see, Quattro Pro automatically added an apostrophe (') to the beginning of the label. That's a *label prefix,* which we'll discuss later.

Now that you have a title for your spreadsheet, let's add some other labels. Use the ↓ key to move the cell selector to cell A6. Check the input line to make sure that the cell selector is in the correct cell.

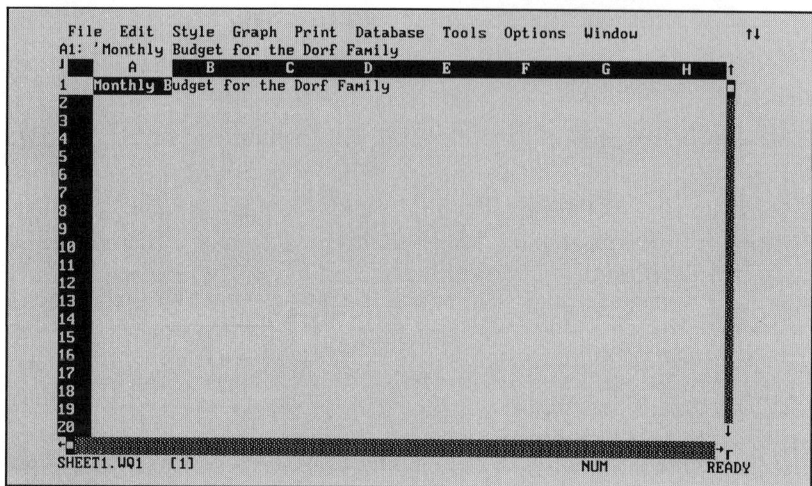

Figure 2.1: A label entered into cell A1

Simplifying Data-Entry with the Arrow Keys

Your next task is to enter labels that identify the numbers you will begin entering in the cells. In a family budget, there is a source of income—normally from jobs—and several expenditures. In this example, assume that both the husband and wife work. In cell A6 type **Income**. Then press the ↓ key.

As you can see on your screen, the label **Income** is now in cell A6, and the cell selector has moved down to cell A7 to await another entry. Are you wondering why we told you to press ↓ rather than Enter, as you have done so far? It's because Enter would have left the cell selector at position A6. Making many sequential entries this way—a row of column headings or a list of data—would involve many wasted keystrokes: Enter, arrow, Enter, arrow, etc. Better, then, to use just an arrow key, if you know in advance the direction you want the cell selector to move.

For a little more practice, press ↓ to move the cell selector to cell A8, and type the label, **Ralph, job**. Press ↓ again to move the cell selector to cell A9 and enter **Alice, job**.

Move the cell selector to cell A11, type the label **Total Income**, and press ↓. At this point, your screen should resemble Figure 2.2.

Then enter the labels shown in Figure 2.3 onto your spreadsheet. When you get to row 20, just keep using the ↓ key in the usual manner to move the cell selector to rows 21, 22, and 24. If you make any errors along the way, try to correct them using some of the techniques listed above. (Note that the label **JUNE** is in cell C6, **JULY** in cell D6, and **AUGUST** in cell E6.)

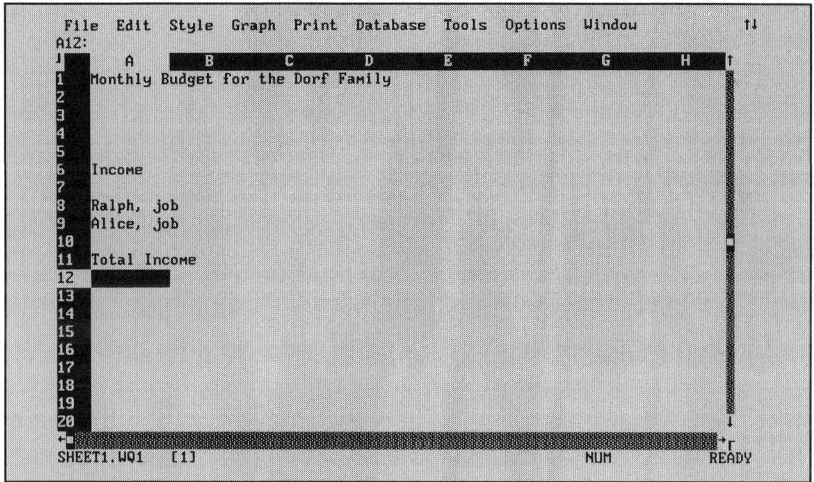

Figure 2.2: Sample spreadsheet with several labels

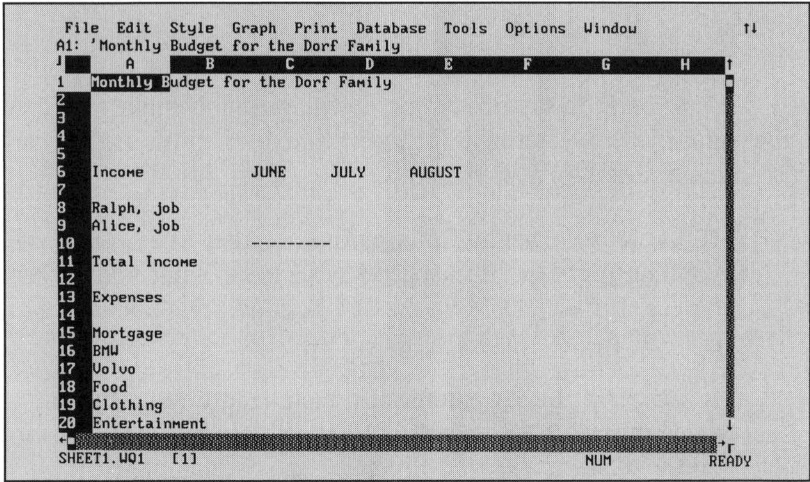

Figure 2.3: Sample spreadsheet with many labels

Underlining Text

The hyphen (–), which you might want to use to draw underlines in a spreadsheet, has a special meaning in Quattro Pro—it is used to subtract numbers or identify negative numbers. Therefore, you cannot enter an underline into a cell simply by typing -----. Try it and you'll get the Error message: **Incomplete formula**. (To cancel, hit the Escape (Esc) key twice.)

You can, however, enter underlines by using the repeat-character label *prefix,* which is a backslash (\). Follow the backslash with the character you wish to repeat. For example, to place an underline in cell C10, follow these steps:

1. Move the cell selector to cell C10.
2. Type \-.
3. Press Enter.

Cell C10 will fill with hyphens: ---------. Now move the cell selector to C23 and enter \- once again to put in another underline. (Remember to hit Enter or an arrow key after typing \-.)

Correcting Mistakes

Unless you are a superb typist, you will probably make mistakes quite regularly while entering information into a spreadsheet. You can correct these mistakes in several ways:

1. If you *have not* yet hit Enter or an arrow key after your typo, you can press the Backspace key to erase what you've just typed. Or else hold down the Ctrl key and press Backspace to erase all the characters at once. Or just press Escape.
2. If you *have* already entered the mistake into the cell, simply place the cell selector back on that cell and reenter the information. The new entry will replace the old completely.

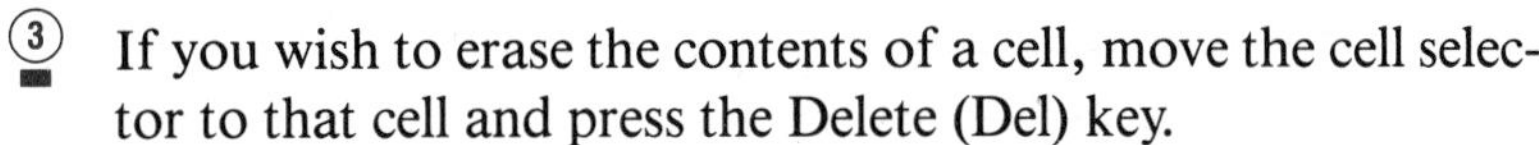

③ If you wish to erase the contents of a cell, move the cell selector to that cell and press the Delete (Del) key.

There are some other ways to correct errors and make changes, which we'll discuss later.

Entering Numbers

Entering numbers into cells is no different from entering labels. Be aware, though, that for the computer to recognize an entry as a number (and not a word), it must begin with either a digit (0–9), a minus sign (–)for negative numbers, or a decimal point. You cannot put commas in numbers. For example, you can type *20000*, but not *20,000*. (Later, you'll see how to display numbers with the commas inserted.)

Let's put some numbers now into the sample spreadsheet for practice. Suppose Ralph earns $2000 per month, which you wish to show in cell C8. Use the arrow keys to move the cell selector to cell C8 and type **2000**. Then press the ↓ key. Ralph's salary will appear in cell C8.

Furthermore, suppose that Alice earns $4000 per month, which you wish to put in cell C9. Since you entered the previous salary with the ↓ key, the cell selector should already be on cell C9, so just type **4000** and press Enter. Your screen should look like Figure 2.4.

Now you can enter some more expenses into column C. Remember, you can use the techniques discussed earlier to correct any mistakes. Enter the following values into the cells below:

Enter **1550** into cell C15

Enter **330** into cell C16

Enter **275** into cell C17

Enter **400** into cell C18

Enter **200** into cell C19

Enter **75** into cell C20

Enter **50** into cell C21

Enter **300** into cell C22

Figure 2.5 shows how the sample spreadsheet should look. Now, you don't have to add up these numbers on a calculator and enter the sum in cell C4; we will later use a formula to find the total expenses instead.

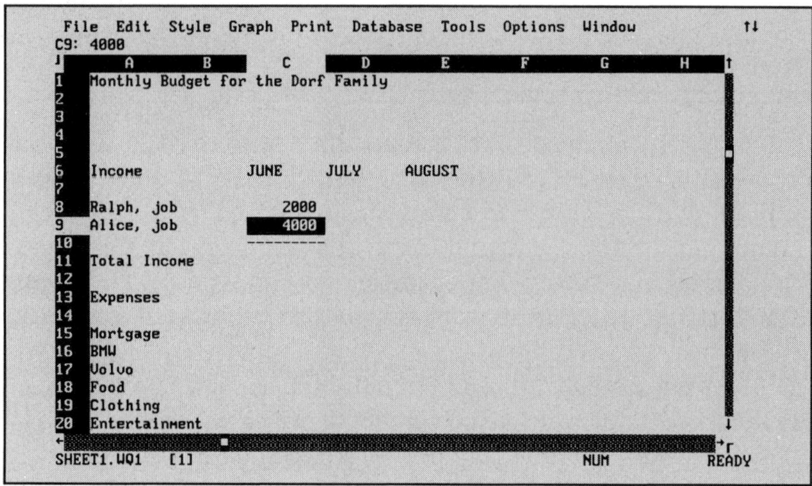

Figure 2.4: Salaries entered in the sample spreadsheet

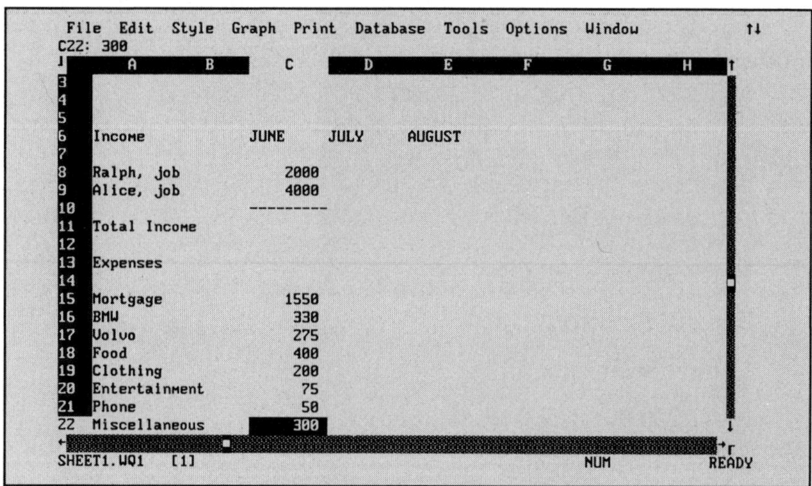

Figure 2.5: Income and expenses in the sample spreadsheet

Entering Dates

There are several methods for entering dates into spreadsheet cells, but only a few techniques will allow you to perform *date arithmetic,* which means treating dates as numbers so you can use them in formulas. The best (and easiest way) is to use the command Ctrl-D and type the date in a *month/day/year* format.

Suppose, for example, you wish to put the current date near the upper-right corner of the sample spreadsheet in cell F1:

1. Move the cell selector to cell F1 using the arrow keys or the F5 (Goto) key.
2. Hold down the Ctrl key and type the letter **D**. (Note that **DATE** replaces **READY** at the right end of the status line.)
3. Enter today's date in *mm/dd/yy* format (for example, 12/1/92 for December 1, 1992).
4. Press the Enter key.

See the date appear in cell F1. But on the input line (while the cell selector is still at cell F1), there's a five-digit number, such as 33208. This is a *serial date* that Quattro Pro uses for date arithmetic.

Serial Dates

Serial dates are calculated based on the number of days elapsed since December 31, 1899, which is assigned the number 1. Thus the serial date 2 is January 1, 1900 and the serial date 33423 is July 4, 1991. The farthest date in the future that Quattro Pro accepts is 12/31/2099 (serial date 73050). To enter dates past 12/31/99, enter the year in full, as in 7/4/2036. (Doing so, though, will fill the cell with asterisks, indicating that the column is too narrow to accomodate all the numbers. Chapter 3 will show you how to change a column's width, so you can display such an entry properly.)

You can also enter dates from the last century, if you want. These have negative serial dates, since they came before December 31, 1899.

Thus the serial date 0 is 12/30/1899 and −24756 is 3/20/1832. The farthest date in the past that Quattro Pro accepts is 3/1/1800 (serial date −36463).

Serial dates are very handy. Here are just a few of the tasks you can perform with them:

- Calculate how many days there are between two dates by subtracting one from the other.
- Fill a row of cells with dates that are all one week (or 5 days or 63 days) apart.
- Find a date 90 days in the future (or past) by taking today's date and adding (or subtracting) 90.

Using Simple Formulas

Formulas are cell entries that perform calculations on other cells. The operators you use in formulas are similar to the operators you use in everyday math. These are the most common ones:

+	Adds
−	Subtracts
*	Multiplies
/	Divides

To help Quattro Pro distinguish formulas from labels, numbers, and dates, most spreadsheet users begin a formula with a plus sign (+). Other characters are allowed, but for now just try to remember to begin all formulas with a plus sign.

Now let's look at a simple formula to add Ralph and Alice's incomes and display the result next to the **Total Income** label on the spreadsheet. When creating formulas, it is better to have them refer to the addresses of cells that contain numbers, rather than the numbers themselves. That way, if you change one of the numbers in a cell, the formula will automatically recalculate the answer. More on this a bit later.

To display the sum of Ralph and Alice's income in cell C11, follow these steps:

1. Move the cell selector to cell C11.
2. Type the formula *exactly* as shown below:

   +C8+C9
3. Press Enter.

You should see that cell C11 now displays **6000**—the sum of Ralph and Alice's income. If you look at the input line near the top of the screen (as in Figure 2.6), you'll see that the cell actually contains the formula +C8+C9.

The formula +C8+C9 says to Quattro Pro, "In this cell, display the sum of the contents of cells C8 and C9." Note that if you had omitted the leading plus sign and entered the formula as C8+C9, Quattro Pro would have interpreted the entry as a label (because it begins with a letter), not as a formula.

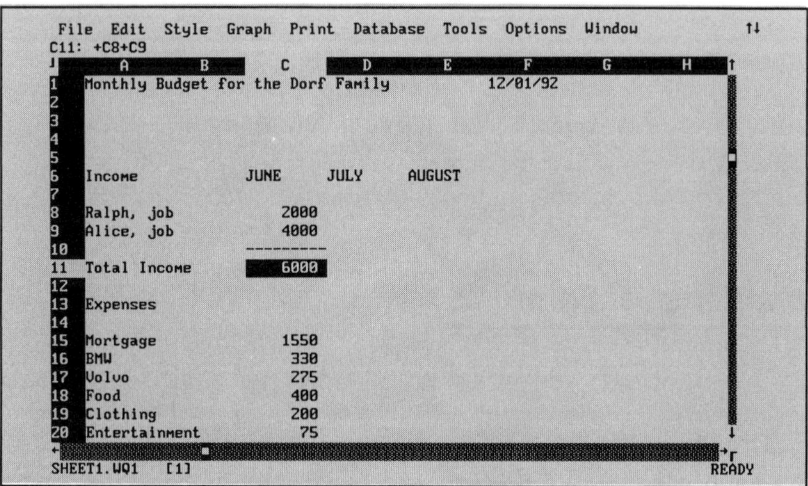

Figure 2.6: Total income calculated with a formula

Recalculating a Formula with Different Data

Suppose Ralph suddenly gets a raise and is now earning $3000 per month. Do you need to enter a new formula? Absolutely not, because the formula +C8+C9 says, "Add whatever is in cell C8 to whatever is in cell C9." Hence, when you move the cell selector to cell C8, type **3000**, and hit Enter, the total income will immediately be recalculated, and cell C11 will display the correct result: **7000**. (See Figure 2.7)

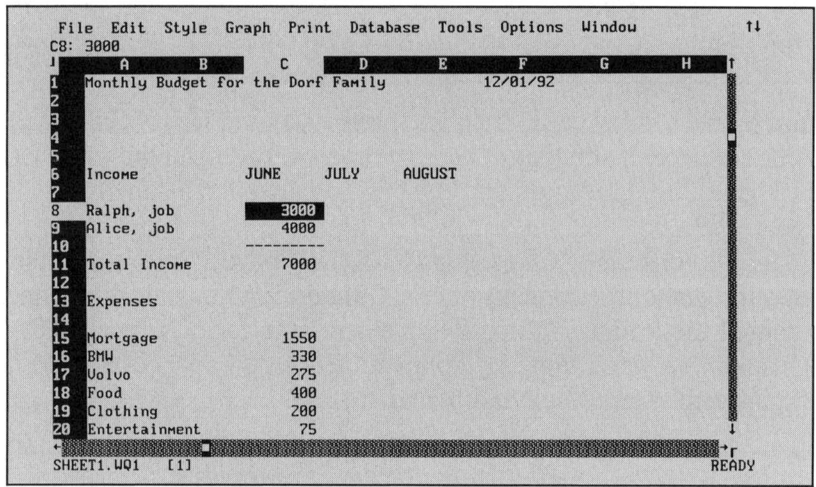

Figure 2.7: *Total income automatically recalculated*

For the time being, however, let's assume that Ralph did not get a raise. Move the cell selector back to cell C8, type **2000**, and press Enter. The total income immediately returns to **6000**.

Functions vs. Formulas

The formula you just created added the total value of two income cells. Looking at the Expenses section of the Dorfs' budget, you can see that there are many cells that need to be totaled in order to determine the couple's expenses. You could take the time to enter the address of every cell (+C15+C16+C17... and so on), but that would be laborious and prone to error. It is simpler to total the cells as a group, or *block*. Before you can sum a large group of numbers, however, you need to know how to define a block of data.

What Is a Block?

A block is any rectangular group of cells on the spreadsheet. It is designated by the cell addresses of its upper-left and lower-right corners, with two periods in between. For example, the block A1..B3 consists of the row of cells A1 through A3 and the row of cells B1 through B3. The smallest possible block is a single cell, such as A1..A1. The largest block is the entire spreadsheet, A1..IV8192. Figure 2.8 shows examples of several blocks on a spreadsheet.

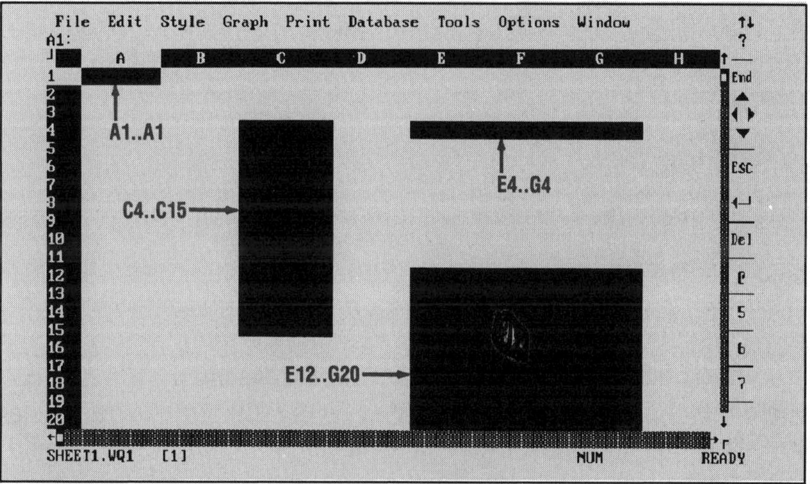

Figure 2.8: Examples of blocks on a spreadsheet

Note that all the sample blocks have an even, rectangular shape. You *cannot* define blocks that have any other shape, such as an **L**, **U**, **T**, triangle or pear. This is important to remember when you are deciding how to enter and list your data.

Using a Function to Sum a Block of Numbers

Rather than write your own formulas, you may be able to use one of Quattro Pro's preprogrammed functions, which are far too numerous to discuss right now. (But we will discuss them in Chapter 5.) You only need the @SUM function to accomplish your present goal.

Notice that the function name begins with the @ (at) sign. All Quattro Pro functions begin with an @ sign, followed by a word and a pair of parentheses that enclose the *argument* of that function. Arguments are the data that the function uses in its calculation. (*Argument* may sound strange, but it is a term that mathematicians use regularly.) After the function finishes its calculation, it *returns* a result.

The @SUM function uses the general syntax @SUM(*block(s)*), where *block(s)* is the block (or blocks) of numbers to be summed. For example, @SUM(C15..C22) says, "Sum all the numbers in the block of cells from C15 to C22." Let's go ahead and use @SUM to total the Dorfs' expenses. You'll want to display the sum in cell C24, so follow these steps:

1. Move the cell selector to cell C24.
2. Type in the function exactly as shown below:

   @SUM(C15..C22)
3. As usual, press Enter when you're through.

You should see the answer, 3180, in cell C24, and the actual function on the input line, as shown see in Figure 2.9. Of course, if you were to change any of the expenses in block C15..C22, @SUM would calculate the new results immediately. You'll get much more experience with formulas and Quattro Pro's functions in future chapters.

Do you want to take a break? Before you walk away from the computer, save your work so that you can use this sample spreadsheet in later chapters.

Saving Your Work

All the work you have done so far on your spreadsheet is stored in the computer's main memory (also called *random access memory,* or RAM). Unless you take specific steps to save a copy of this spreadsheet on the computer's disk as a file, it will be erased completely when you exit from Quattro Pro or turn off the computer. To save your

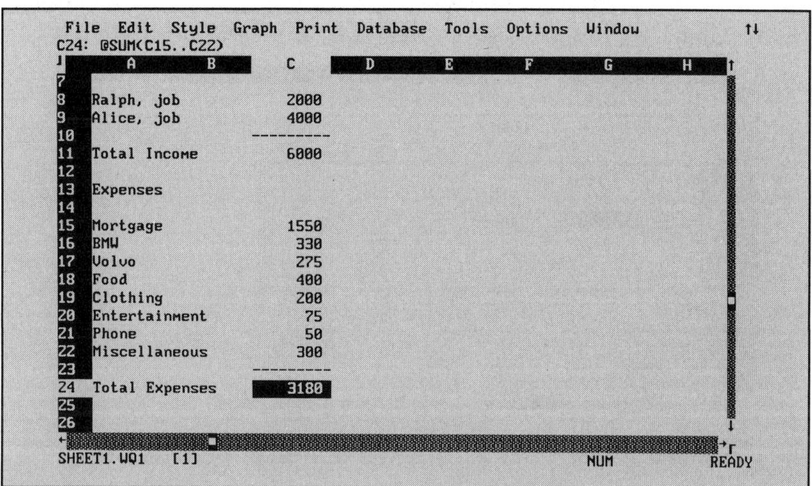

Figure 2.9: Cell C24 showing the sum of the expenses

work, you need to set some options (or commands) from the Quattro Pro menu system.

To access the Quattro Pro menu bar, simply press the forward slash (/) key. The highlight will appear on the menu name File by default. Hit Enter, and the File menu will drop down from the top of the screen.

At the end of Chapter 1, you opened the File menu and used the Exit command to leave Quattro Pro. Remember, to select an option on any menu, you can use ↑ or ↓ to move the highlight to the option you want, or type the option's highlighted access letter.

To save this spreadsheet as a file on your disk, you need to select the Save option. Again, you can do so either by typing **S** or by moving the highlighter to the Save option and pressing Enter. Quattro Pro version 3.0 includes a new command on the File menu, Save All. It is discussed in Chapter 9.

Naming Your Spreadsheet

After you've selected File and Save from the menus, Quattro Pro will display a prompt in the message window, as seen in Figure 2.10. The names you see in the window are the files that came with Quattro Pro. The format for file names is as follows:

drive:\directory*.WQ1

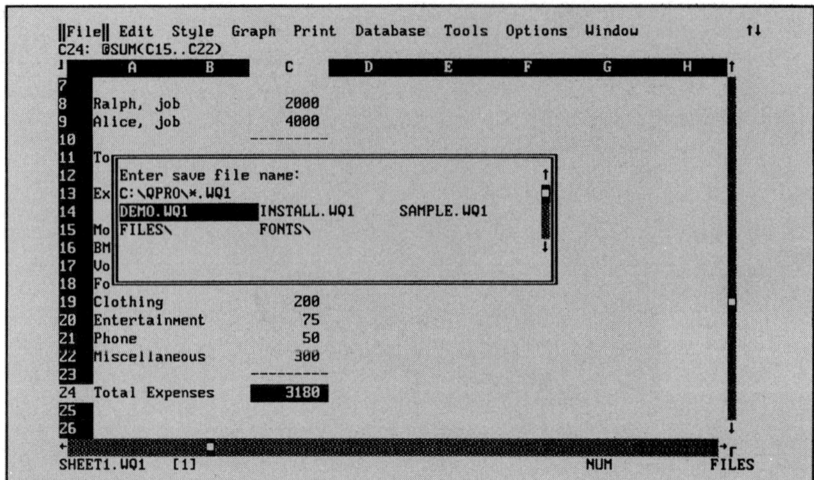

Figure 2.10: *The File Save message window*

The exact description of the *drive:\directory* portion depends on where you installed Quattro Pro. If it is installed on the C drive in the QPRO subdirectory, the screen will read as in Figure 2.10.

The name you enter for the spreadsheet can be no more than eight characters long, must not contain any blank spaces, and should not contain any punctuation marks other than the underline character (_). To make the name of the file easy to remember in this example, simply type **DORF** and press Enter.

You may notice that a disk-drive light comes on as Quattro Pro saves the file. After you've completed the steps for saving your work, a copy of the spreadsheet will remain on the screen.

Congratulations! You have successfully built a Quattro Pro spreadsheet that includes several types of entries: labels, numbers, a date, and formulas. Before moving on to more advanced techniques, you'd be wise to become familiar with the different data types. Take some time to read the rest of this chapter, and by all means feel free to experiment on a new blank spreadsheet if you like.

One important point to note here is that you should save files regularly during the course of your work. If the power goes out, the work you sweated over could be gone in an instant. Exiting from Quattro Pro without saving your work will also cause a spreadsheet's demise.

At this point, with the spreadsheet safely stored on disk, you can exit Quattro Pro if you like. The routine way of doing this is to call up the File menu and select Exit: i.e., type /, hit Enter and select Exit. Alternatively, you can shortcut this route by simply pressing Ctrl-X.

Aligning Labels

As we mentioned earlier, Quattro Pro automatically places the apostrophe label prefix in front of any label you enter. This prefix tells Quattro Pro to left-justify the label within the cell. Label prefixes and their effects are listed below:

' (apostrophe)	Left-justifies label
^ (caret)	Centers label
" (quotation mark)	Right-justifies label
\ (backslash)	Repeats label

To use a label prefix, simply type it in before you type the first letter of the label. For example, to center the letters *ABC* within a cell, position the cell selector to the appropriate cell and type **^ABC**. Then press Enter.

Figure 2.11 shows examples of labels entered with various prefixes. Note that any label that is long enough to spill over into adjoining cells will always be left-justified within its cell, regardless of the label prefix you assign. Also note that long labels will spill over only into empty cells. For example, in Figure 2.11, cell A10 contains the label **This is a long label**. But because cell B10 contains the number **999**, the fragment *long label* spilling out of A10 is cut short at the beginning of cell B10.

Cell A6 contains the label \=. Because the backslash label prefix fills the cell with whatever character(s) follow it, cell A6 is filled with equal signs.

Cell A12 contains a long label that appears to be centered within cell A12. It isn't, though. Instead, there are simply blank spaces between the label prefix and the label itself. The cell actually contains the phrase, *This is a long label indented with leading spaces,* with

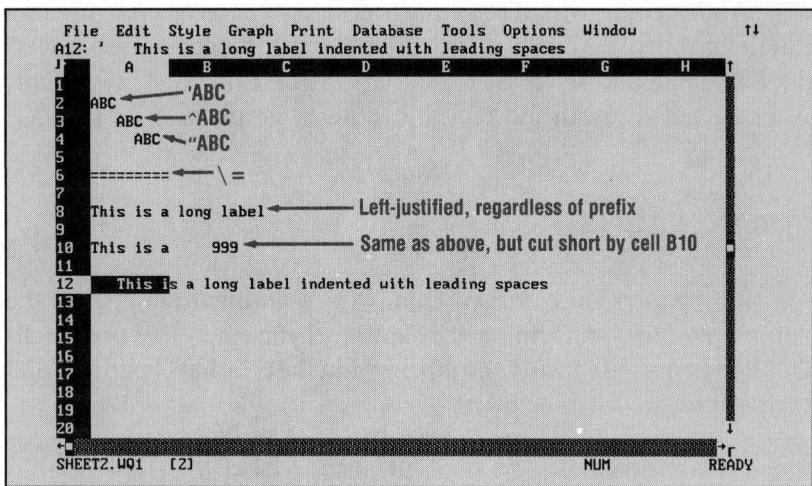

Figure 2.11: Sample labels in a spreadsheet

some blank spaces in front of it. To enter such a label, simply position the cell selector, press the space bar a few times to insert blank spaces, type in the label, and hit Enter.

Entering Labels That Start with a Number

In some cases, you'll want to enter labels that do not begin with a letter—for example, an address such as 123 Oak Tree Lane. If you simply enter this text, Quattro Pro will beep and display the error message

Invalid cell or block address

because it does not know whether the entry is a number (123) or a label (Oak Tree Lane). (Hit Escape to clear the message.) Labels that begin with a number *must* be entered with a label prefix. Thus you should enter the street address as **'123 Oak Tree Lane** (or **^123 Oak Tree Lane** or **"123 Oak Tree Lane**).

Rectify the problem now by pressing the Home key to move the cursor to the beginning of the label, typing an apostrophe (or ^ or "), and pressing Enter. This puts the prefix where it belongs and stores the corrected label in the cell.

Rules for Entering Numbers

Here are the rules you need to keep in mind when entering numbers into a spreadsheet:

- A number can contain only digits (0–9), a leading plus (+) or minus (–) sign, and a decimal point (.). A trailing percent (%) sign is also acceptable. Commas, blank spaces, dollar signs, and other nonnumeric characters are not allowed.
- A number can contain only one decimal point.
- If you have a habit of using the letter *l* for the number *1* and the letter *O* for the number *0* on a standard typewriter, you'll need to break that habit now. Quattro Pro distinguishes between the two and will not accept any letters as numbers. Use the number keys on the top of the keyboard or on the numeric keypad to enter all numbers.
- The number you enter into a cell can be extremely large or small, as long as it does not exceed 254 digits. If you enter a number that is too wide for a cell, the number will not spill over into an adjacent cell. Instead, the cell will display the number in scientific notation. You can use the Column Width option from the Style menu to widen the cell so that a lengthy number can fit. Unlike labels, numbers are automatically right-justified.
- You can include a % sign at the end of a number to indicate percentage values. Quattro Pro will convert the number to a decimal value. For example, if you type **9.375%** into a cell, Quattro Pro will display it as **0.09375** (unless you change the display, discussed in Chapter 6).

Examples of Valid and Invalid Numbers

If all those rules for entering numbers are confusing you, take a look at examples of valid and invalid numbers in Table 2.1. It will help summarize the rules for you.

Table 2.1: Example of Valid and Invalid Number Entries

NUMBER	VALID OR INVALID?
1	Valid, nothing unusual about this number
123.45	Valid, nothing unusual about this number
+123.45	Valid, same as 123.45
−123.45	Valid, a negative number
22%	Valid, displayed as **0.22**
12 3/4	Invalid, contains a space (12 + 3/4 is okay, though)
12,345	Invalid, contains a comma
$123.45	Valid, though Quattro Pro will ignore the dollar sign
640K	Invalid, contains a letter
6.3E+9	Valid, the letter *E* (or *e*) can be used to express scientific notation—which is 6.3×10^9 in this example

In the next chapter, you'll learn some more advanced techniques for using the Quattro Pro menus and simplifying the development of larger spreadsheets.

3

LEARNING BASIC EDITING TECHNIQUES

FEATURING

Retrieving a Spreadsheet
Editing Cell Entries
Inserting and Deleting Rows and Columns
Erasing Blocks of Data

If you exited from Quattro Pro in the last chapter, be sure to get it up and running on your computer again. If you did not exit from Quattro Pro (but did indeed save the DORF spreadsheet), type /**FE**. This activates the menu bar, opens the File menu and selects the Erase command. When Quattro Pro asks you if you want to lose your changes, type **Y** for Yes. That way, you can start this chapter with a clean slate.

Retrieving Your Spreadsheet

Recall from the last chapter that you used the Save command from the File menu to save a spreadsheet as a file named DORF. Quattro Pro always adds the *extension* .WQ1 to any file name you provide, so your spreadsheet is actually stored under the file name DORF.WQ1 in the QPRO directory on your computer's hard disk.

Go ahead and retrieve DORF now:

1. Type /**FR** to select the Retrieve option from the File menu. Quattro Pro will open the file window with a list of the saved file names and display the prompt:

   Enter name of file to retrieve:
   C:\QPRO*.W??

(The asterisk and question mark are DOS *wild-card* specifications, * standing for any number of characters and *?* standing for any single character. Thus *.W?? represents all files in the QPRO directory whose extension begins with *W*.)

2 To select the file you want to retrieve, either type its name (DORF in this example) or use the ↑ or ↓ keys to highlight the name (DORF.WQ1). Then press Enter.

You'll see the spreadsheet reappear on the screen as in Figure 3.1. (Depending on where you positioned the cell selector when you last saved the spreadsheet, you may see a different range of rows than what is shown.)

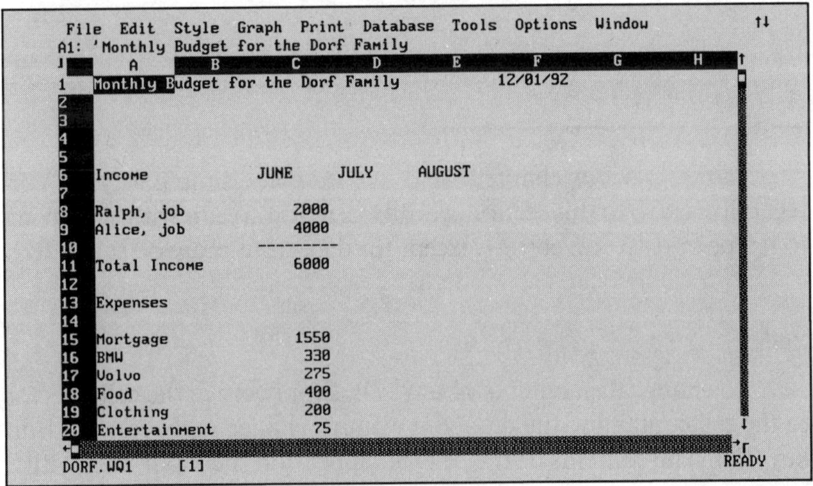

Figure 3.1: The DORF file retrieved from disk

Retrieving vs. Opening

Retrieve and Open are not the same. Notice that when you highlight Retrieve in the File menu, the status line reads, **Load a spreadsheet into the current window**. This means that whatever is in the current window will be erased to make room for the newly loaded spreadsheet. This wasn't a problem just a moment ago when you retrieved DORF, because you were just loading it into an empty spreadsheet. If you had been in danger of losing your current screen, Quattro Pro would have asked you, **Lose your changes?**, to which you could have answered Yes or No.

By contrast, selecting Open lets you **Load a file into a new spreadsheet window**, as per the status line. This means that your newly loaded spreadsheet will fill a new window that overlays the current window. You can open quite a number of different spreadsheets in this way—in fact, up to 32. This "stacking" feature is not only handy, but probably essential for many tasks you wish to accomplish.

Setting up a particular group of spreadsheets in a certain manner is called *configuring the worksheet*. Once you establish a configuration of windows that suits your work best, you can save your workspace for later use. For now, you'll be working with just one spreadsheet.

Editing a Cell Entry

In the previous chapter, we discussed some simple ways to correct cell entries. In this section, you'll learn how to edit without having to retype or delete an entry—except for dates (but more on that later).

Exploring the Edit Mode

To change the contents of any cell, simply move the cell selector to the cell containing the data you want to change and press the Edit key (F2). The contents of the cell will appear on the input line, with a large cursor at the end of the entry. And the word **EDIT** will appear at the far right of the status line.

Table 3.1 lists the special keys you can use while in this Edit mode to control the cursor and make changes to the cell entry. If your arrow keys are on the numeric keypad, be sure that Num Lock is off.

Let's get some hands-on practice with the Edit mode right now. Start with the label in cell A1 and change *Dorf* to *Smith*:

1. Press the Home key to move the cell selector to cell A1.

Table 3.1: Special Keys in Edit Mode

KEY	WHAT IT DOES
←	Moves the cursor left one space
→	Moves the cursor right one space
Backspace	Moves the cursor left one space, and erases in the process
Insert (or Ins)	Toggles between Insert and Overwrite modes
Delete (or Del)	Deletes the character at the cursor's position
Tab	Moves the cursor five spaces to the right
Ctrl-→	Does the same as Tab
Shift-Tab	Moves the cursor five spaces to the left
Ctrl-←	Does the same as Shift-Tab
Home	Moves the cursor to the first character in the entry
End	Moves the cursor one space past the last character in the entry
Enter	Sends the entry on the input line to the cell
Escape (or Esc)	Abandons changes made on the input line and retains the original cell entry

(2) Press the Edit (F2) key. The input line will then read

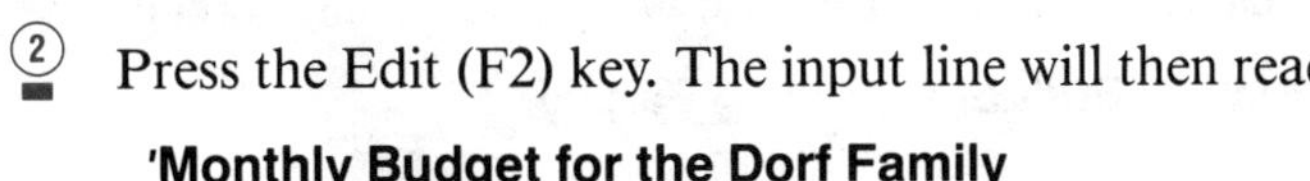

'Monthly Budget for the Dorf Family_

where _ denotes the cursor's position. (If you have the mouse driver installed, you'll see that **[Enter][Esc]** precedes the label. These words will appear whenever you enter something into a cell or edit a cell's contents—and, again, only if you are using a mouse with Quattro Pro.)

(3) Press ← 11 times to move the cursor to the *D* in Dorf, like so:

'Monthly Budget for the Dorf Family

4. Hit Insert to switch from Insert to Overwrite mode. The Overwrite indicator (**OVR**) will appear on the status line, meaning that whatever you type now will replace the characters ahead of the cursor.

5. Type **Smit** and you will notice that the *S, m, i,* and *t* replaced the *D, o, r,* and *f*:

   'Monthly Budget for the Smit_Family

6. If you insert the *h* in *Smith* now, you'll overwrite the blank space and end up with **SmithFamily**. To avoid this run-on, first return to the Insert mode by pressing Insert again. The Overwrite indicator will disappear.

7. Now type **h**. Note that the blank space and the word *Family* shifted to the right, making room for the new letter:

   'Monthly Budget for the Smith_Family

8. Hit Enter to complete the change.

After you press Enter, the modified label will return to cell A1.

Now let's practice deleting some text from a cell entry. With the cell selector still on cell A1, follow these steps:

1. Press F2 to bring the cell entry back to the input line.

2. Press ← 12 times to put the cursor under the *S* in *Smith:*

   'Monthly Budget for the Smith Family

3. Hit Delete five times to erase *Smith,* so the label reads:

   'Monthly Budget for the _Family

4. Make sure that you are in the Insert mode.

5. Type **Dorf** so the label reads:

   'Monthly Budget for the Dorf_Family

6. Press Enter. The original label will be back in cell A1.

Of course, you're not limited to editing labels; you can edit any kind of entry you like.

Editing Dates: A Special Case

Cells that contain dates entered with the Ctrl–D key combination require a slightly different technique for editing. For example, in the previous chapter you entered a date into cell F1. If you move the cell selector to cell F1 and press the Edit key, the serial date will appear on the input line. Unless you happen to know the serial number for the new date you wish to place in the cell, this method won't do you much good. Press Escape to cancel the edit.

To enter a new date, it is easier to follow the same procedure you used to enter the date in the first place. Move the cell selector to the cell containing the date, press Ctrl–D, and enter the new date in *mm/dd/yy* format. Then press Enter or an arrow key.

The Automatic Edit Mode

Whenever you enter an incorrectly syntaxed number, formula, function, etc., into a cell, Quattro Pro will beep and display an error message. After you hit Escape, it will automatically put you in the Edit mode. At this point, you can use all the keys listed in Table 3.1 to make corrections.

You saw an example of this when you attempted to enter the label *123 Oak Tree Lane* in Chapter 2. Quattro Pro rejected the entry because you put letters in a number—and so it thought you were entering an invalid cell or block address. (You weren't, but it thought you were.) You corrected the entry by pressing Home to move the cursor to the beginning of the label, typing an apostrophe to identify the entry as a label, and then hitting Enter.

Changing a Column Width

By default, Quattro Pro sets the width of all columns in the spreadsheet to nine spaces. But you can easily change that width. Recall from Chapter 2 that if you enter a number that is too long to fit into a cell, Quattro Pro will display it in scientific notation, such as **1.23E+08** for 123,000,000. Widening the column will allow the software to display the number in the more familiar format.

To widen or narrow a single column, first move the cell selector to the column you wish to change. Then select the Column Width option from the Style menu. In the following steps, we'll change the width of column D to demonstrate how this works:

1. Move the cell selector to cell D5.
2. Type /**SC** to access the Column Width option from the Style menu. The screen will display the prompt:

   Alter the width of the current column [1..254]: 9

   where 1..254 is the range of acceptable widths and 9 is the current width.

At this point, you can press ← and → to experiment with various widths. Each time you press ←, the column will narrow one space. Each time you press →, the column will widen one space. Alternatively, you can choose a number to indicate the width of the column. For now, type **4** and press Enter.

As you can see in Figure 3.2, column D is just wide enough to accommodate the July heading.

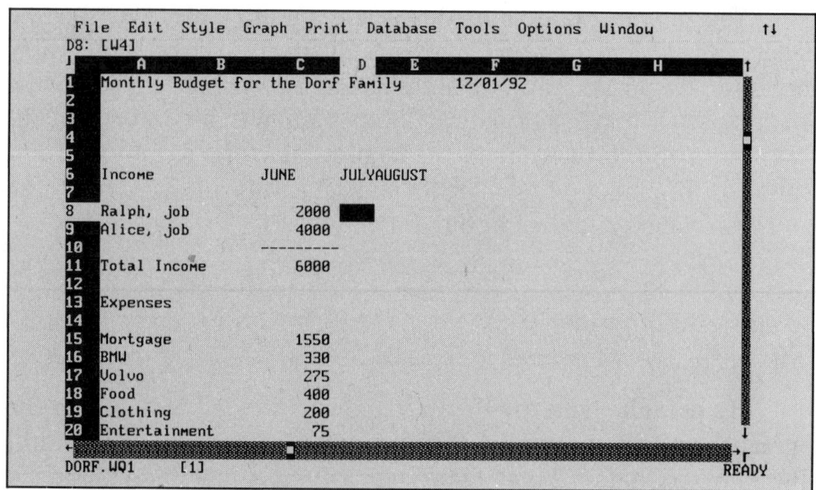

Figure 3.2: Column D narrowed to four spaces

Reinstating a Column Width

If you change your mind about a column width and wish to revert to the default width of nine spaces, move the cell selector to the appropriate column and type **/SR** to select the Reset option from the Style menu. (You do not have to hit Enter; the column will be reset before you know it.)

Changing All Column Widths

If you prefer to adjust the widths of all columns in the spreadsheet simultaneously, select the Global Width option, rather than the Column Width option, from the Style menu. For example, to set all the columns in your spreadsheet to a width of 15 spaces, follow these steps:

1. Type **/OFG** to access the Global Width option on the Formats submenu under the Options menu.
2. Type **15**.
3. Hit Enter.
4. Hit Escape twice.

To reset the columns to their width of nine spaces, type **/OFG9**, hit Enter once, and Escape twice. (Because you widened the columns globally, typing /SR will not work.)

Inserting a Row

Suppose you wish to add some new categories to the Expenses portion of the spreadsheet. To do so, you first need to add some blank rows to the spreadsheet to accommodate the new information. The Edit-menu option called Insert will allow you to do this. Let's try this by inserting a few rows beneath the row labeled *Phone* (row 21) in the current spreadsheet:

1. Move the cell selector to the row above which you wish to place a new row. In this case, move it to position A22.

2. Type **/EI** to select the Insert option under the Edit menu. The screen will display your options in a box (with **Rows** highlighted) and, on the status line:

   Insert row(s) above the current row

3. Press Enter. The input line at the top now reads:

   Enter row insert block: A22..A22

4. Press ↓ twice to "stretch" the cell selector to cell A24. The input line now reads

   Enter row insert block: A22..A24

   indicating that new rows A22, A23, and A24 will be inserted.

5. Hit Enter to complete the job.

Three new rows will appear beneath row 21, as shown in Figure 3.3. (You may have to scroll down a few rows to see them.)

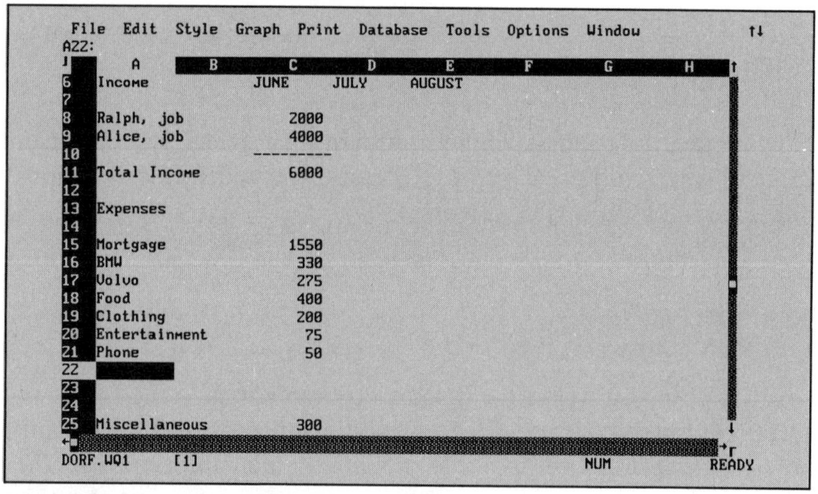

```
File  Edit  Style  Graph  Print  Database  Tools  Options  Window      ↑↓
A22:
     A            B         C         D         E        F        G        H
6  Income                 JUNE      JULY     AUGUST
7
8  Ralph, job             2000
9  Alice, job             4000
10                     ---------
11 Total Income           6000
12
13 Expenses
14
15 Mortgage               1550
16 BMW                     330
17 Volvo                   275
18 Food                    400
19 Clothing                200
20 Entertainment            75
21 Phone                    50
22
23
24
25 Miscellaneous           300
DORF.WQ1     [1]                                          NUM        READY
```

Figure 3.3: Three new rows entered in DORF

Inserting a Column

The technique for inserting new columns is identical to that for inserting new rows, except that you use the Column Insert command.

To demonstrate, we'll insert a new column between **JUNE** and **JULY** on the current spreadsheet:

1. Move the cell selector to column D. (In this example, move the cell selector specifically to cell D6, so you will be able to see the results better.)
2. Type **/EIC** to get at the Columns option on the Insert submenu under the edit menu. The input line will display the following prompt:

   Enter column insert block: D6..D6

3. To insert a single column at the current position, just hit Enter. (To insert several new columns, keep pressing the → or ← key to extend the cell selector to as many columns as you want before pressing Enter.)

The new column is inserted to the left of the previously highlighted column as shown in Figure 3.4.

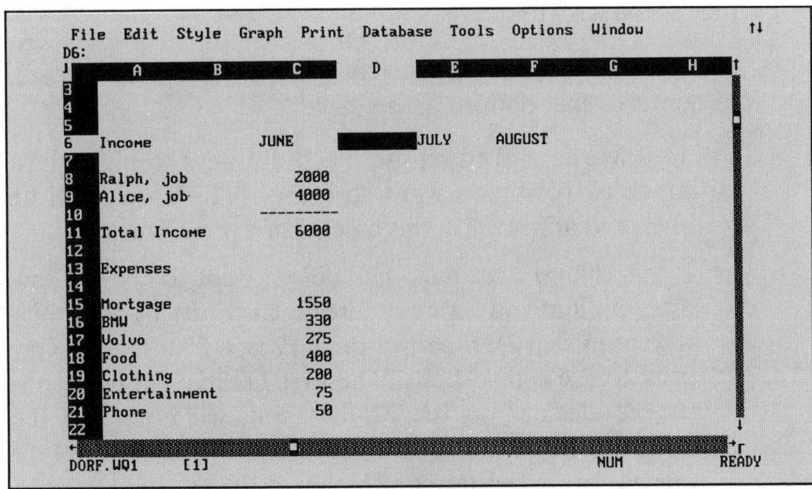

Figure 3.4: A column inserted between **JUNE** and **JULY**

Deleting a Row

Before you delete a row from a spreadsheet, remember that you will dump the *entire* row, from column A to column IV. Afterwards, all rows beneath will move up to replace the deleted one. (To erase only the *contents* of a row, or a portion thereof, you can use the Erase Block option under the Edit menu, which is discussed later in this chapter.)

To delete a row, then, position the cell selector at the row you wish to delete (or the top-most row if you wish to delete several) and select the Delete option under the Edit menu. Remove row 22:

1. Move the cell selector to any cell in row 22.
2. Type /**ED** to get at the Delete option under the Edit menu. The screen will display your options in a box (with **Rows** highlighted) and, on the status line:

   Delete all rows in the selected block
3. Press Enter. The input line will ask you to enter the block of rows you wish to delete.
4. Press Enter to delete the current row only (for this exercise). There are other options at this stage:
   - To delete several rows, use the ↑ or ↓ keys to highlight a block of rows you want to erase. (The block will be anchored at row 22 in this case.) Then press Enter.
   - If you change your mind and do not want to delete a row after all, and you have not already hit Enter by this point (except in step 3), then just press Escape four times to get back to the spreadsheet. (The first Escape will unanchor the cell selector from row 22; the second will bring back the box with **Rows** highlighted; the third will reveal the Edit menu with the Delete option highlighted; and the fourth will bring back the spreadsheet.)

Deleting a Column

When you erase a column from a spreadsheet, beware that you will trash the *entire* column, from row 1 to row 8192. Afterwards, all columns to the right will shift left to replace the deleted one. (To erase only the *contents* of a column, or a portion thereof, use the Erase Block option, discussed next.)

Go ahead and delete the new column D that you just inserted:

1. Move the cell selector to any cell in column D (though preferably to cell D6 in this example, so that you can best see the results).
2. Type /**ED**.
3. From the Delete box, select **Columns**. Hit Enter.
4. To delete the current column only (i.e., column D), just press Enter. To delete several columns, use the → or ← keys to highlight a block of columns you want to erase. Then hit Enter. To cancel and back out to the spreadsheet, press Escape four times.

Erasing a Block of Data

As we mentioned above, deleting an entire row or column affects a very large portion of the spreadsheet—well beyond what you see on the screen. To limit the erasure to a particular block of cells, use the Erase Block option under the Edit menu.

Erasing portions of a spreadsheet used to be hazardous work—you might have accidentally erased the wrong block and been stuck. Fortunately, Quattro Pro has a built-in safeguard against just that problem, called Undo. When you take any action that changes the spreadsheet, and find that it was not as you intended, you can press Alt-F5 to "undo" the previous action. It's like pretending the error never happened. In the following example, you will erase a block and then invoke Undo to return the spreadsheet to its prior state.

Enabling Undo

Before erasing anything, make sure that the Undo option is enabled—i.e., set to work.

1. Type **/OO** to call up the Other submenu under the Options menu.
2. From this submenu,you should check to see whether Undo is set to Enable or Disable.
   - If it is disabled, press Enter when Undo is highlighted. A box will open. Enable should already be highlighted, so just press Enter. Then hit Escape to close the menu and bring you back to the spreadsheet.
   - If it is enabled, just hit Escape twice to back you out of the Options menu and into the spreadsheet.

Erasing the Block

Now you can use the /EE feature—i.e., the Erase Block option under the Edit menu—with impunity. The first step is to move the cell selector to the upper-left corner of the block you want to erase. Then start selecting menu options. For this exercise, erase the labels and expenses from rows 15 through 21.

1. Move the cell selector to position A15.
2. Type **/EE**. At this point the input line will read:

   Block to be modified: A15..A15

   Quattro Pro is "suggesting" the currently highlighted block, A15..A15 (which is actually just cell A15). You can use the arrow keys to stretch the cell selector over other cells and expand the area you want to erase.
3. Press → twice to extend the cell selector to cell C15.

4 Press ↓ six times to extend the cell selector down to row 21. (Or else hold ↓ down while the selector highlights the rows automatically.) At this point, the entire block of cells from A15 to C21 is highlighted and the prompt reads

Block to be modified: A15..C21

as shown in Figure 3.5.

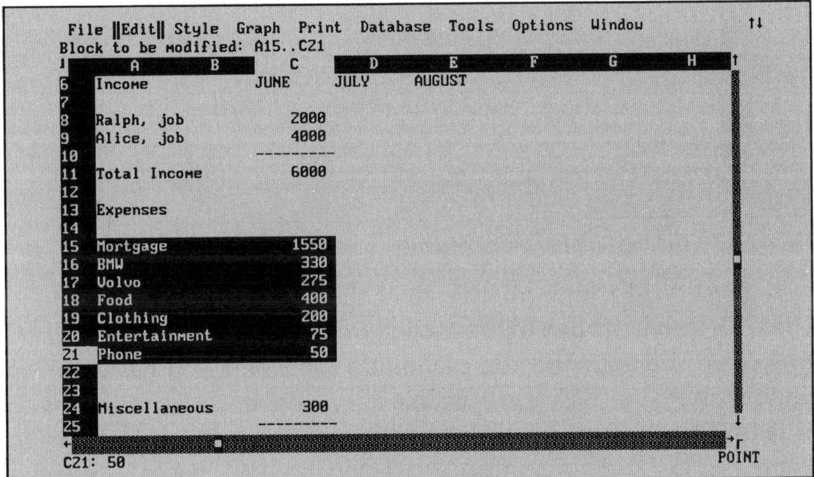

Figure 3.5: Block of highlighted cells to be erased

5 Hit Enter after you have finished highlighting.

As soon as you press Enter, the area that was highlighted will be completely erased, as shown in Figure 3.6.

Recovering from Disaster with Undo

But wait a minute. Suppose you change your mind and realize that you didn't want to change this large block of cells after all. No need to worry: Quattro Pro knows what you did, and can reverse the action with Undo.

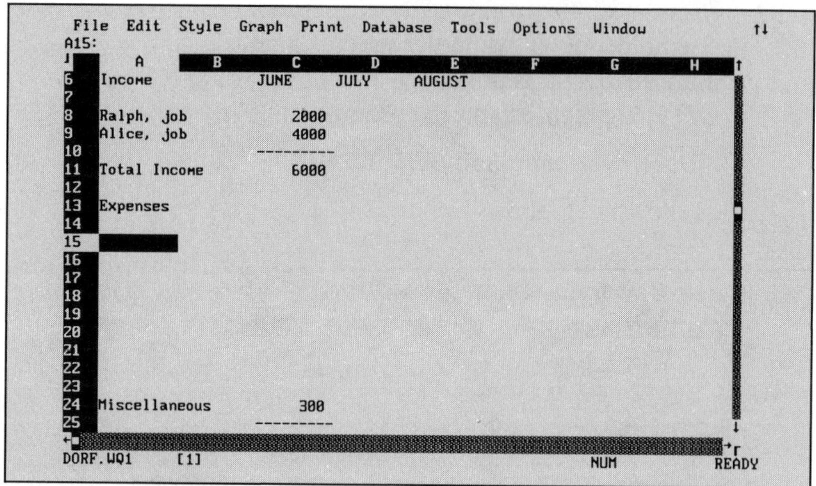

Figure 3.6: The highlighted block erased

Press Alt–F5. Immediately, all of the cells are restored as before. Undo is a wonderful tool for recovering from a mistake—whether a deletion or an addition. You can even undo something you have already undone! But you must either enable it when you start a session with Quattro Pro or change the default setting. You can do this by selecting Update from the Options menu after Undo has been enabled. Resetting the Update will make Quattro Pro enable Undo whenever the program is started.

A note of caution: Undo only works on your most recently issued command. So if you erase a block of cells and then delete a row, pressing Alt–F5 will only return the deleted row. When you make a mistake, undo it *immediately!*

Erasing the Entire Spreadsheet

If at any time you want to erase the spreadsheet screen completely and start with a "clean slate," just access the Erase option from the File menu. Quattro Pro will double-check your intentions by presenting the prompt:

Lose your changes?
No
Yes

Select Yes if you don't mind losing the spreadsheet that is on the screen at the moment (and that extends beyond it as well); select No if you do.

As with Erase Block and all Quattro operations, the Erase option only affects the copy of the spreadsheet that is currently in memory. It has no effect on the most recently saved disk copy. Therefore, if you've recently saved your spreadsheet and then accidentally erased the entire thing, you can still get your work back by typing **/FR**, for File menu and Retrieve option. If Undo is enabled, you can also reverse the accidental erasure by pressing Alt-F5, provided that you have not done anything else in the meantime.

The Importance of Saving Your Work

In this chapter you've seen some general techniques for changing, adding to, and deleting segments of your spreadsheet. You've also learned that enabling the Undo option is crucial if you wish to restore accidental erasures.

Undo is helpful, but even it cannot save your work during the past hour (or more) if there is a sudden power failure—in which case you will certainly lose all your work since the last time you saved the spreadsheet. To avoid such a catastrophe, then, save your work often. This ensures that you won't lose more than 15–20 minutes' worth of your work, or whatever time interval you choose.

Before leaving this chapter, be sure to save the spreadsheet. Type **/FS**, as before, to select the Save option under the File menu. Quattro Pro will come to the realization that (a) you want to save your file as DORF, and (b) there is already a file on disk with the same name. So it will display a box with these words:

File already exists:
  Cancel
  Replace
  Backup

What are these options about?

- **Cancel** closes the box and sends you back to the spreadsheet, as though you had never asked to erase anything.

- **Replace** saves your spreadsheet as DORF and, in so doing, throws away the old version.
- **Backup** saves your spreadsheet as DORF, but also keeps the old version. It manages this by changing the extension of the old file from .WQ1 to .BAK. Now you'll have two files on disk, DORF.WQ1, the most recent version of the Dorfs' family budget, and DORF.BAK, the version of the spreadsheet before you made the changes that are now in DORF.WQ1.

Making backups of your spreadsheets is always a good idea. It ensures against losing vital information that perhaps you once thought was not important. However, you have not really created any vitally important documents now, so just choose Replace to save your modified DORF spreadsheet.

In the next chapter, you'll learn some more advanced techniques for copying and moving blocks of data on the spreadsheet, and get a little more practice with formulas as well.

4

COPYING AND MOVING BLOCKS OF DATA

The Pointing Method
Copying Information
Moving Information
Relative and Absolute Cell References

Simplifying Your Work with the Pointing Method

As you know from Chapter 2, you can place cell addresses and block references (such as A1..C5) in functions. But *pointing* allows you to do that by highlighting a cell or block, rather than typing the address itself. You have already been exposed to the pointing technique when, in the previous chapter, you "stretched" the cell selector to highlight a group of cells for erasing.

You can use this same pointing technique to create functions and copy and move information easily. Because it is so visually oriented, you don't have to waste time looking up the address of a cell or block and then keying it in—and erasing typos. With pointing, you enter the address as you look it up.

Creating a Function with the Pointing Method

Recall that in Chapter 2 you entered the useful function @SUM(C15..C22) to sum the expenses on the spreadsheet. You entered this function simply by typing it in. And if you were lucky you didn't have to retype it. But look at the other way you can create this function.

Move the cell selector to C26, where the function is located, and erase it. The cell should be empty now. To reenter the function:

1. Move the cell selector to C26, if it is not already there.
2. Type the beginning of the function:

   @SUM(

   Capital letters are not important, so **@sum(** would work as well. (Quattro Pro just converts the letters to uppercase later on anyway.) It is more important to include the open parenthesis.
3. Begin the Point mode by pressing ↑. Notice that the function on the input line reads **@SUM(C25** and the mode indicator in the lower-right corner reads **POINT**. You are in Point mode, and now you'll see how to stretch the cell selector over the cells you wish to include in the function.
4. Press ↑ ten times to move the cell selector to cell C15, or hold it down until the selector moves to C15 by itself.
5. Now you want to "anchor" the cell selector to this cell before stretching it over the numbers you want to sum. To do this, press the period (.) key. The function on the input line now reads **@SUM(C15..C15)**.
6. To stretch the cell selector, press ↓ nine times. Each time you press ↓, the cell selector will stretch downward another row until all the numbers are highlighted, as in Figure 4.1.
7. Complete the function by typing the closed parenthesis. The function on the input line now reads **@SUM(C15..C24)**. Notice that the cell selector jumps back to its original location, cell C26.
8. Press Enter to complete the function.

The sum of the expenses, 3180, now appears in cell C26. You can see the actual function, @SUM(C15..C24), on the input line, as shown in Figure 4.2.

After learning a few rules about pointing, you can employ some fancy tricks. Both are discussed in the rest of the chapter.

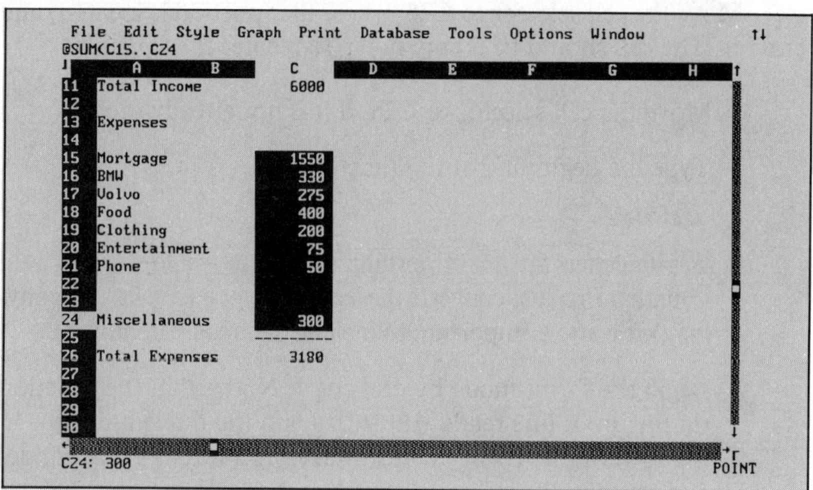

Figure 4.1: The cell selector highlighting the numbers being summed

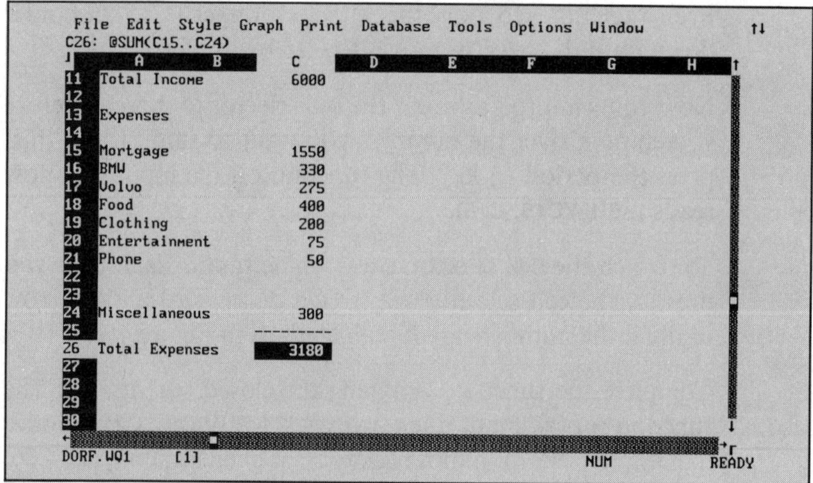

Figure 4.2: An @SUM function in cell C26

Entering the Point Mode

Pointing works only while you are entering or editing a function or formula, or when you are entering certain commands that operate on blocks. (You'll see examples of the latter in a moment.) If you are entering a function, you can begin pointing immediately after you've typed the open parenthesis that follows the function name, or the comma that separates the arguments. If you are entering a formula, you can begin pointing immediately after you've typed one of the arithmetic operators (+, −, *, or /).

To point, simply press the appropriate arrow key to start moving the cell selector. The mode indicator at the right end of the status line will read **POINT** and the input line will show the address of the cell at which you're pointing.

If you are entering a simple formula, just type whatever the next operator is and then move the selector to the next cell you want to include in the formula. Your pointing will enter the cell addresses in the formula automatically; all you have to do is type the necessary math symbols and nesting parentheses to make the formula complete. (When you're done, hit Enter to view the result.)

If you are entering a block of cells into a function's argument instead, you'll first need to tell Quattro Pro where the block begins and ends.

Anchoring the Cell Selector

When the cell selector gets to the upper-left corner of the block you wish to highlight, anchor it by pressing the period key. The input line will show a block address rather than a cell address.

Stretching the Cell Selector

Once you have anchored the cell selector, press the arrow keys, End, Home, Page Up, Page Down, Tab, Shift-Tab, Ctrl-→, or Ctrl-← in the usual manner to stretch the cell selector.

Unanchoring the Cell Selector

Now suppose that things get a little out of hand while you are pointing and you want to start again. As usual, Escape will get you out of a jam—this time by immediately "unanchoring" the cell selector so that you can move it to a new starting position. As soon as the cell selector is no longer anchored, the input line will show a cell address rather than a block address.

Alternatively, you can hit the Backspace key to unanchor the cell selector. This will send the cell selector back to its original location.

Moving the Free Cell

Whenever the cell selector is anchored and you are stretching it to highlight an area of the spreadsheet, you'll notice that one corner contains a small blinking cursor. This corner is called the *free cell* and is the corner that moves as you press the arrow keys.

In some cases, you may prefer to stretch the cell selector from a different corner. To do so, just press the period key. Each time you do this, the free cell will jump to the next corner in the block, allowing you to stretch the cell selector from any corner.

Exiting the Point Mode

When you're through stretching the cell selector over the block of cells you wish to include in your function, just continue typing in the other arguments. (If you are not entering a function but are instead using a menu command, just press Enter to complete your pointing.) The cell selector will shrink back to its normal shape, highlighting just a cell, and the address of the block you highlighted will appear on the input line.

You'll have a chance to practice some of these techniques in the examples that follow.

Copying Information from One Cell to Several

Up to this point, the spreadsheet has contained information just for the month of June. Now it needs data for July and August as well. To speed things along, we'll show you how to copy entries rather than type them in again.

Copying data, such as numbers, labels, and dates, is a relatively straightforward operation. Position the cell selector on the cell(s) you wish to copy, or on the upper-left corner of the block of cells you're copying. Access the Copy option from the Edit menu. Specify the *source cell(s),* the one(s) you want to copy from, and the *destination cell(s),* the one(s) to copy to. Press Enter. The following example demonstrates this procedure.

Suppose you want to copy Ralph's income from cell C8 to D8 and E8:

1. Move the cell selector to cell C8. The number 2000 will be highlighted.
2. Type **/EC** to access the Copy option from the Edit menu.
3. The input line reads:

   Source block of cells: C8..C8

   Quattro Pro is suggesting the current block, C8..C8 (actually just cell C8).
4. Press Enter to accept the suggested block. Now the input line reads:

   Destination for cells: C8

   In this example, you want to copy Ralph's income to cells D8 and E8.
5. Press → to move the cell selector to cell D8. The input line now reads:

   Destination for cells: D8
6. Press the period key to anchor the cell selector to cell D8. The input line reads:

   Destination for cells: D8..D8

   You know the cell selector is anchored now because this prompt is showing a block address (D8..D8) rather than a cell address (D8).
7. Press → to stretch the cell selector over to cell E8. The line now reads

   Destination for cells: D8..E8

   and the cell selector is highlighting cells D8..E8, as shown in Figure 4.3.

8. Press Enter to complete the copy.

Immediately, the contents of the source block (cell C8) are copied to the cells in the destination block (D8..E8), as shown in Figure 4.4.

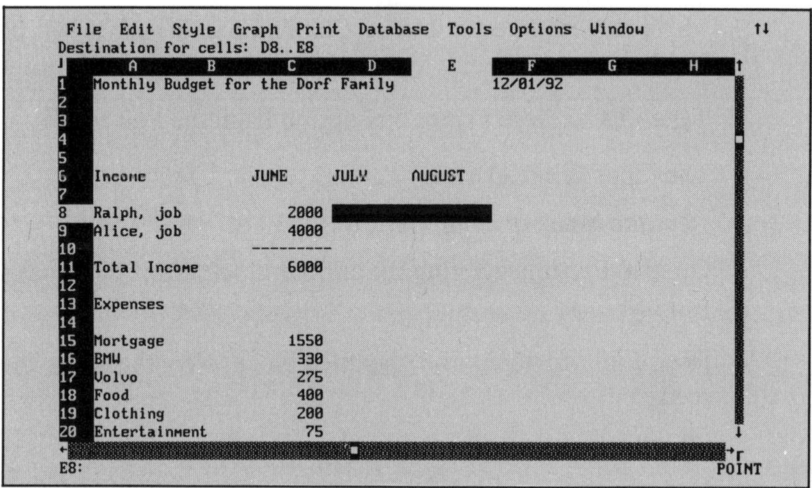

Figure 4.3: Cell selector highlighting block D8..E8

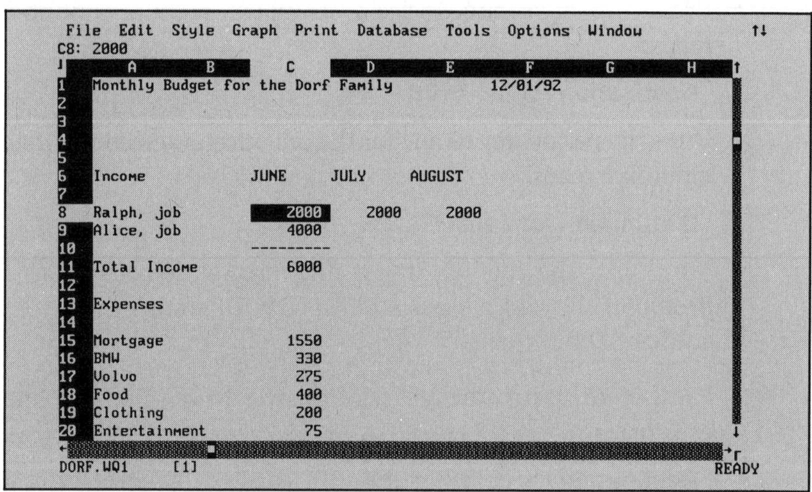

Figure 4.4: Cell C8 copied to cells D8 and E8

Copying Blocks of Information

In the last example, you copied a single cell's contents to two other cells. You can also copy the contents of several cells at once.

Suppose that the monthly expenses in cells C15 through C24 are fairly constant, so you wish just to copy June's expenses to the July and August columns:

1. Move the cell selector to cell C15.
2. Type /**EC** as before. The prompt on the input line reads:

   Source block of cells: C15..C15

   As before, the cell selector is already anchored. You can tell this because a block address (C15..C15) rather than a cell address (C15) is displayed in the prompt.
3. Press the End key and then ↓ to stretch the cell selector quickly over all the filled cells below. Then press ↓ five times to stretch the cell selector down to the total in cell C26, as shown in Figure 4.5. Note the prompt:

   Source block of cells: C15..C26

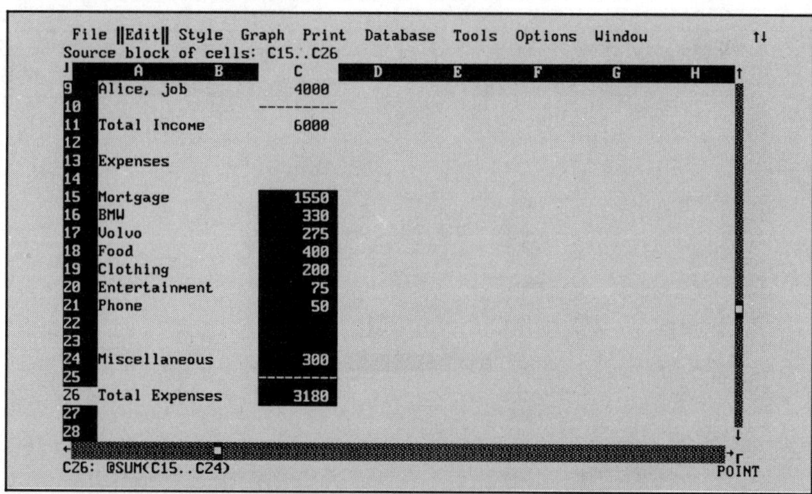

Figure 4.5: The block of cells C15..C26 highlighted

4. Press Enter and Quattro Pro will ask you on the input line where you want to copy these cells:

   Destination for cells: C15

5. Press → to move the cell selector to cell D15. The prompt reads:

   Destination for cells: D15

6. Anchor the cell selector by pressing the period key. The prompt now reads:

   Destination for cells: D15..D15

7. Press → to stretch the cell selector over to cell E15. The prompt now reads

   Destination for cells: D15..E15

   and the cell selector is stretched across columns D and E, as shown in Figure 4.6. At this point, you could press ↓ 11 times to highlight the entire destination block, D15..E26—but that is not necessary. The next step will do it for you.

8. Press Enter to complete the copy operation.

Your screen should now match Figure 4.7.

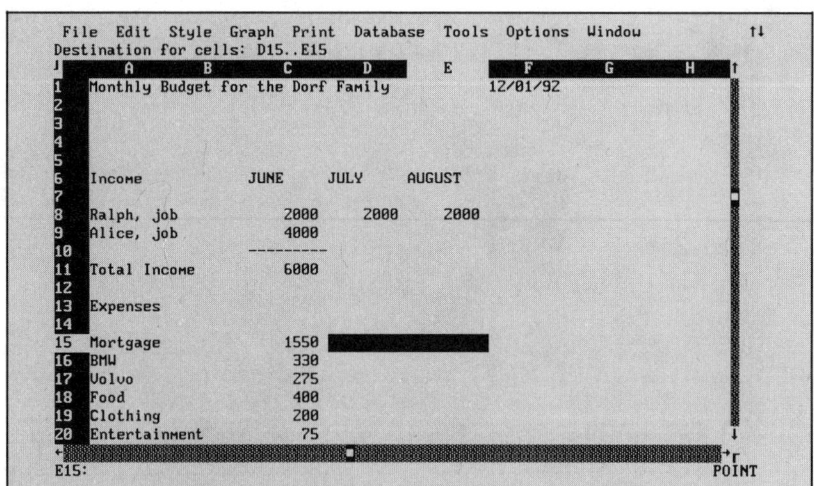

```
 File  Edit  Style  Graph  Print  Database  Tools  Options  Window
Destination for cells: D15..E15
      A          B          C          D          E          F          G          H
1  Monthly Budget for the Dorf Family                       12/01/92
2
3
4
5
6  Income                  JUNE      JULY      AUGUST
7
8  Ralph, job               2000      2000      2000
9  Alice, job               4000
10                       ---------
11 Total Income             6000
12
13 Expenses
14
15 Mortgage                 1550
16 BMW                       330
17 Volvo                     275
18 Food                      400
19 Clothing                  200
20 Entertainment              75
E15:                                                                     POINT
```

Figure 4.6: The block D15..E15 highlighted

```
 File  Edit  Style  Graph  Print  Database  Tools  Options  Window          ↑↓
E26: @SUM(E15..E24)
      A        B         C          D          E          F        G        H
9  Alice, job           4000
10                    --------
11 Total Income         6000
12
13 Expenses
14
15 Mortgage             1550       1550       1550
16 BMW                   330        330        330
17 Volvo                 275        275        275
18 Food                  400        400        400
19 Clothing              200        200        200
20 Entertainment          75         75         75
21 Phone                  50         50         50
22
23
24 Miscellaneous         300        300        300
25                  ------------------------------
26 Total Expenses       3180       3180       3180
27
28
DORF.WQ1     [1]                                              NUM        READY
```

Figure 4.7: The Expenses section copied to July and August

Notice that Quattro Pro was rather clever about copying the expenses. Even though you did not specify the entire destination block D15..E26, Quattro Pro performed the copy flawlessly. Quattro Pro always copies the entire source block, even if the destination block you specify contains fewer cells than the source block. For example, if you highlighted a large block as the source, but highlighted only a *single* cell as the destination, Quattro Pro would still copy the entire source block. (The single cell at the destination would just become the upper-left corner of the copied block.)

This may sound a little confusing at first, but you'll find that with a little practice the procedure becomes intuitive. Let's move on to some more topics concerning copying.

A Shortcut for Copying

In the examples above we have always instructed you to open the Edit menu and select the Copy option in order to copy a cell or block. There is nothing wrong with choosing this route to perform a copy. But there is a shortcut you may prefer to know about.

The next time you want to copy something—say, cell A1—to another part of the spreadsheet, move the cell selector to that cell and simply press Ctrl–C. Quattro Pro will respond with the same message on the input line as the one it gave you after you entered /EC in the previous examples: **Source block of cells: A1..A1**. From here you can proceed with your copying as before.

A Slight Diversion

Alice's income is expected to increase by 10 percent in August, so you can't just copy her income from column C. Instead, you can calculate her August income with a formula.

To begin with, move the cell selector to cell D9 and enter July's income—4000. (We could have copied 4000 from cell C9, but in this example it is probably easier to type **4000**.) Now to calculate August's income, you need to increase July's income by 10 percent.

To increase a value by a percent, multiply the value by one plus the percentage. For example, Alice's new income will equal 1.10 times her July income. So enter the appropriate formula:

1. Move the cell selector to cell E9.
2. Type the formula **+D9*1.10**.
3. Press Enter to complete the formula.

The result, 4400, appears in cell E9.

It is a simple matter to calculate the 10 percent increase without using the spreadsheet; however, this example serves to illustrate the use of a formula that refers to another cell.

Now, let's get you back to the main topic of this chapter—copying.

Copying a Formula

The menu selections and the steps for copying formulas are the same as those for copying data. Quattro Pro treats formulas a little differently, however, in that it attempts to retain their meaning as it copies them. (You actually got a hint of this in the previous example, but let's deal with this topic independently here.)

Suppose you want to copy the summing formula in cell C11 to cells D11 and E11. Here are the steps to do so:

1. Move the cell selector to cell C11.
2. Type **/EC** to access the Copy option from the Edit submenu. (Or else just press Ctrl–C.)
3. Press Enter to specify C11..C11 as the source for the copy.
4. Press → to move the cell selector to cell D11.
5. Press period (.) to anchor the cell selector.
6. Press → again to stretch the cell selector to cell E11. At this point, the highlighter is stretched across cells D11 and E11, and the input-line prompt reads:

   Destination for cells: D11..E11

7. Press Enter to complete the copy.

See that 6000 appears in cell D11, but 6400 in E11. You may have thought that Quattro Pro would simply copy the formula +C8+C9 to each of these cells. But this is not exactly the case. If you move the cell selector to E11, you will see on the input line that it actually contains the formula +E8+E9! So the copied formula was adjusted to apply to column E, which contains Ralph's income and Alice's recently increased income. If you move the cell selector to cell D11, you'll see that cell D11 has also been adjusted. It contains the formula +D8+D9. Figure 4.8 shows the "logic" Quattro Pro used to copy the formulas.

(To copy cell C10 to cells D10 and E10—i.e., extend the underline through column E—follow the exact procedure described above, good for replicating a cell any number of times.)

In other words, Quattro Pro did not copy the formulas *exactly*. Instead, it made sure that the copied formulas would retain their original meaning in a different context, which in this example was to "display the sum of the numbers in the two rows above." This copying

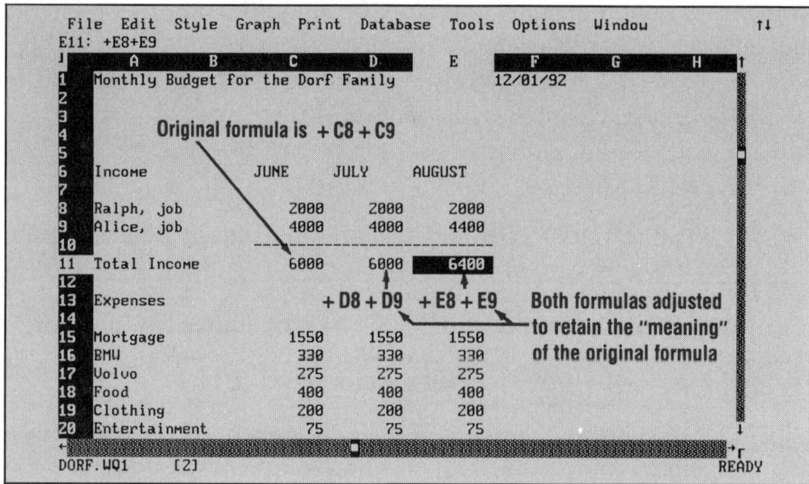

Figure 4.8: *Quattro Pro's adjustment of the formulas as it copied them*

feature is handy because a spreadsheet often contains several copies of a given formula.

The formula you just copied may have been simple, and the cells it worked on easy to find, but this feature of retaining a formula's "meaning" applies even to complicated formulas nested in a complex spreadsheet.

Understanding Relative and Absolute Cell References

In the previous example, you saw how Quattro Pro adjusted the cell addresses inside a formula as it copied the formula to two cells. In some cases, however, you will not want Quattro Pro to adjust such *cell references.* For example, if cell B2 contained a 15 percent discount rate, any formulas that included that discount would have to refer always to cell B2, no matter where they were situated in the spreadsheet.

To prevent Quattro Pro from adjusting such a reference while it is copying a formula, you must change it from a *relative* to an *absolute* reference. You've seen what a relative reference is: it refers not to one specific cell's address, but to a cell that is located *relative* to the formula's position. In the previous section's example, the formula you copied summed "the two numbers above"—i.e., 2000+4000 in July's column and 2000+4400 in August's column.

But an absolute reference—indicated by a dollar sign ($) in front—always refers to a *specific* cell's address, no matter where the formula is located.

Imagine you have the formula +B2*C3 in cell C2. As written, it multiplies two numbers together—the number in the cell to the left of the formula by the number in the cell underneath. That is what the formula really means. But these references are relative, so if you relocate the formula to cell K25, Quattro Pro will have to rewrite it as +J25*K26 to keep its original "meaning" intact.

Now, if you make the references absolute—so the formula reads +$B$2*$C$3—the formula will take on a different, more specific meaning altogether: "multiply the number in cell B2 by the number in C3." No matter where this formula is actually situated, it will always generate the same answer (unless, of course, you change the numbers in cells B2 or C3).

Creating Absolute References

There are two ways to put a dollar sign in a cell reference to make it absolute. One is simply to type it as you enter the formula. The second is to press the Absolute (Abs) key (F4) to change the reference from relative to absolute automatically. This latter method is preferable when you are creating a formula with the pointing method.

Each time you press the F4 key, Quattro Pro will adjust the cell reference. For example, if you begin a formula with a reference such as +C9 on the input line and then press the Abs key, the reference will change to +$C$9. If you press F4 again, the reference will turn to +C$9, in which case column C is relative but row 9 is absolute. Pressing F4 again will change the reference to +$C9, in which case the column is absolute and the row is relative. Pressing F4 one more time will bring the formula back to the fully relative +C9.

In the example above, the Abs key produced two *mixed references* in its cycle: +C$9 and +$C9. In mixed references, one part of the reference is relative and the other is absolute. Hence, if you were to copy the formula +C$9 to a new cell in a different column, the column reference would adjust itself to the new cell's column but the row would still refer to row 9. Alternatively, copying the formula +$C9 to a new cell in a different row would adjust the row but leave the column referring to column C.

Let's test the F4 key. Suppose the Dorf family has an outstanding, interest-free loan from their friends of $1000. They want to see how paying off 25 percent of this loan each month will affect their finances.

First, set up a couple of columns in which to store the loan information:

1. Move the cell selector to cell A22 and enter the label **Loan %**. Then press →.
2. With the cell selector in cell B22, type the label **Loan $**.
3. Move the cell selector to cell A23 and type in the percentage that the Dorfs will pay off each month—**25%**. (It will appear as **0.25** in the cell.) Press →.
4. With the cell selector in cell B23, type in the loan amount—**1000**—and press Enter.

Now you can begin entering the formulas to see what happens if the Dorfs pay off 25 percent of their loan each month:

1. Move the cell selector to cell C23.
2. Type + to start entering a formula.
3. Press ← twice to move the cell selector to cell A23. The formula on the input line now reads **+A23**.
4. To make this cell reference absolute for copying, press the Abs key (F4). The formula now reads **+$A$23**.

5. Type * (for multiplication) to continue entering the formula. The formula now reads **+$A$23*** and the cell selector jumps back to cell C23.

6. Press ← once to move the cell selector to cell B23. The formula now reads **+$A$23*B23**.

7. Press F4 to make *that* reference absolute as well. The formula now reads **+$A$23*$B$23**.

8. Press Enter.

Cell C23 now contains the formua +$A$23*$B$23, and the cell displays **250** (because 25 percent of 1000 is 250).

Now copy this formula into the columns for July and August:

1. With the cell selector still on cell C23, type **/EC** to access the Copy option from the Edit menu. (Or just press Ctrl–C.)

2. Press Enter to accept the suggested source block, C23..C23.

3. Press → to move the cell selector to cell D23.

4. Press period (.) to anchor the cell selector. The prompt now reads:

   Destination for cells D23..D23

5. Press → again to stretch the cell selector over to cell E23, so the prompt reads:

   Destination for cells D23..E23

6. Press Enter to complete the copy.

At this point, your spreadsheet should look like Figure 4.9.

Nothing is ever immutable in a spreadsheet. Suppose the Dorfs decide to pay off only 10 percent of the loan each month. To see what effect this has on their monthly expenses, simply move the cell selector to cell A23. Type in the new percentage figure, **10%**, and press Enter. (The 10% appears as **0.1** in the cell.)

Quattro Pro immediately recalculates the monthly payments on the loan so that each month displays **100**, rather than **250**. Figure 4.10 shows this.

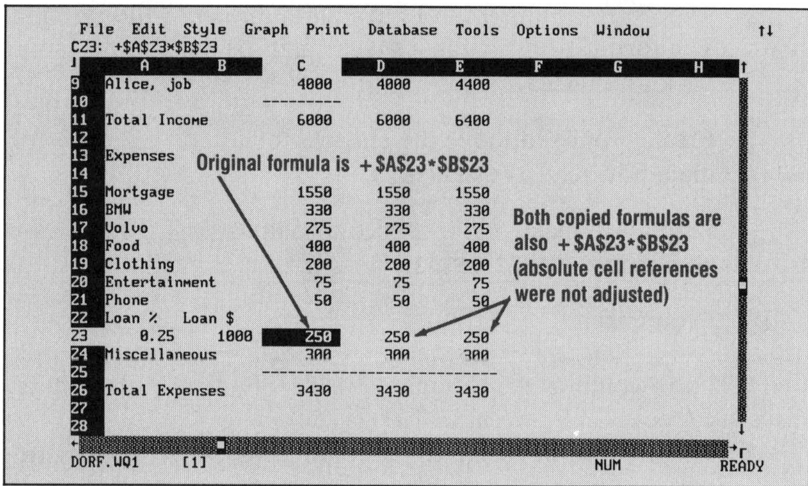

Figure 4.9: *Formulas calculating 25 percent loan payments in row 23*

```
 File  Edit  Style  Graph  Print  Database  Tools  Options  Window
A23: 0.1
      A          B          C          D          E          F          G          H
9   Alice, job             4000       4000       4400
10                     ---------
11  Total Income           6000       6000       6400
12
13  Expenses
14
15  Mortgage               1550       1550       1550
16  BMW                     330        330        330
17  Volvo                   275        275        275
18  Food                    400        400        400
19  Clothing                200        200        200
20  Entertainment            75         75         75
21  Phone                    50         50         50
22  Loan %   Loan $
23       0.1     1000       100        100        100
24  Miscellaneous           300        300        300
25                     ----------------------------
26  Total Expenses         3280       3280       3280
27
28
DORF.WQ1      [1]                                      NUM          READY
```

Figure 4.10: *Loan payments reduced to 10 percent in cell A23*

Changing Existing References

As mentioned in Chapter 3, you can use the Edit key (F2) to change any existing cell entry, including formulas. If you wish to modify a formula by converting one of its references to a relative, absolute, or mixed reference, you can still use the F2 key. This saves you from having to retype the formula.

For example, suppose you want to change the existing absolute reference in the formula in cell C23 to either a mixed or relative reference. That is, get rid of some of the dollar signs in +$A$23*$B$23. It is not hard to do in the Edit mode.

Move the cell selector to cell C23 and press the Edit key (F2). The formula will appear on the input line as such:

+$A$23*$B$23_

where the underline at the end of the formula (_) represents the cursor's position on the input line. Next, to change the way that $A$23 is referenced, move the cursor with the ← key to anywhere in that reference (i.e., under the first $, the A, the second $, the 2, or the 3). Then press the Abs key (F4).

Notice how that part of the formula becomes a mixed reference: A$23. Hit F4 again and it will change to $A23. Hit F4 again and you'll see A23, a fully relative reference. Hit F4 once more and the reference will revert back to $A$23.

Move the cursor to the second half of the formula, $B$23, and hit F4 a few times. The same changes will occur, in a cycle, from absolute (both dollar signs) to mixed (one dollar sign) to relative (no dollar signs). Be sure that the formula returns to the state that you found it in (i.e., with four dollar signs in it) before reading on.

Moving Data

Moving information around a spreadsheet is much like copying, except that you use the Move option, rather than the Copy option, under the Edit menu. Let's give it a whirl.

First press Home to move the cell selector up to cell A1. You'll notice that there are several blank rows near the top of the spreadsheet, as shown in Figure 4.11.

To move the data beneath the blank rows upwards, you could either delete rows 3, 4, and 5 (using the Edit menu's Delete option described in Chapter 3) or else move all the information below row 6

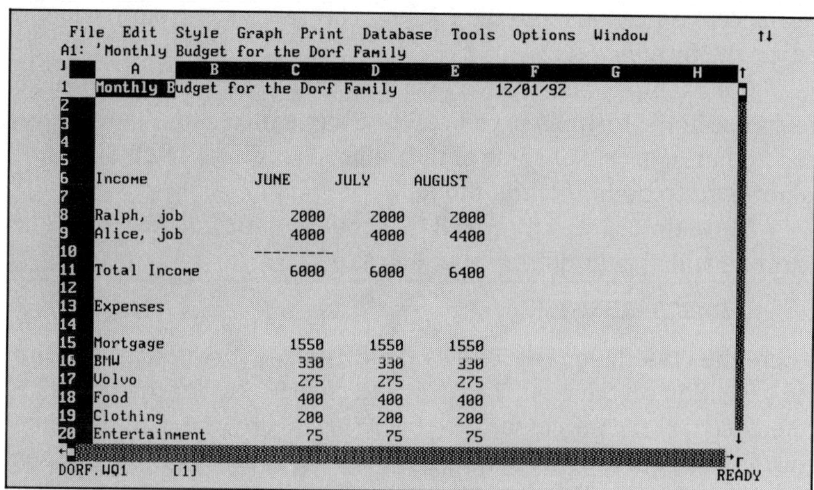

Figure 4.11: The spreadsheet with a few blank rows

up a few rows. Let's try the latter method:

1. Position the cell selector in the upper-left corner of the block being moved (cell A6 in this example).

2. Type **/EM** to access the Move option in the Edit menu. The input line displays the prompt:

   Source block of cells: A6..A6

3. Press → four times to stretch the cell selector over to cell E6. The prompt now reads:

   Source block of cells: A6..E6

4. Press the Page Down key to stretch the cell selector downward 20 rows. The prompt now reads:

   Source block of cells: A6..E26

5. Press Enter. The prompt now reads:

   Destination for cells: A6

6. Press ↑ to move the cell selector up to A3, the future address of the upper-left corner of the block being moved. The prompt

now reads:

Destination for cells: A3

7. Hit Enter to complete the move.

You've just moved a significant block of cells! If you ever have the sudden realization that you moved a block to a wrong part of the spreadsheet, do not panic. As with all commands, this one can be undone with Undo (Alt–F5). Try it with the block you've just moved. Provided that the Undo option was already set to Enable, and you didn't do anything else since the move, you'll see the block jump back to its original position. Press Alt–F5 again and see your undone move undone! Keep pressing Alt–F5 to see the block jump back and forth between the two positions. Be sure to put the block in its new location (starting at row 3) before reading on.

As Figure 4.12 shows, the entire highlighted block moved up and closed the gap beneath the spreadsheet title in cell A1. If you scroll around the spreadsheet and look at the calculations, you'll see that all formulas still display correct results. That is because the Move command always adjusts formulas, even those with absolute references, to their new location. With Move, you can rely on Quattro Pro to adjust all formulas within the moved block automatically.

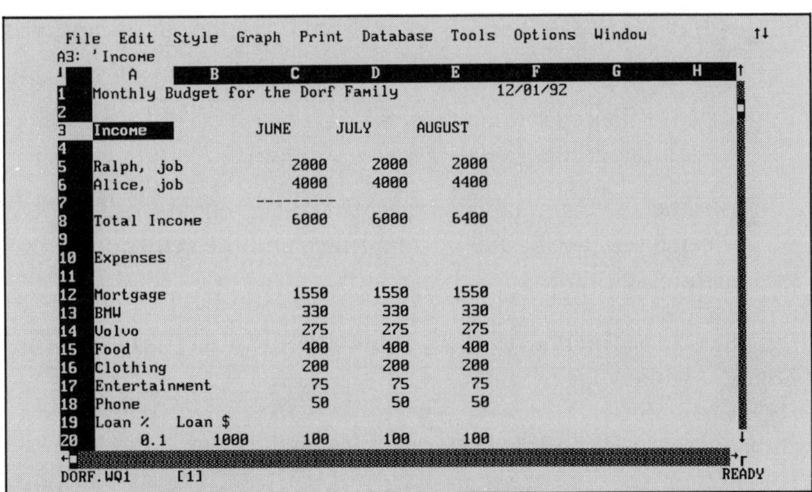

Figure 4.12: Data moved up on the spreadsheet

A Shortcut for Moving

In the example above we instructed you to open the Edit menu and select the Move option in order to move a block of cells. There is nothing wrong with choosing this route to perform a move. But there is a shortcut you may prefer to know about.

The next time you want to move something—say, cell A6—to another part of the spreadsheet, move the cell selector to that cell and simply press Ctrl–M. Quattro Pro will respond with the same message on the input line as the one it gave you after you entered /EM in the previous example: **Source block of cells: A6..A6**. From here you can proceed with your moving as before.

Some Finishing Touches

On a budget spreadsheet, you'll probably want to know how much cash remains after all expenses have been paid. You can easily add the appropriate formulas to DORF.WQ1 using techniques we have already discussed so far in this book. The first steps required to do this are as follows:

1. Move the cell selector to cell A25, and type the label **Remainder**. Press Enter.
2. Move the cell selector to cell C24, and type \= to fill the cell with underlines (=========). Press ↓.
3. Enter the formula to subtract the total income from the total expenses: **+C8−C23**. Press Enter and the cell should show the result: **2720**.

To extend the underline and copy the formula to the July and August columns, follow these steps:

1. Move the cell selector to cell C24.
2. Press Ctrl–C. This puts Quattro Pro in the Point mode for copying.

3. Press ↓ to highlight the source block, C24..C25.
4. Press Enter.
5. Press → to move the cell selector to cell D24.
6. Press period (.) to anchor the cell selector.
7. Press → to extend the cell selector to cell E24.
8. Press Enter.

Now the total remaining cash is displayed at the bottom of each column, as shown in Figure 4.13.

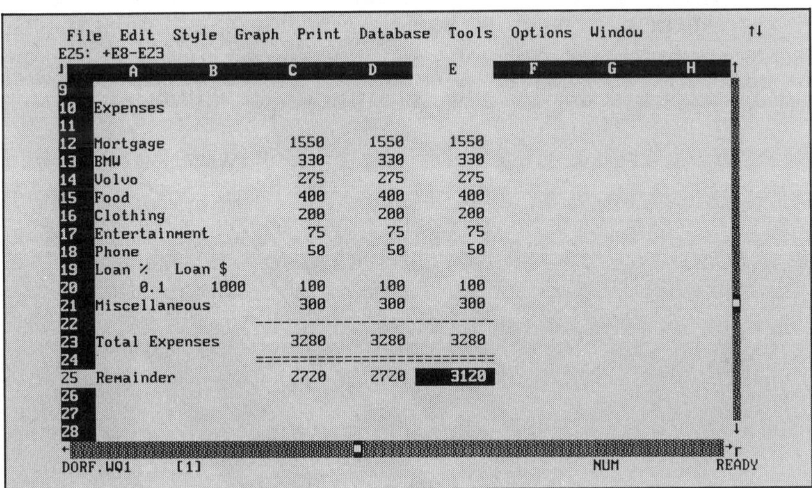

Figure 4.13: *Remaining cash calculated in row 25*

Saving the Modified Spreadsheet

Since you've made quite a few changes to DORF.WQ1 so far, save this new version of the spreadsheet for future use. As at the end of Chapter 3, you can use the usual Save command to do so. So type **/FS**. Since this is just a sample spreadsheet, select Replace so that you don't have to deal with a backup file lurking about your disk.

Now that you have saved the file safely, feel free to experiment with the numbers in the spreadsheet—the income and expenditure values, the loan-repayment percentage in cell A20, and the loan amount in cell B20—to try out various fanciful "what if" scenarios: e.g., what if Ralph or Alice earned more or less money, what if they traded in their BMW for a VW, etc. Don't type values directly into the cells in rows 8 or 23, however, as these contain formulas. (You'll learn about a way to protect such cells from accidental changes in Chapter 8.) When you're through playing around, be sure that you do *not* save the spreadsheet as DORF.WQ1. Choose a name of your own.

So far, you've learned a great deal about building spreadsheets—not only how to enter data and formulas, but also advanced techniques for changing spreadsheets, copying information, and using the pointing method. In the next chapter, we'll show you more advanced techniques for creating formulas and overview the complete range of functions (such as @SUM) that Quattro Pro has to offer.

FORMULAS AND FUNCTIONS

FEATURING

- *Types of Function Arguments*
- *Quattro Pro Functions*
- *Nesting Functions and Formulas*
- *Developing Powerful Business Spreadsheets*

In this chapter, we will explore different types of functions and their uses with and within formulas. The key difference between a function and a formula is that a *function* is a condensation of a complex *formula*. A function also always begins with an @ symbol. Start out by opening an empty spreadsheet so you can try out some of the functions and formulas that we describe in this chapter. To do so, type /**FN**.

Why a Function?

In previous chapters, you saw how we used the @SUM function to total a long column of numbers, because @SUM(C12..C24) was much simpler than entering the longer formula +C12+C13+C14+C15+C16+C17+C18+C19+C20+C21+C22+C23+C24. All of Quattro Pro's many functions are similarly designed to simplify your work.

Suppose, for example, you want to calculate the monthly payments on a loan when you know the principal, interest rate, and term. The formula for calculating the payments is fairly complex, so to simplify matters Quattro Pro offers the @PMT function, which calculates the payment directly from the known information. If cell A1 contains the principal amount of the loan, cell A2 the monthly interest rate, and cell A3 the term of the loan (in months), then the function

@PMT(A1,A2,A3) will calculate and display the monthly payments on the loan.

Types of Function Arguments

Most functions require at least one *argument,* enclosed in parentheses, to perform their calculations. Some functions use several arguments, while others need none. A function can also be another function's argument. There are four types of arguments:

- Numeric
- Label
- Date
- Block

In addition, some functions support *lists* as arguments. Each of the argument types is discussed below.

Numeric Arguments

Many functions expect to work on numbers and no other type of data. A numeric argument must be one of the following:

- A number
- A formula that results in a number
- A reference to a cell that contains a number—or a formula or function that results in a number (A1, for example, if A1 contains the formula 200*4 or function @COS(37))

The @SQRT function *returns* (i.e., calculates and displays) the square root of a number. Therefore, @SQRT expects to operate on a number. Entering @SQRT(Smith) or @SQRT(31-DEC-90) will not result in anything, since trying to find the square root of a name or date is rather nonsensical.

When Quattro Pro cannot perform a requested calculation because the argument is of the wrong type, you will see an error message appear:

Invalid cell or block address

But when the argument is of the right type, yet still mathematically invalid—as in @SQRT(– 5)—the function will return the word

ERR

in its cell. (Quattro Pro does not recognize complex numbers.)

Label Arguments

Some functions expect labels (also called *character strings* or just *strings*) as their argument. For example, the @UPPER function converts all lowercase letters in a label to uppercase letters. A label argument can be one of the following:

- A label enclosed in quotation marks
- A label function
- A reference to a cell that contains a label—or a formula or function that results in a label

For example, the function @UPPER("Hello there") returns **HELLO THERE**. If cell A1 contains the label **Joe Smith**, the function @UPPER(A1) will return **JOE SMITH**. If cell B7 contains the label **Welcome**, and cell B9 contains the label **Quattro Pro Users**, the function @UPPER(B7&B9) will return **WELCOMEQUATTRO PRO USERS**. (The & operator connects labels, so cell B7 will need a blank space after *Welcome* in order for the function to space all the words out properly.)

Obviously, you cannot convert a number to uppercase; hence, a function such as @UPPER(123.45) would return only **ERR**. (But if the number were enclosed in quotes, the function would simply echo the number.)

Date Arguments

As we mentioned in Chapter 2, dates entered using the Ctrl–D key combination are displayed on the screen as dates, though they are actually stored by Quattro Pro as serial dates (which are just numbers). Technically speaking, then, any function that operates on numbers will also operate on dates. But practically speaking, some functions are designed to work specifically on dates.

The @DAY function, for example, takes a serial date argument and returns the day of the month as a number between 1 and 31. So @DAY(33298) tells you that serial date 33298 (i.e., March 1, 1991) falls on the first of the month.

Block Arguments

Some Quattro Pro functions operate on entire groups or blocks of cells. For example, the @SUM function calculates the sum of all the numbers in a block of cells. (Chapter 7 discusses blocks in detail.)

Figure 5.1 shows a sample spreadsheet with several numbers in the block of cells A1 to C5. The total of all the numbers in that block is calculated in cell C8 with the function @SUM(A1..C5). Of course, changing any number in the block would instantly recalculate the total.

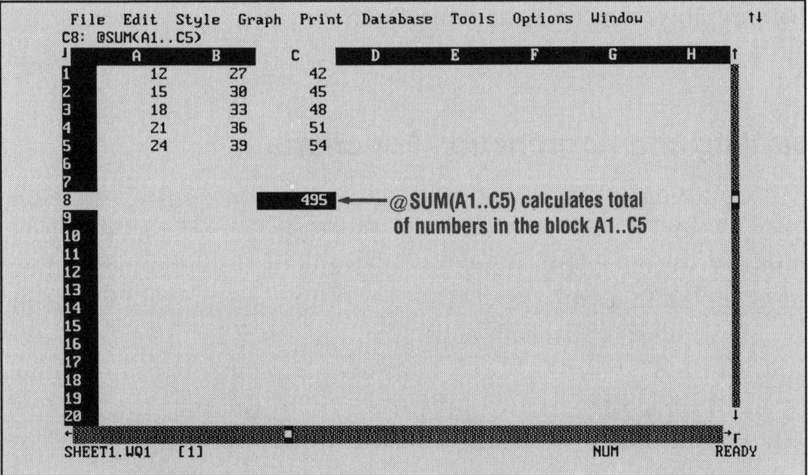

Figure 5.1: Sample spreadsheet with the @SUM formula

List Arguments

Some functions allow lists of items as function arguments. Such a function can have any number of arguments, separated by commas: values, formulas, functions, cell references, and even blocks. The only restrictions are that (1) the entire function size cannot exceed 254 characters, and (2) all the data types must match.

For example, the @SUM function also accepts lists. Therefore, the function @SUM(100,C99,A1..C8) calculates the sum of the number 100 plus the number stored in cell C99 plus all the numbers in the block of cells from A1 to C8. Note that each of the three arguments is separated by a comma, as required in all functions that work on lists or multiple arguments.

Summary of Quattro Pro Functions

This section presents a brief description of most functions that Quattro Pro offers, categorized by the type of task they perform. There is no need for you to memorize the entire list; instead, just note those functions that might prove useful in your own work with Quattro Pro. (Quattro Pro offers far more functions than most individuals will ever use.)

Later in this chapter, we'll demonstrate techniques for building very powerful formulas that employ a variety of Quattro Pro's functions.

Counting and Aggregation Functions

Counting and aggregation functions perform calculations on groups (blocks) of cells. All these functions accept blocks, lists, numbers, formulas, functions, and cell references as arguments. For example, the function @SUM(A1..Z28) sums all numeric values in the block of spreadsheets cells from A1 to Z28. The function @SUM(A1,B3..R9,200,J22/2) adds up the number in cell A1, plus the numbers in the block of cells from B3 to R9, plus the number 200, plus one-half the quantity in cell J22. Any non-numeric entries that these functions come across will be counted as zero.

The following are some of Quattro Pro's counting and aggregation functions:

@AVG(*list*)	Averages the numbers in a *list*
@COUNT(*list*)	Counts the number of nonblank cells in a *list*
@MAX(*list*)	Selects the highest number (or latest date) from a *list* of numbers (or dates)
@MIN(*list*)	Selects the lowest number (or earliest date) from a *list* of numbers (or dates)
@STD(*list*)	Calculates the standard deviation of a *list* of numbers
@SUM(*list*)	Adds a *list* of numbers together
@VAR(*list*)	Calculates the variance of a *list* of numbers

Financial Functions

Financial functions perform calculations that are commonly used in financial work, such as computing the payment on a loan, future value, present value, and depreciation. When using financial functions, you must make sure that the various arguments have matching units.

For example, to calculate the *monthly* payment on a loan when you know only the *annual* interest rate and the *years* of the term, you must first divide the annual interest rate by 12 (to get the monthly interest rate) and multiply the number of years by 12 (to get the total number of months).

Not that there's anything special about monthly payments. Suppose you're keen to know the *daily* payment on a home loan with a principal of $100,000, an annual interest rate of 9.75 percent and a term of 30 years. You would first need to divide the rate by 365 and multiply the term by 365. With time expressed in the same unit, the function @PMT(100000,9.75%/365,30*365) could then operate successfully.

The following are several of Quattro Pro's financial functions:

@CTERM(*interest, future,present*)	Determines the number of compounding periods required for an investment at a *present* value to reach a *future* value, given a fixed *interest* rate
@DDB(*cost,salvage, life,period*)	Calculates the depreciation allowance for a given asset at a certain *period* in the investment, given the initial *cost, salvage* value, and *life* of the asset (using the double-declining balance method)
@FV(*payments, interest,term*)	Returns the future value of a series of regular *payments* at a fixed *interest* rate, for a specified *term*. (This function is included in Quattro Pro for compatibility with Quattro and Lotus 1-2-3.)
@FVAL(*rate,nper,pmt, <pv>,<type>*)	Returns the future value of a series of regular payments at a fixed interest *rate,* for a specified term. This is a more accurate version of the future value calculation above. The arguments in < > are optional.
@IRR(*guess,block*)	Returns the internal rate of return for a *block* of cash flows, based on an initial *guess* (estimate)
@PMT(*principal, interest,term*)	Calculates the payment on a loan with a given *principal, interest* rate, and *term*

Mathematical Functions

These functions perform mathematical operations on numbers—and all expect numeric arguments, except for @PI and @RAND, which do not use any arguments.

The following are many of Quattro Pro's mathematical functions:

@ABS(x)	Converts the number x to its absolute (positive) value
@COS(x)	Determines the cosine of x
@DEGREES(x)	Converts x radians to degrees
@EXP(x)	Calculates e to the x power
@INT(x)	Lops off the decimal portion of x, leaving an integer value
@LN(x)	Calculates the natural logarithm of x
@LOG(x)	Calculates the base-10 logarithm of x
@PI	Gives the value of π to as many places as the cell is wide (13 maximum—or 3.1415926535898)
@RADIANS(x)	Converts x degrees to radians
@RAND	Returns a random decimal number between 0 and 1
@ROUND(x,y)	Rounds the number x to y decimal places of accuracy
@SIN(x)	Determines the sine of x
@SQRT(x)	Calculates the square root of x
@TAN(x)	Determines the tangent of x

Date and Time Functions

Date and time functions operate on Quattro Pro *serial date* and *time* values. Serial dates, described in detail in Chapter 2, are calculated based on the number of days elapsed since December 31, 1899. Serial times are calculated as the percentage through the day, from 0 (for midnight) to 0.999999 (11:59:59 PM). For example, 0.50 is noon, exactly halfway through the day. Serial times can be tacked onto serial dates, so 33298.5 is noon on March 1, 1991.

Date and time functions accept a variety of arguments, and they can be used to convert numbers or labels to serial dates and times. (In the list, *serialdate* means serial date *and* time.)

@DATE(*year, month,day*)	Converts a given *year, month,* and *day* into a serial date
@DATEVALUE ("*datestring*")	Returns a serial date from a label or character *string,* in quotes, in an acceptable date format (*dd-mmm-yy, dd-mmm*, or *mmm-yy*)
@DAY (*serialdate*)	Reveals the day of the month (1 to 31) of a given *serial date*
@HOUR (*serialtime*)	Reveals the hour (0 to 24) of a given *serial time*
@MINUTE (*serialtime*)	Reveals the minute (0 to 59) of a given *serial time*
@MONTH (*serialdate*)	Reveals in which month (1 to 12) a given *serial date* lies
@NOW	Prints the current date and time as a serial number (no argument needed)
@SECOND (*serialtime*)	Reveals the second (0 to 59) of a given *serial time*
@TIME(*hour, minute,second*)	Converts an *hour, minute,* and *second* into a serial time
@TIMEVALUE ("*timestring*")	Returns the serial time from the time value stored as a label
@TODAY	Gives the current date (no argument needed)
@YEAR (*serialdate*)	Gives the year of a given *serial date* as a value between 0 (for 1900) and 199 (for 2099)

Logic Functions

Logic functions study the existence of an item, or the relationship between two items, and decide whether it is true or false. Following the universal standard, Quattro Pro signifies "true" by the number 1 and "false" by the number 0.

The function @IF is the only logic function that does not directly answer true or false. Instead, @IF returns whatever you want it to, based on the result of a comparison. It uses the basic structure @IF(*this is true, then return this, otherwise return that*). For example, when translated into plain English, the function @IF(A1<10,"Less than","Greater than") says, "If the number in cell A1 is less than 10, then display 'Less than' in the cell; otherwise display 'Greater than'." We will give examples of how you can apply this useful function later in this chapter.

The following are a few of Quattro Pro's logic functions:

@FALSE	Returns the logical decision of false (0) automatically (no argument needed)
@IF(*condition, true,false*)	Returns whatever is in the *true* argument if the comparison in *condition* proves true; otherwise returns whatever is in the *false* argument
@TRUE	Returns the logical decision of true (1) automatically (no argument needed)

String Functions

String functions operate on labels (nonnumeric data). Most use at least one label type of argument, and many also use numeric arguments. For example, the @REPEAT function repeats a character a certain number of times, using the syntax @REPEAT(*character,n*). Thus, the function @REPEAT(=,80) prints 80 equal signs across the screen. If cell A1 contains the character **A**, and cell A2 contains the number **20**, then the function @REPEAT(A1,A2) will display twenty A's: **AAAAAAAAAAAAAAAAAAAA**.

Following is a partial list of Quattro Pro's string functions:

@CHAR(*x*)	Returns the ASCII character of *x*
@HEXTONUM ("*string*")	Converts the hexadecimal number stored as *string* to a decimal value
@LENGTH("*string*")	Returns the length of *string*

@LOWER("*string*")	Prints all letters in *string* as lowercase
@NUMTOHEX(*x*)	Converts the decimal number *x* to a hexadecimal value
@PROPER("*string*")	Prints *string* with the first letter of each word in uppercase, and all other letters in lowercase
@REPEAT ("*string*",*n*)	Prints *string n* times
@TRIM("*string*")	Removes all blank spaces from *string*
@UPPER("*string*")	Prints all letters in *string* as uppercase
@VALUE("*string*")	Returns numeric characters stored as numeric data in *string*

Miscellaneous Functions

These miscellaneous functions perform a variety of advanced tasks. Many are used only in macros or extremely sophisticated spreadsheets. However, @VLOOKUP and @HLOOKUP might be useful to you right away.

The following are a sampling of Quattro Pro's miscellaneous functions:

@@(*cell address*)	Prints the contents of the cell at *cell address*
@CHOOSE(*n,list*)	Prints the *n*th item from the *list* of options
@COLS(*block*)	Prints the number of columns in the specified *block*
@HLOOKUP (*x,block,n*)	Looks up the value *x* in *block,* and prints the value from *n* rows down

@MEMAVAIL	Reveals the amount of RAM memory currently available
@MEMEMSAVAIL	Returns the amount of expanded memory (EMS) available (no argument needed)
@ROWS(*block*)	Counts and displays the number of rows in *block*
@VLOOKUP (*x,block,n*)	Looks up the value *x* in *block,* and prints the value from *n* columns across

Database Statistical Functions

The database statistical functions listed below are similar to the counting and aggregation functions listed earlier, but they are used specifically with Quattro Pro databases. All need three arguments to run: the database *block,* database *field* (or *column* therein), and *criterion* range. (For more information about databases, see Chapter 13.)

Here are some of Quattro Pro's database statistical functions:

@DAVG(*block,field, criterion*)	Calculates the average of numbers in *field,* given a *block* and *criterion* range
@DCOUNT(*block,field, criterion*)	Counts the number of nonblank cells in a *field,* given a *block* and *criterion* range
@DMAX(*block,field, criterion*)	Selects the highest number (or latest date) from a *field,* given a *block* and *criterion* range
@DMIN(*block,field, criterion*)	Selects the lowest number (or earliest date) from a *field,* given a *block* and *criterion* range
@DSUM(*block,column, criterion*)	Sums the numbers in a *column* of a *field* that meet the *criterion* range

Getting Help with Functions

Let's face it—it's hard to remember which arguments go where in functions, especially when you're first learning. But you can use the Quattro Pro Help system to get a quick reminder at any time. Just press the Help key (F1). (You may have to press F1 a second time to get the Help Topics screen.)

At the Help Topics screen, press → to highlight the Functions category; then press Enter. This brings you to the Function Topics screen, shown in Figure 5.2. From there, you can select the Function Index to see a list of individual functions that you might need help with. Or you can select Function Arguments to get help with the topic of arguments. Or you can select a specific function category—say, Financial—to find out which functions are of particular interest at the moment.

As usual, you can press Escape at any time to leave the Help system and return to your work.

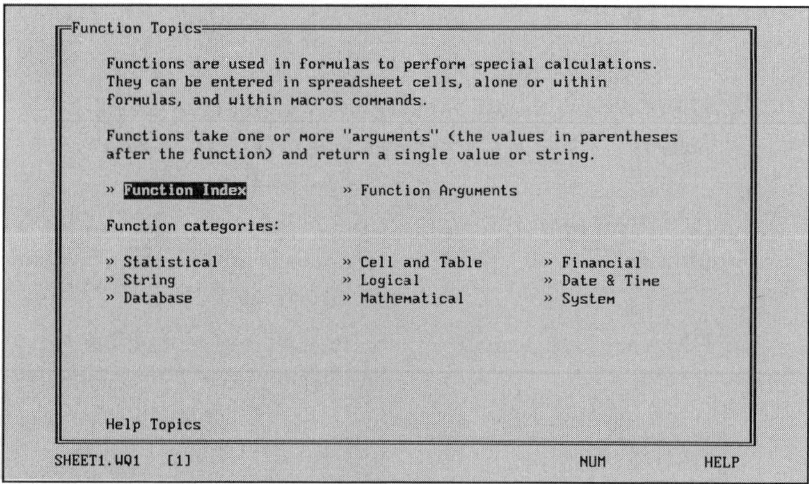

Figure 5.2: *The Function Topics help screen*

A Shortcut for Entering Functions

A handy technique for entering functions is to use the Functions key (Alt–F3). Suppose you wanted to calculate the average of the numbers in the block A1..A13. You would use the @AVG function to calculate the average as follows:

1. Type the numbers into column A, as per Figure 5.3.
2. Move the cell selector to cell B15.
3. Press Alt–F3 to bring up the menu of Quattro Pro functions, as shown on the right of the column of numbers in Figure 5.3.

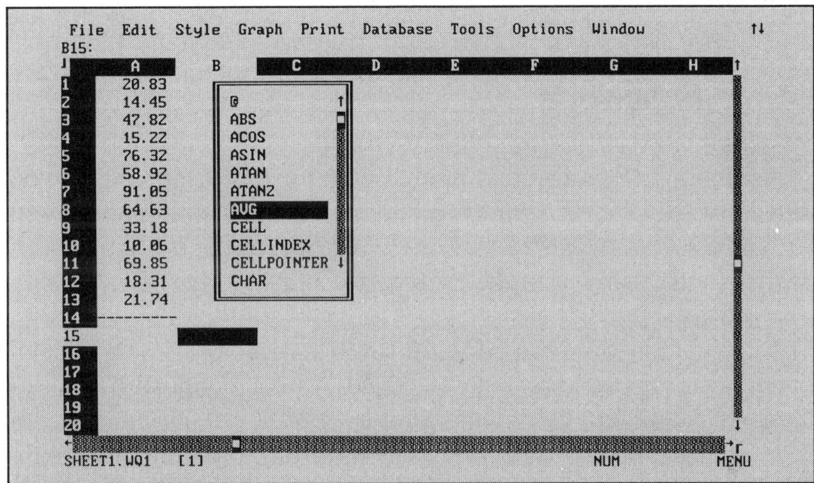

Figure 5.3: *Calling up the Functions menu*

4. Press ↓ six times, to highlight the @AVG function.
5. Press Enter to select the function. **@AVG(** appears on the input line.
6. Press Home to move the cell selector to cell A1. The function now reads **@AVG(A1**.
7. Press the period key to anchor the cell selector. The function now reads **@AVG(A1..A1**.
8. Press End and then ↓ to extend the cell selector to cell A14.
9. Now, you don't want to include the cell with the dashes in it, so press ↑ to shrink the cell selector by one row. The function on the input line now reads **@AVG(A1..A13**.

10. Type) (closed parenthesis) to complete the function as **@AVG(A1..A13).**

11. Press Enter to insert the function into the cell.

Cell B15 now displays **41.72154**, the average of the numbers in the block A1..A13. On the input line, you can still see the actual function, @AVG(A1..A13).

If you want to save this spreadsheet now, go ahead (though you don't have to).

Nesting Functions

You can *nest* functions inside other functions, as long as you remember to include a complete pair of parentheses for each function. In fact, all Quattro Pro functions must have an equal number of opening and closing parentheses to be acceptable; otherwise, Quattro Pro returns an error message.

Nested functions can be helpful even in relatively simple calculations. For example, the @SQRT function works only with positive numbers, so @SQRT(A1) would return **ERR** if cell A1 contained a negative number. You can avoid such an error by nesting the @ABS function, which ensures that an argument remains or becomes positive, inside the @SQRT function: i.e., @SQRT(@ABS(A1)).

Because Quattro Pro always calculates by starting with the innermost parentheses and working its way out, this function *first* returns the absolute value of the number in cell A1, and *then* the square root of that absolute value. For example, if cell A1 contained −81, the @ABS function would convert it to +81 and the @SQRT function would return a 9, which would be displayed in the cell that contained the function.

Another function that commonly has other functions nested within it is @ROUND, which rounds a number to a specified number of decimal places. Suppose you want to know the monthly payment on a loan, with the result rounded to two decimal places. The principal for the loan (say, $50,000.00) is stored in cell B1. The annual interest rate (10 percent) is stored in cell B2. The term (30 years) is stored in cell

B3. The function @ROUND(@PMT(B1,B2/12,B3*12),2), then, displays the monthly payments to two decimal places.

How so? The innermost function, @PMT(B1,B2/12,B3*12), calculates the monthly payment by dividing the annual interest rate by 12 to get the monthly interest rate, and multiplying the years by 12 to get the number of months. This function returns the value 438.785785 and substitutes it into the function @ROUND(438.785785,2). The actual value returned by the entire function is 438.79—that is, the monthly payment on the loan rounded to the nearest penny is $438.79.

Even though these examples show only two levels of function nesting, you can actually nest functions as deeply as you wish. In fact, a single function can contain any number of nested functions, as long as it does not exceed the 254-character limit and the number of open parentheses matches the number of closed parentheses.

Advanced Use of Operators

In our examples so far, you've seen the use of the basic arithmetic operators: + (addition), – (subtraction), * (multiplication), and / (division). Quattro Pro actually offers quite a variety of operators, listed in Table 5.1 in descending order of precedence.

Operators that have the same level of precedence are calculated in order of left to right as they appear in a formula. Any natural order of precedence can be overridden by the use of parentheses, just as in everyday mathematics. That is, any operator enclosed in parentheses will be used first in the calculation. (The logical operators =, <>, <, >, <=, >=, #AND#, #OR#, and #NOT# are special operators used with logical functions.)

The order of precedence of operators can affect the results of a formula dramatically. For instance, the formula 12+2*100 equals 212 because the multiplication (2*100) takes place before the addition, according to the order of precedence. However, using parentheses to group the addition, as in (12+2)*100, forces the addition to take place before the multiplication, so the result is 1400 (i.e., 14*100).

By natural order of precedence, exponentiation takes place before addition, subtraction, multiplication, or division. Therefore,

Table 5.1: Quattro Pro Operators and Their Order of Precedence

OPERATOR	DESCRIPTION	PRECEDENCE
^	Exponentiation	7
−, +	Negative, positive	6
*, /	Multiplication, division	5
−, +	Subtraction, addition	4
>=	Greater than or equal to	3
<=	Less than or equal to	3
<,>	Less than, greater than	3
=,<>	Equal, not equal	3
#NOT#	Logical NOT	2
#AND#, #OR#	Logical AND, logical OR	1
&	Links two labels (strings)	1

10^3 + 17 equals 1017—that is, 10 cubed (1000) plus 17. Using parentheses to group the addition, as in 10^(3 + 17), yields the much larger number of 10 to the 20th power because now the addition takes place before exponentiation. Similarly, the formula 4096^1/4 first raises 4096 to the power of 1, then divides that result by 4 to yield the result 1024. However, 4096^(1/4) raises 4096 to the power of 1/4, which equals the 4th root of 4096, or 8.

Keep in mind that if you leave out parentheses for grouping, Quattro Pro will follow the order of precedence specified in Table 5.1. If you are not sure how Quattro Pro will perform a complex calculation, just add parentheses as required to ensure that it performs as you want it to.

For example, the formula 2*(43*(5 + 10) + (4*7)) will first add the 5 and 10 in the middle, since they are surrounded by parentheses. Then it will multiply the result (i.e., 15) by 43, add that result (645) to 28 (the product of 4 by 7), and finally multiply *that* result (673) by 2, yielding a total of 1346. Note that the parentheses around 4*7 are redundant; the formula 2*(43*(5 + 10) + 4*7) works as well. Since the * operator between the 4 and the 7 has precedence over the + to the left of the 4, the formula would never have added 43*(5 + 10) to 4 before multiplying by 7. Still, it doesn't hurt to add too many parentheses if you're not sure; it'll only take a little more time to type the formula out.

Sample Applications of Formulas

In this section, we'll discuss and demonstrate some practical applications of the concepts we've discussed so far. Open an empty spreadsheet now; you'll want to save it for the next chapter. To do so, type /**FN**.

Suppose you are responsible for developing financial scenarios. Your task is to determine the feasibility of expanding the plant and facilities to meet expected increases in sales. The sample formulas and functions below will help your decision-making.

Calculating the Mortgage Payment

The spreadsheet in Figure 5.4 contains some loan information, including the monthly payback and total payback. The values in cells C1, C2, and C3 were typed in simply as numbers. The payment and payback were calculated with a function and formula, respectively.

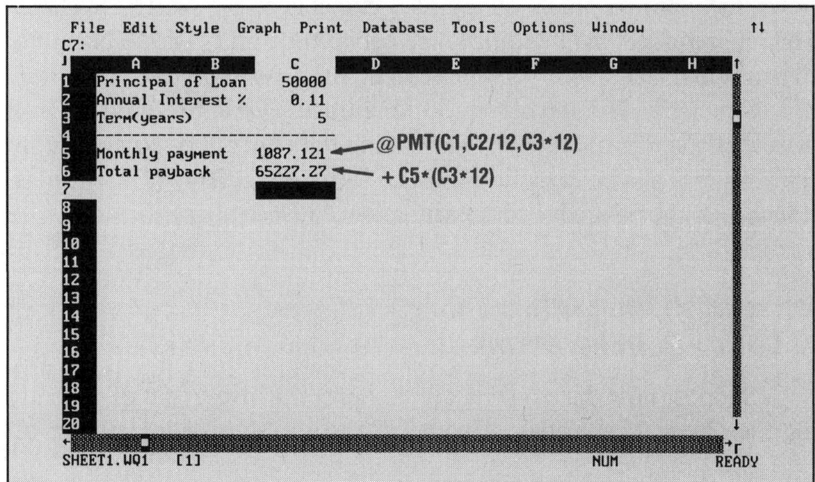

Figure 5.4: Spreadsheet that calculates the payment on a loan

The financial function that calculates the monthly payment, @PMT(C1,C2/12,C3*12), is stored in cell C5. As mentioned before, because the loan parameters are expressed in years (e.g., an 11 percent *annual* interest rate and a 5-*year* term), the function divides the annual interest rate in cell C2 by 12 to calculate the monthly interest rate and multiplies the term in cell C3 by 12 to calculate the number of months in the loan. The result is the monthly payment on the loan.

The formula that calculates the total payback simply multiplies the monthly payment in cell C5 by the number of months required to pay off the loan (the years in cell C3 multiplied by 12). The formula +C5*C3*12 in cell C6 calculates this value.

The monthly payment on the mortgage can now be used in some other calculations. Save the spreadsheet now (in case you make accidental deletions later) and read on.

Calculating the Internal Rate of Return

The next step is to calculate the rate of return on net sales in order to make a viable return on the capital outlay. Cash flows are based on the capacity of the plant and equipment. The initial entry is negative, since it corresponds to the capital outlay. Monthly cash flows are then reduced by monthly carrying costs to determine the net operating income.

To calculate the internal rate of return, input the block of cash flows, including the initial outlay, as arguments of the @IRR function. The rate returned will be somewhere between 0 and 1, with 0 being no return and 1 being 100 percent return. (It is possible to have a rate of return higher than 100 percent.) In Figure 5.5, @IRR(C16,C14..O14) calculates the internal rate of return using the estimate of 50 percent in cell C16 and all the cash flows in the block C14..O14. (The months extend past the right edge of the screen out to December.)

Computing the Future Value of a Lump-Sum Investment

Suppose now that you want to compare the investment of expanding the physical capacities of your firm to the simpler investment of

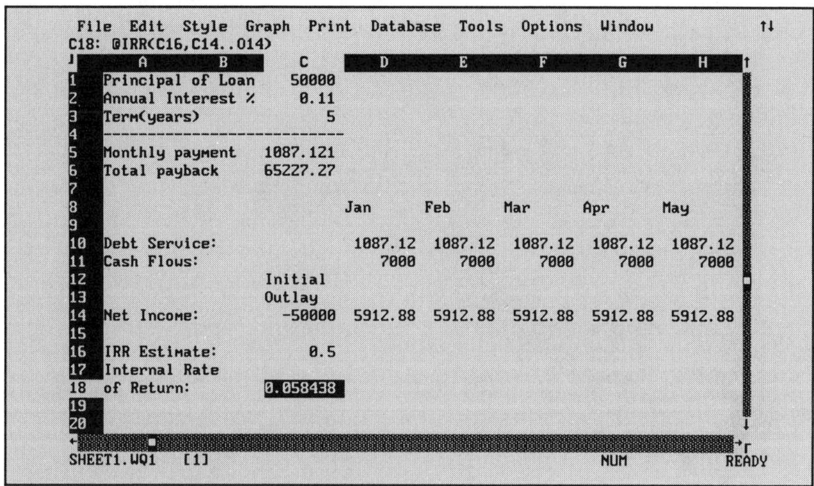

Figure 5.5: The internal rate of return

depositing the return in an interest-bearing account.

Quattro Pro does not have a function that calculates the future value of a lump-sum investment directly, but you do not need such a function if you know which formula to use. The future value of a lump-sum investment can be calculated with the formula Inv*(1+(APR/Per))^(Term*Per), where *Inv* is the dollar amount of the lump sum investment, *APR* is the annual percentage rate, *Per* is the number of compounding periods per year, and *Term* is the number of periods in the investment.

Figure 5.6 shows a lump-sum investment calculation, given an interest rate of 7.6 percent compounded monthly and a 3-year term. Cell D24 contains 0.0765 (the annual interest rate), cell D25 contains 3 (the number of years of the investment), cell D26 contains 12 (the number of compounding periods per year), and cell D27 contains 50000 (the single lump-sum investment). The formula in cell D29, +D27*(1+(D24/D26))^(D25*D26), returns **62852.74**—or $62,852.74, the future value of the initial investment after three years.

Save the spreadsheet now. Then open up a clean slate (by typing **/FN**) in case you want to recreate some of the following sample spreadsheets.

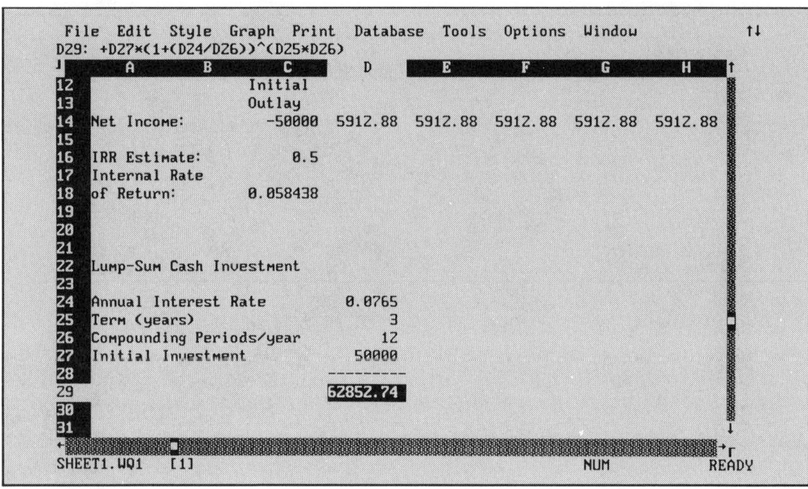

Figure 5.6: The annual return on an investment

Sample Counting and Aggregation Functions

Figure 5.7 shows a spreadsheet with sample counting and aggregation functions. Cell B14 contains @SUM(B1..B12), which displays the sum of the numbers in the block B1..B12. Cell B15 contains the function @AVG(B1..B12), which displays the average of these numbers. The cells beneath contain @MAX, @MIN, @VAR, @STD, and @COUNT, which display the results of other calculations.

Date Arithmetic and a Logic Function

Figure 5.8 shows a spreadsheet that demonstrates some date arithmetic and a logic function. Near the top of the spreadsheet are two dates—11/01/91 and 12/15/91—each of which was previously entered by first pressing Ctrl–D. Cell C4 calculates the number of days between the two dates by using the formula +C2 – C1 to subtract the later date from the earlier date.

The bottom half of the spreadsheet demonstrates the use of the logic function @IF to calculate a payment due, based on whether or not the payment is late. Cell C8 contains 100, the amount due. Cell C9 contains 11/01/91, the due date. Cell C12 contains 0.1, the percent added to

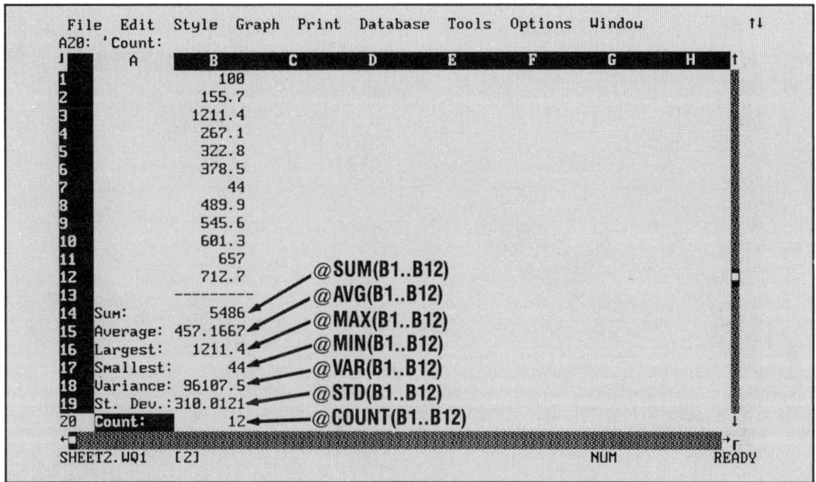

Figure 5.7: Sample counting and aggregation functions

the amount due if the payment is not made within 30 days (i.e., a 10 percent late fee). Cell C15 contains the current date, 12/15/91. (Both dates were entered using Ctrl–D.)

Cell C17 shows 110, the amount due. Note that the spreadsheet has added 10 percent to the amount due because more than 30 days elapsed. The function @IF(C15 – C9< =30,C8,C8*(1 + C12)) figured out the amount due. In English, it says, "If the number of days between today and the due date is less than or equal to 30 [C15 – C9< =30], then display the amount due [,C8]; otherwise, display the amount due with the appropriate percentage added [,C8*(1 + C12)]."

Note that, as all Quattro Pro formulas and functions require, there is an equal number of open and closed parentheses in the function.

If you need to enter a date directly into a function, you cannot use Ctrl–D. Instead, you must use the @DATE function with the syntax @DATE(*yy,mm,dd*), where *yy* is the year (last two digits), *mm* is the month (1–12), and *dd* is the day.

The function in cell A19, @IF(@DATE(91,12,15)=C2, "Same","Not the same"), shows an example. This formula says, "If @DATE(91,12,15) is equal to the date in cell C2, then display the word 'Same'; otherwise, display 'Not the same'." As you can see in cell A19, the formula displays **SAME**, indicating that the date 12/15/91, entered into cell C2 with Ctrl–D, is the same as the date expressed by @DATE(91,12,15).

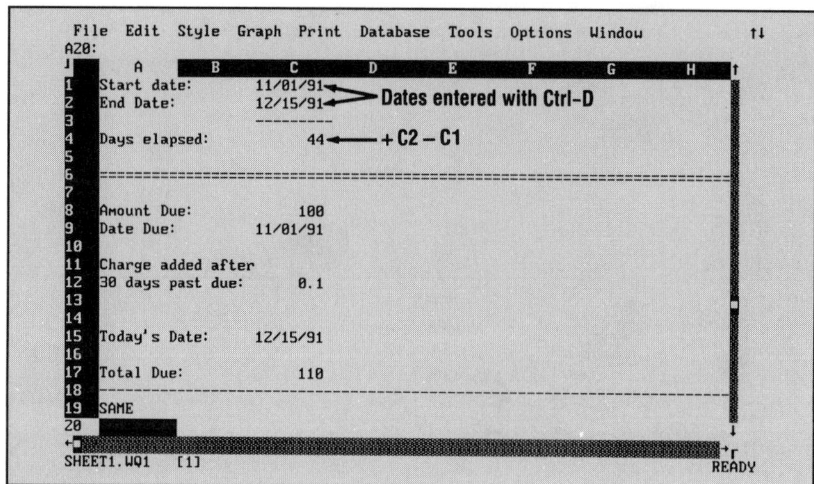

Figure 5.8: Spreadsheet with date arithmetic and a logic function

Solving for X

So far, you've been shown only one way to use a Quattro Pro function—namely, plug in its arguments and let it calculate an answer. There are many times, however, when you'll need to use a function "in reverse," i.e., solve for an argument when you know the result.

As you know, the financial function @PMT calculates the monthly payments on a loan, given the principal, interest rate, and period. But suppose you would rather figure out the *principal,* given a monthly payment plan of your own design. That way, you *know* you'd be able to pay it off. Rather than chance upon the loan amount by trial and error—repeating *what if* scenarios that haphazardly hit or miss your desired monthly-payment amount—run the @PMT function backwards and solve for it directly.

Figure 5.9 shows a loan-calculation spreadsheet. The function in cell B4 is @PMT(B1,B2/12,B3*12). It says that monthly payments of $438.79 will pay off a loan of $50,000 over 30 years at an interest rate of 10 percent.

Now, it so happens that you can afford to part with $700 per month, so you know you are able to take out a larger loan. The question

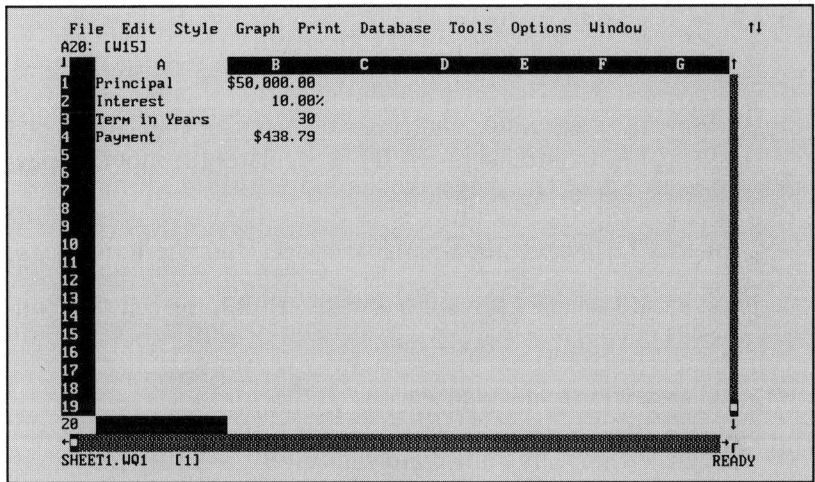

Figure 5.9: A loan-calculation spreadsheet

is, how much larger? To calculate the principal of such a loan:

1. Type /**T** to select the Tools menu.
2. From the menu, select the Solve For option.
3. Since the function is in cell B4, highlight the Formula Cell option and press Enter. Then highlight cell B4 and press Enter.
4. Choose the Target Value option and enter **700** in the box, since that is the payment you know you can afford. Press Enter to go back to the submenu.
5. Designate which cell is the variable. In this example, you want to calculate the principal (situated in cell B1), so choose the Variable Cell option, highlight cell B1, and press Enter.
6. Select Go to solve for the principal.

The answer appears immediately in the cell where the principal of $50,000 used to be; the loan you can pay off in monthly installments of $700 over 30 years at 10 percent interest is $79,765.57.

Try another variation of this feature by changing the principal in cell B1 to $100,000, leaving the target value as $700, and solving for the *interest:*

1. Press Escape twice to leave the menus and enter the spreadsheet.
2. Move the cell selector to cell B1 and enter **100000**. Notice that the @PMT function in cell B4 recalculates the monthly payments right away as $877.57.
3. Type /**TS** to select the Solve For option from the Tools menu.
4. Choose Variable Cell and highlight cell B2, the cell that contains the interest. Press Enter.
5. Choose Go from the submenu.

The answer appears immediately in cell B2; in order for you to make monthly payments of $700 on a $100,000 loan over 30 years, the rate of interest has to be 7.5 percent.

This Solve For feature can be incorporated into many different situations. You can also refine the calculation if you want. Choose the Parameters option to specify how many times Quattro Pro should iterate the function it uses to solve for *x* (1 to 99), and to decide how close to the Target Value it should attempt to get. The default settings should be adequate for most techniques.

The use of functions and formulas to create powerful and flexible spreadsheets is limited only by your creativity and understanding of the functions themselves. Virtually any calculation that can be done in any other manner can be translated into the spreadsheet format.

In the next chapter, we will use the spreadsheet created in this chapter to show examples of a variety of formatting techniques.

6

ENHANCING YOUR SPEADSHEET'S APPEARANCE

FEATURING

Formatting Numbers
Formatting Dates and Times
Formatting Labels

When you enter numbers, dates, times, and labels in a cell, they don't "just appear"; they are displayed in a default format of some sort. This chapter shows you how to change the way that data are displayed in your spreadsheet, without changing the data themselves.

Before reading on, open up an empty spreadsheet so you can experiment with some of the formatting styles discussed in this chapter.

Formatting Numbers

By default, numbers (including the results of numeric calculations) are automatically displayed to as many decimal and integer places as fit into a cell. To change the format of a number (or block of numbers), follow these steps:

1. Position the cell selector on the cell or upper-left corner of the group of cells you wish to format.
2. Type **/SN** to access the Numeric Format option from the Style menu.
3. Select the appropriate format from the options displayed (described in Table 6.1).

4. If requested, enter the number of digits to the right of the decimal point that you want displayed, in the range from 0 to 15. Press Enter.

5. Highlight the cell or block of cells you want to format and press Enter to complete the job.

We'll provide some exercises for you at the end of this chapter. For now, just take a moment to review the various format options for numbers, as listed in Table 6.1. (Note that you can modify currency settings and numeric punctuation for foreign countries with the international settings discussed in Chapter 14.)

Table 6.1: Format Options for Displaying Numbers

FORMAT	DESCRIPTION	EXAMPLES
Fixed	Displays numbers to a fixed number of decimal places, rounded as appropriate (can specify 0–15 decimal places)	– 123.00 123.46 12345678.90
Scientific	Displays numbers in scientific notation	– 1.2E + 02 123E + 02 1.23E + 07
Currency	Displays leading currency sign, commas in thousands places, and negative numbers in parentheses	($123.00) $123.46 $12,345,678.90
, (comma)	Shows commas in thousands places, and displays negative numbers in parentheses	(123.00) 12,345,678.90
General	Displays numbers as entered or calculated and rounds to nearest decimal value as space permits in cell	– 123 123.45678 12345678.9
+ / – (plus/minus)	Transforms numbers to miniature bar graphs, with + for each positive integer, – for each negative integer,	+ + + – – . + + + +

Table 6.1: Format Options for Displaying Numbers (continued)

FORMAT	DESCRIPTION	EXAMPLES
	and . for zero (examples show the numbers 3, −2, 0 and 3.9999 formatted)	
Percent	Displays numbers as percentages	12.75% 9.38% 12.00%
Date	Displays numbers as per specified date format (see Table 6.2 on these different formats)	
Text	Displays formulas rather than the values they calculate	+C6−C4 @IF(A4=20,50,0)
Hidden	Hides values or text from view	
Reset	Displays numbers as determined by the Global Format setting from the Options menu	

Formatting Dates and Times

When you enter a date by pressing Ctrl–D, Quattro Pro automatically formats the cell to display the date in *mm/dd/yy* format. When you enter dates or times with the functions @DATE, @DATEVALUE, @NOW, @TIME, @TIMEVALUE, or @TODAY, Quattro Pro only displays their serial numbers. For example, if you type **@DATE(91,12,30)** into a cell, Quattro Pro returns the serial date **33602** rather than **12/30/91**. If you enter **@TIME(12,30,0)**, it returns **0.520833** rather than **12:30 PM**.

To display *mm/dd/yy* dates or serial dates and times in different formats, follow these steps:

1. Move the cell selector to the cell or upper-left corner of the block containing the date(s) or time(s) you want to format.
2. Type **/SND** to access the Date option under the Numeric Format submenu. (If you are formatting a serial time, go one step further and select the Time option. Total keystrokes: **/SNDT**.)
3. Select the format you want (see Table 6.2). Press Enter.
4. Highlight the cells you wish to format with the usual pointing method.
5. Press Enter.

Descriptions and examples of various date and time formats are listed in Table 6.2. (Again, note that all international formats can be modified using the international settings discussed in Chapter 14.)

Table 6.2: Date and Time Formats

FORMAT	DESCRIPTION	EXAMPLES
Date 1	*dd-mmm-yy* format	23-Dec-87 01-Jan-00 27-Jul-20
Date 2	*dd-mmm* format	23-Dec 01-Jan 27-Jul
Date 3	*mmm-yy* format	Dec-87 Jan-00 Jul-20
Date 4	Long International format	12/23/87 87-12-23 12.23.87
Date 5	Short International format	12/23 12-23 12.23

Table 6.2: Date and Time Formats (continued)

FORMAT	DESCRIPTION	EXAMPLES
Time 1	*hh:mm:ss* a.m./p.m. format	01:20:31 AM 01:20:31 PM 12:00:00 AM
Time 2	*hh:mm* a.m./p.m. format	01:20 AM 01:20 PM 12:00 AM
Time 3	Long International format	13:20:31 13.20.31 13,20,31 13h20m31s
Time 4	Short International format	13:20 13.20 13,20 13h20m

Formatting Labels

As you may recall from Chapter 2, you can use label prefixes to left-justify, right-justify, or center a label within a cell. Using the Alignment option, you can change the label alignment in an entire group of cells. The steps for formatting labels are as follows:

1. Move the cell selector to the cell or upper-left corner of the block containing the label(s) you want to format.
2. Type /**SA** to access the Alignment option from the Style menu.
3. Highlight the format you want:
   - General (for labels left-justified and numbers right-justified within the cell)
   - Left (for labels and numbers left-justified within the cell)

- Right (for labels and numbers right-justified within the cell)
- Center (for numbers and labels centered within the cell).

4. Press Enter.
5. Highlight the cell(s) you wish to align.
6. Press Enter.

Any label that is too wide for its cell will automatically be left-justified. Typing **/SA** only realigns labels that are already in a block; subsequent entries will appear in the default label-alignment format.

Reformatting Entries on a Sample Spreadsheet

In Chapter 5, we showed a sample spreadsheet with various formulas. This same spreadsheet, before formatting, is shown in Figure 6.1. Now we'll format the spreadsheet to give a much neater display.

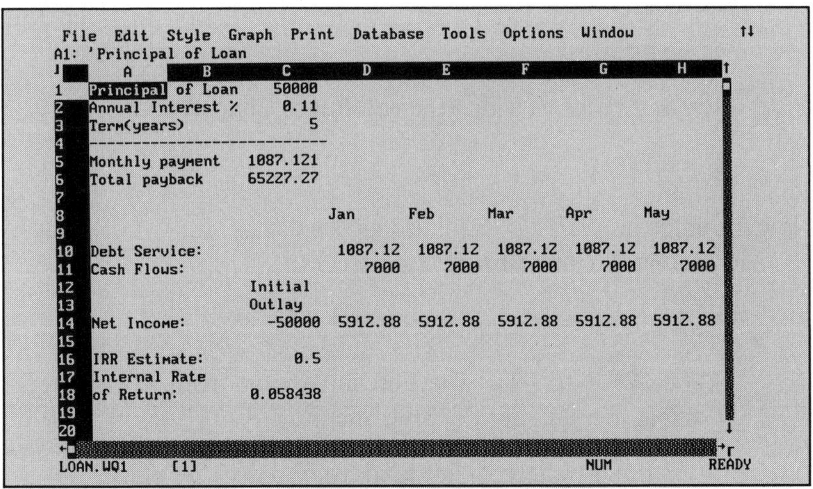

Figure 6.1: The loan-analysis spreadsheet from Chapter 5

Formatting the Loan Numbers

Suppose you wish to format the numbers in the loan portion of the spreadsheet as currency and percentage values. Here are the steps to do so:

1. Move the cell selector to cell C1.
2. Type /**SN** to access the Numeric Format option from the Style menu.
3. Select Currency.
4. Press Enter to select the suggested decimal width, 2.
5. Press Enter to select the suggested block (in this case, cell), C1..C1.

The cell displays *********. This is because the number is too big to fit into the cell in Currency format.

To widen the column, follow these steps:

1. Leave the cell selector in column C.
2. Type /**SC** to access the Column Width option from the Style menu.
3. Press → twice to widen the column to 11 spaces.
4. Press Enter.

Now the value in cell C1 is displayed as **$50,000.00** rather than **50000**.

To format the interest rate as a percent:

1. Move the cell selector to cell C2.
2. Type /**SNP** to select the Percent option from the Numeric Format menu under the Style menu.
3. Press Enter to accept the standard two decimal places.
4. Press Enter again to accept the suggested block (in this case, cell), C2..C2.

Now the percentage is displayed as **11.00%** rather than **0.11**.

To format the loan-payment values:

1. Move the cell selector to cell C5.
2. Type /**SNC** to select the Currency option from the Numeric Format menu under the Style menu.
3. Press Enter to accept two decimal places.
4. Press ↓ once to extend the cell selector to cell C6.
5. Press Enter.

Now the monthly payment and total payback are displayed as **$1,087.12** and **$65,227.27**, respectively, rather than as **1087.121** and **65227.27**.

You might want to right-align the month names in row 8 so that the numbers within each column line up better. Here are the steps to do so:

1. Move the cell selector to cell B8.
2. Type /**SAR** to select Right from the Alignment option under the Style menu.
3. Press the End key and then → to extend the cell selector all the way to the right of the month names.
4. Press Enter.

Now the month names in row 8 are shifted to the right so that they align better with the numbers below.

Figure 6.2 shows the sample spreadsheet completely formatted. Besides the formatting discussed above, the block D10..G14 was formatted with /**SNF2**, cell C14 was formatted with /**SNF**, and cells C16 through C18 were formatted with /**SNP3**.

With a little practice, you'll find that formatting is not only easy but fun. Once again, feel free to experiment on your own. You can't do any harm, and you'll find practice is the quickest way to master this valuable Quattro Pro feature. When you're through, either save the spreadsheet under a name of your own, or throw it away.

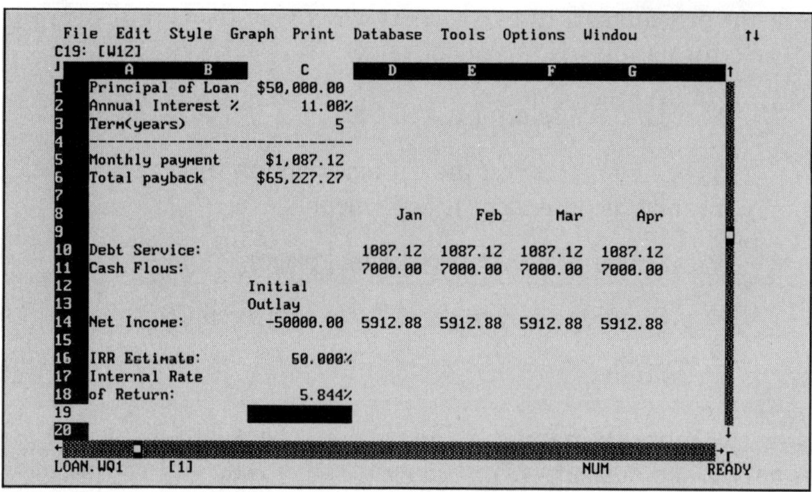

Figure 6.2: Sample spreadsheet after some formatting

7

EFFECTIVE MANAGEMENT OF BLOCKS

FEATURING

Filling blocks with data
Giving blocks names
Moving named blocks

In Chapter 4 you learned the basics of copying and moving blocks of data. This chapter will show you some more techniques of handling blocks so that you can make them an integral part of your work with ease.

Filling a Block

Block filling is a very useful technique that can help speed spreadsheet development. The Fill option under the Edit menu lets you fill blocks of cells with numbers or dates and also lets you increment (and decrement) values along the way. The basic technique for using the Fill option is as follows:

1. Position the cell selector at the upper-left corner of the block you wish to fill.
2. Access the Edit menu, and select the Fill option.
3. Specify a block you want to fill, either by using the pointing method or by entering block coordinates.
4. As requested on the input line, enter a *start value,* a *step value,* and a *stop value.* (Press Enter after typing each one.)

To try this out yourself, start with a blank spreadsheet and follow the steps below. (If you have any other work on your screen, save it first (keystrokes /**FS**). Then either erase the screen with /FE or open an empty, new spreadsheet with /FN.) Suppose now that you wish to type in the years 1990 to 1993 across row 2 of the blank spreadsheet. Here are the steps:

1. Move the cell selector to cell B2.
2. Type /**EF** to access the Fill option from the Edit menu.
3. When the input line prompts **Destination for cells: B2**, highlight the block of cells you want to fill. In this case, press the period key to anchor the cell selector, press → three times to extend it to cell E2, and then press Enter to finish defining the block.
4. The screen will show you a new box, asking you for a start value. Type **1990** and press Enter.
5. For the step value, just press Enter to use the suggested value, 1.
6. For the stop value, type **1993**.
7. Press Enter to complete the fill operation.

You'll see the years appear across row 2, as in Figure 7.1. (To add the underlines, type \- into cell B3 and use the usual Copy option from the Edit menu to copy the contents of cell B3 into cells C3, D3, and E3.) Save this spreadsheet now, so you can use it later in the chapter. Now open another empty spreadsheet so you can try some of the examples mentioned below for yourself.

When using Fill, you should keep a few simple points in mind. For one, the step value need not be 1; it can be any positive or negative number. For example, if you enter 100 as the start value, −25 as the step value, and 0 as the stop value, Fill will generate the numbers 100, 75, 50, 25, and 0 (provided the block contains at least five cells—i.e., enough room to accept the entire fill).

If you do not know the exact stop value for a fill operation, just enter any large number (or accept the suggested value of 8192—the maximum number of rows in the spreadsheet) and the operation will

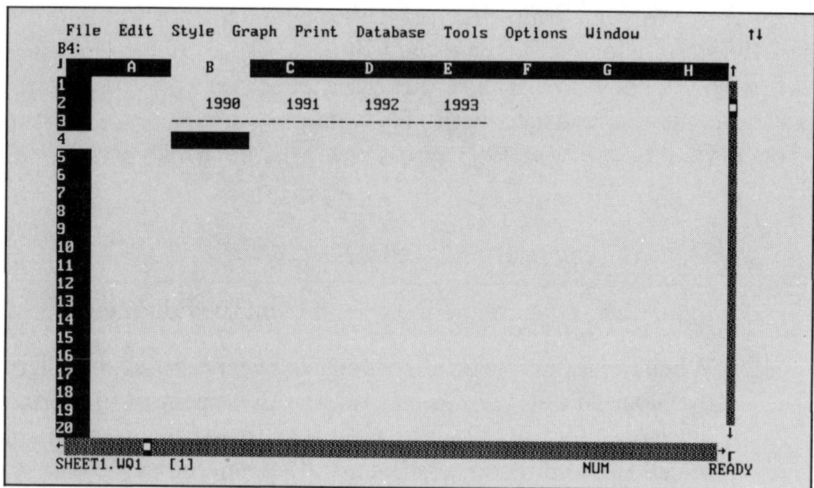

Figure 7.1: Years in row 2 entered with the Fill command

automatically stop when the specified block is filled or the ending number for the fill is reached. When decrementing past zero, enter a very large negative number for the ending value.

To fill a block of cells with dates, you can enter any date function, such as @TODAY or @DATE, or use any Ctrl–D-created date for the start and stop values and use any step value you like. (A step value of 1 would increment each date by one day.) Keep in mind, however, that the suggested stop value of 8192 will not be high enough for most dates because it's the serial date for June 5, 1922. Since you're probably interested in dates that come much later in the century, you should enter a much larger number instead.

After Quattro Pro has filled in the serial dates, type **/SND** to convert the serial dates to a more familiar date format.

When you do a fill for a second time on the same spreadsheet, you'll notice that Quattro Pro highlights the block it filled the last time. To fill a new block, press the Backspace key to unanchor the cell selector. Specify the coordinates of the new block you want to fill and press Enter. Notice that Quattro Pro then suggests the same start, step, and stop values as before. Type over these values as you wish to proceed with the fill.

If you fill a block that consists of several rows and columns, the Fill option will automatically start at the top-left corner of the block, fill that column, and then proceed to the top cell of the next column—continuing until all the columns are filled.

Figure 7.2 shows the result of two fill operations. The first example filled the block A1..A20 with dates. The function @DATE(91,5,19) was entered as the start value, 1 as the step value, and 99999 as the stop value. Then we formatted the block A1..A20 into the particular date format by typing **/SND2.**

In the second example, the block D14..G19 was filled with the number 4500 as the start value, – 50 as the step value, and 0 as the stop value. (Here we chose a stop value much smaller than 4500 because the step value was a large negative number—i.e., decrementing quickly from 4500.)

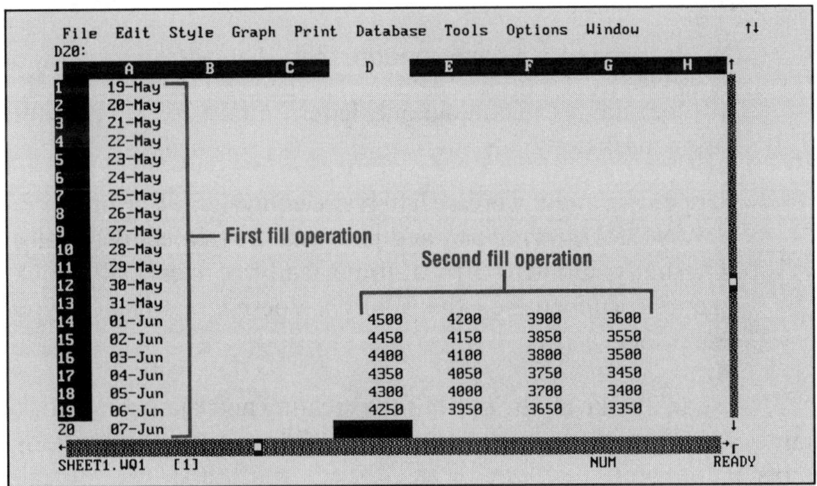

Figure 7.2: Results of the two fill operations

Simplifying Your Work with Named Blocks

Although it is never actually *necessary* to name blocks in your work, giving blocks names makes it easier to build and utilize a single spreadsheet.

You can use block names (which can refer to a single cell as well) within functions and formulas (in place of cell references), in response to the Go To key (F5), and in other places. For example, suppose you assign the names *Principal, Interest,* and *Term* to cells containing the principal, interest, and term of a loan. You could then calculate the payment on the loan using the more readable function @PMT(*Principal,Interest,Term*) rather than one with cell references, such as @PMT(B1,B2,B3). Furthermore, from anywhere on the spreadsheet you could press the F5 key and enter the cell's name to move the cell selector quickly to that cell. This is a very handy technique if you want to manage a large spreadsheet efficiently.

Valid Block Names

There are a few simple rules to keep in mind when creating block names:

- A block name can have no more than 15 characters.
- A block name can contain only letters, numbers, and punctuation marks.
- Uppercase and lowercase letters are equivalent. For instance, *PRINCIPAL, Principal,* and *principal* are treated identically. (Actually, Quattro Pro automatically converts all block names to uppercase—that's why it doesn't matter how you enter them.)

You can invoke all the options for creating and managing block names from the Names submenu on the Edit menu. The options under Names are:

- Create
- Delete
- Labels
- Reset
- Make Table

We'll discuss each of these options for creating and managing named blocks in the sections that follow.

Naming a Block

Naming a block is quite easy:

1. Move the cell selector to the upper-left corner of the block you want to name.
2. Select the Names and Create options from the Edit menu. That is, type /**ENC**.
3. When prompted, enter a name for the block and press Enter.
4. When prompted, highlight the block to be named and press Enter again.

To see the benefit of giving a block a name, press the Go To key (F5) and enter the block name directly on the input line. The cell selector will jump to the first cell in that block from anywhere on the spreadsheet.

Now, add some numbers and additional underlines to the spreadsheet you saved before (shown in Figure 7.1), so that it looks like Figure 7.3. To assign the name FIRSTYEAR to the data in column B (currently highlighted in the figure):

1. Move the cell selector to cell B4.
2. Key in /**ENC**. Quattro Pro will display a window with the prompt:

   Enter name to create/modify:

3. Type in **FIRSTYEAR** (capital letters are not necessary) and press Enter. The input line will display the prompt:

   Enter block: B4..B4

4. Press ↓ four times to highlight the block B4..B8 as shown in Figure 7.3.
5. Press Enter to complete the naming process.

To experiment with the named block, first try entering a function that contains the block's name. For example, move the cell selector to cell B10 and enter the function **@SUM(FIRSTYEAR)**. You will then see the total, 2118, appear in cell B10. To move the cell selector to the upper-left corner of the block, press F5, type **FIRSTYEAR**, and press Enter. The cell selector will move to the top of the named block, as shown in Figure 7.4.

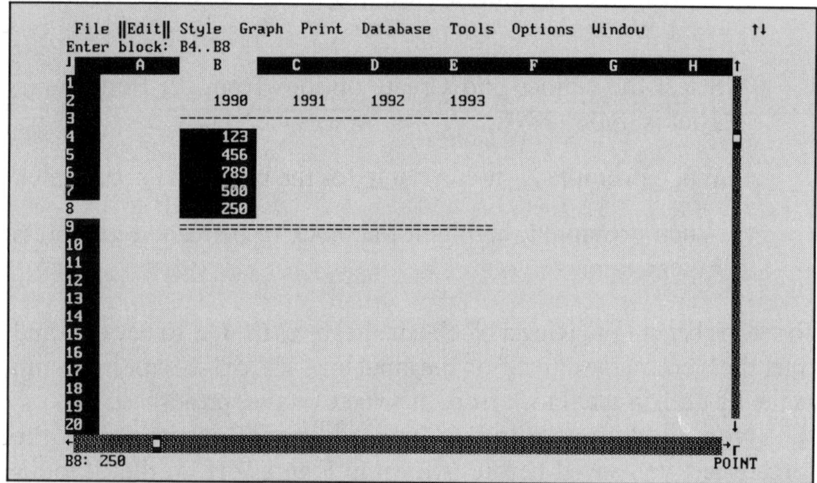

Figure 7.3: *Block to be named FIRSTYEAR, highlighted*

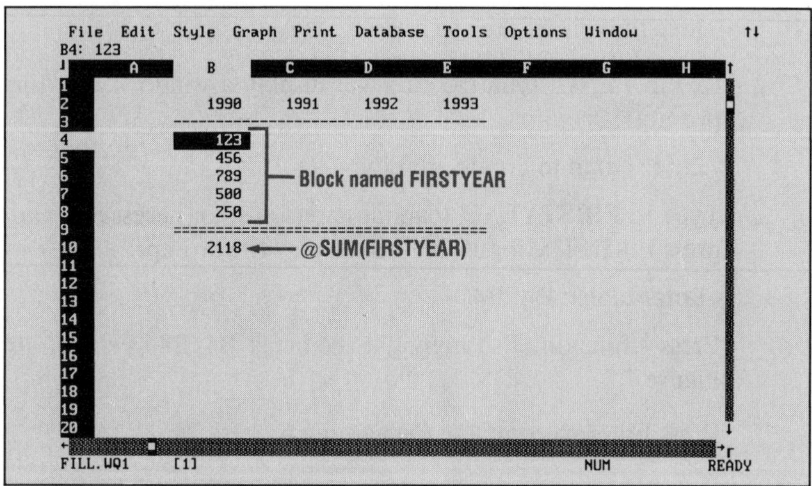

Figure 7.4: *Cell selector sent to FIRSTYEAR by the Go To key*

We discuss the use of block names in functions and in conjunction with the F5 key in more detail below. Save your spreadsheet now and open up a clean one for the examples to come.

Cell Labels as Block Names

Rather than type in block names directly, you can use labels within the spreadsheet as block names. (These labels must conform to the rules for valid block names mentioned above.)

To demonstrate, Figure 7.5 shows a sample spreadsheet with some data for a loan typed in. Column B was set to 15 spaces using the /**SC** command (or the Ctrl–W shortcut), cell B1 was formatted with /**SNC2** (or the shortcut Ctrl–F followed by selecting Currency and 2), and cell B2 was formatted with /**SNP0** (or Ctrl–F followed by Percent and 0 (zero)).

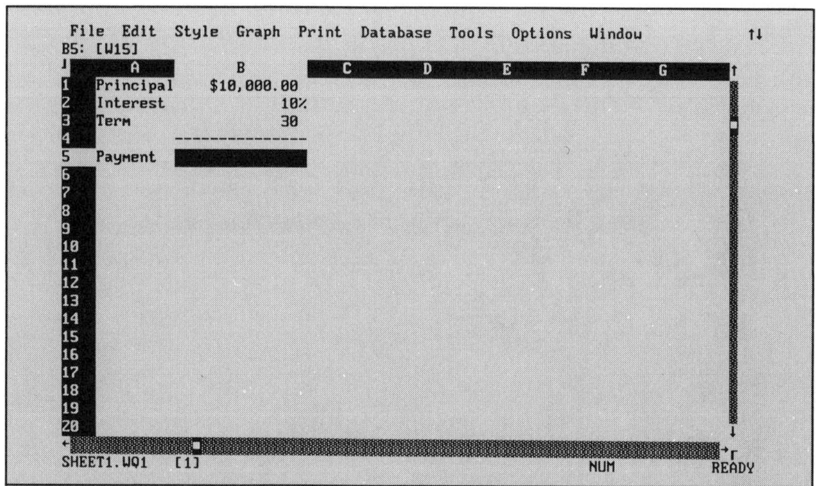

Figure 7.5: Sample spreadsheet with labels and loan values

Now suppose you want to assign the labels in cells A1 through A3 to the corresponding cells B1 through B3:

1. Position the cell selector at the upper-left corner of the block of labels (cell A1 in this example).

2 Key in /**ENL**. The screen will display four options:

Right
Down
Left
Up

Quattro Pro needs to know where the yet-to-be-named cells are in relation to the labels. These cells can be located either one column to the left or right of the labels, or one row above or below the labels. They cannot be farther away.

3 In this example, the cells to be named are to the right, so go ahead and select Right.

4 Quattro Pro will display the prompt

Enter label block: A1..A1

and wait for you to specify the block of cell names.

5 Press ↓ twice to highlight the labels in cells A1 through A3, as shown in Figure 7.6.

6 Press Enter.

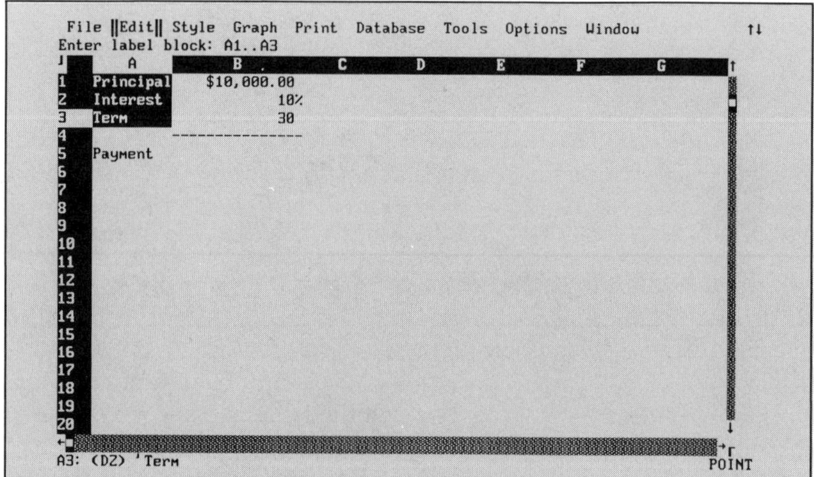

Figure 7.6: Labels used as block names, highlighted

Though not much appears to have happened, you have assigned the name PRINCIPAL to cell B1, INTEREST to cell B2, and TERM to cell B3. You'll see how to use these new names next.

Placing Block Names in a Function

You saw in a previous example how you could type a block name directly into the function @SUM(FIRSTYEAR). You can also use the Names key (F3) as a shortcut for entering block names. Let's experiment with the sample spreadsheet you've been using so far. Suppose you wish to calculate the payment on the loan using the new block names. Here are the steps:

1. Move the cell selector to where you want the function to appear (cell B5 in this example).
2. Type **@PMT(** to begin the function.
3. Press the F3 key. You'll see a window appear with the list of existing block names at the bottom, the function's cell address above that, and the function itself at the top, as shown in Figure 7.7.

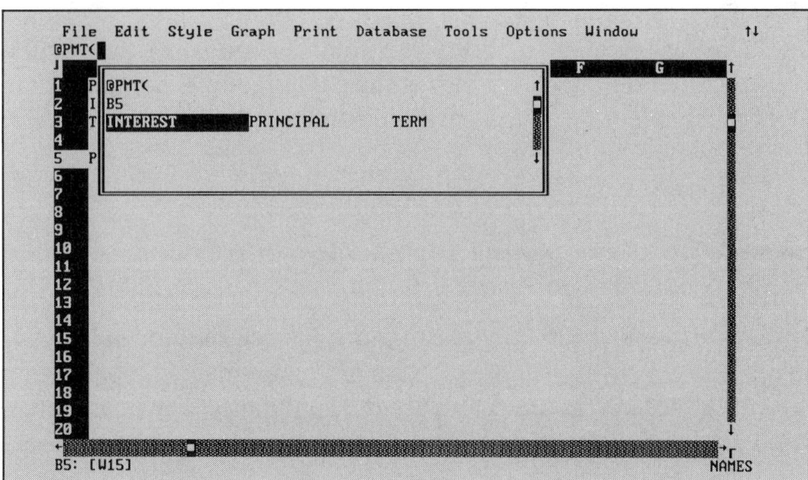

Figure 7.7: The block-name window

4. Highlight PRINCIPAL and press Enter. The function now reads

   @PMT(PRINCIPAL

5. Type **,** (a comma) to continue the function, and press F3 again to call up the block names.

6. Highlight INTEREST and press Enter.

7. Type **/12** to divide the annual interest by 12, and add a comma, so the function now reads

   @PMT(PAYMENT,INTEREST/12,

8. Press F3 to bring back the menu of block names, highlight TERM, and press Enter. The function now reads

   @PMT(PRINCIPAL,INTEREST/12,TERM

9. Finish the function by typing ***12)** to multiply the term by 12 and complete the function. It now reads

   @PMT(PRINCIPAL,INTEREST/12,TERM*12)

10. Press Enter.

The completed formula is placed in cell B5 and displays the calculated monthly payment. Now format cell B5 as in Figure 7.8 (keystrokes **/SNC2**).

This technique of selecting block names and using the Names key (F3) is not only fast, but also ensures that you will not misspell a block name or enter a nonexistent block name while creating a function or formula.

How to Go to a Named Block Quickly

As mentioned earlier, you can move the cell selector quickly to any named cell or to the upper-left corner of any named block using the F5 (Go To) key. You can also use the F3 (Names) key in conjunction with the F5 key to move the cell selector quickly to a named block

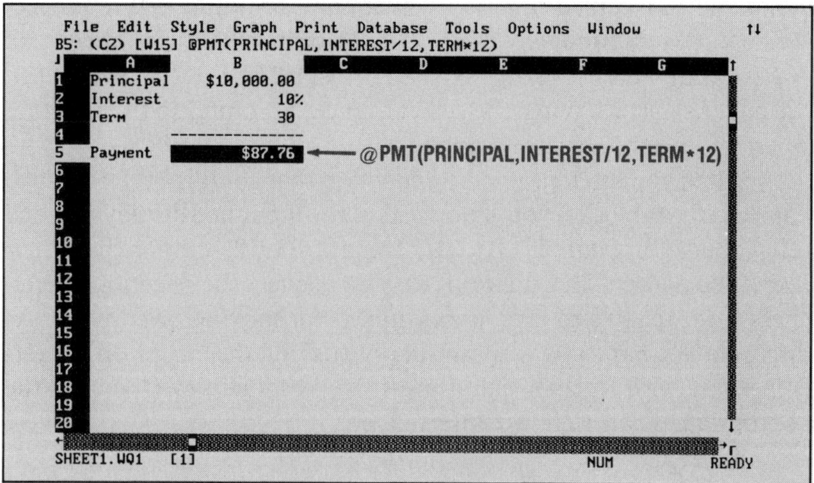

Figure 7.8: The function calculating with block names

(or cell). To try this out on the current spreadsheet, follow these steps:

1. Press F5. The input line will present the instruction:

   Enter address to go to: B5

2. Press F3. The screen will display a menu of block names and the current cell selector location.

3. Highlight any cell or block name and press Enter. The cell selector will jump immediately to the named cell or block.

This simple technique is actually very handy when you're working on a large spreadsheet because it allows you to move quickly to a specific cell from anywhere in the spreadsheet, with minimal typing and little room for error.

Save this spreadsheet now; you'll need it in the next chapter.

Giving Blocks Absolute and Relative Names

Named blocks can be treated as *absolute* or *relative* references when copying functions. For example, if you copy a function such as @PMT(PRINCIPAL,INTEREST/12,TERM*12) with the Ctrl-C command, the copied function will attempt to adjust cell references for their meaning and may produce incorrect results. If, however, you copy or move @PMT($PRINCIPAL,$INTEREST/12,$TERM*12), the dollar signs will make the cell references absolute, so the function will not adjust to its new location.

When you attempt to edit a function that contains references to named cells or blocks, you'll notice that the input line displays the cell references—for example, B1, B2/12, and B3*12—rather than their respective names. This makes it easy to convert the function's references from relative to absolute or mixed for moving or copying. As discussed in Chapter 4, you can simply position the cursor on the reference you wish to change and press the Absolute key (F4) until the appropriate dollar signs are inserted.

Moving a Named Block

Another advantage of named cells or blocks is that their names move with them. Therefore, any functions that refer to named blocks will still refer to them, and so retain their accuracy. For example, in the current spreadsheet, the function @PMT(PRINCIPAL,INTEREST/12, TERM*12) refers to the values in cells B1, B2, and B3. But moving any of these cells around the spreadsheet has no effect on it, so the function still calculates the proper payments.

To test this out for yourself, move the data in block A1..C3 to a new location. You'll notice that the payment function in cell B5, @PMT(PRINCIPAL,INTEREST/12,TERM*12), still calculates the appropriate payment. In addition, if you press the F5 and F3 keys and select a block name to go to, you'll see the cell selector move to the *new* location of the named block.

Block Moves That Overwrite Data

When you move data on a spreadsheet to an area that already contains data, it will completely overwrite (replace) that original data. If you inadvertently overwrite data in this way, they will be lost forever unless you press Alt–F5 to undo your move. An even safer way to ensure that data are not lost is first to save the spreadsheet before you move anything.

Effects of Block Moves on Formulas

Should you move data and/or formulas around on a spreadsheet, Quattro Pro will ensure that the formulas' meanings are retained. For example, if you move a formula such as +A1+A2 from one cell to another, its cell references will remain the same, regardless of whether they are relative or absolute. That is, moving the formula +A1+A2 from cell A3 to C3 leaves the formula as +A1+A2 in the new cell. But if you move the data to which the formula refers—or both the formula and the data—then the cell references will adjust accordingly.

Look at Figure 7.9 to see how this makes sense. Cell A4 contains the formula +A1+A2. If you move only the formula in cell A4 to a new location (say, cell C18), it will still display the sum of cells A1 and A2—as it should. If, however, you move the the entire block of cells A1 through A4, so that both the data and formula are relocated, then the formula in the new location will be adjusted to refer still to the two cells above it— +C11+C12 in this example. And if you move just the data—block A1..A2, in this case—to, say, C1..C2, then the formula in cell A4 will change from +A1+A2 to +C1+C2. In both cases, Quattro Pro has the smarts to retain the original meaning of the formula.

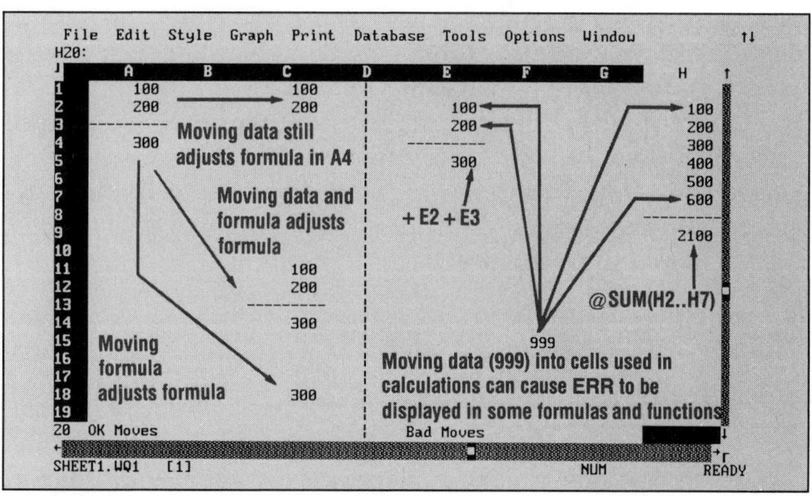

Figure 7.9: Examples of "OK" and "bad" moves

Avoiding Block Moves That Cause Errors

When you move data from somewhere on the spreadsheet to a new area that is already referenced by an existing formula, Quattro Pro may respond by changing the reference in the formula to ERR, which in turn makes the entire formula display **ERR** in its cell. This is a safety device that informs you when a data move might have caused a formula to calculate incorrect data.

For example, if cell E5 contains the formula +E2+E3 and a move of yours replaces the data in cell E2 with a new number, then the formula in cell E5 will become +ERR+E3 and the cell will display **ERR**. Quattro Pro is telling you that as a result of new data being moved into cell E2, the calculation performed by the formula in E5 may now yield an answer you're not expecting. If the move was intentional, you will need to edit or re-enter the formula in cell E5 so that it becomes +E2+E3 again.

If a function refers to an entire block, such as @SUM(H2..H7), then moving data into either of the *coordinate cells* H2 or H7 will change the function to @SUM(ERR). Note that this occurs *only* when you move data into one of the coordinate cells—i.e., those that define the upper-left and lower-right corners of a block. Moving data into any other cell within this block will not cause an error, but simply cause the function to recalculate and display the new value instead. Figure 7.9 shows examples of some "bad" moves that might cause a function or formula to display **ERR**.

Of course, all of this can seem quite confusing until you practice rearranging blocks on a spreadsheet some more. As discussed earlier, you can always type **/FS** to save the spreadsheet before moving anything. You can also press Alt–F5 to undo a move immediately after discovering you've made a mistake.

Reassigning a Block Name

When you name a block on a spreadsheet that already contains named blocks, Quattro Pro will display a list of existing block names and a prompt that awaits your entry. To change the location of an existing block name, enter the name or select it from the menu. Quattro Pro will display the current location of the block. If the block is a single cell, just move the cell selector to the new location and press Enter. If the existing block is larger than one cell, press Backspace or Escape to unanchor the cell selector, and then specify the new location for the block.

Deleting a Block Name

This procedure deletes only the block's *name,* not its data. To select this option, simply type /**END**. Then select the name you wish to delete from the menu of block names that appears on the screen.

If you delete a block name that is used in a function, Quattro Pro will simply adjust the function to use the cell reference rather than the block name. For example, if you were to delete INTEREST from the sample spreadsheet in Figure 7.8, the payment function @PMT(PRINCIPAL,INTEREST/12,TERM*12) would automatically be rewritten as @PMT(PRINCIPAL,B2/12,TERM*12).

Deleting All Block Names

To delete all the block names from a spreadsheet, type /**ENR** to select the Reset option. The screen will display the prompt **Delete all named blocks?** and provide you with the options **No** and **Yes**. To delete all block names, select Yes; to retain all block names, select No.

As with Delete, Reset only removes a block's *name,* not the data within it. The Reset option also replaces *all* references to named blocks within functions with regular cell references. Use this option with caution, therefore. After you have removed all the block names from a spreadsheet, the only way to retrieve them is to enter each one again. The Alt-F5 Undo command will also work, provided it has been previously enabled and that you invoke it immediately after the deletion. (Of course, if you saved the spreadsheet before deleting the block names, you can always retrieve the spreadsheet from the disk.)

Listing Block Names

There are two ways to view a list of block names and the cells that they reference. The first is the same one you used when you created the @PMT function. After making an entry on the input line that includes a function or an operator, press F3. The list of named blocks will appear in a window. Press the + key and the cell references for each named block will be displayed next to the names of the blocks. Pressing the – key contracts the Names window to its narrower width.

A second way of viewing block names and their coordinates is to make a table of block names directly on the spreadsheet. Quattro Pro can do this for you. Type **/ENM** to access the Edit menu and select the Names and Make Table options. When prompted, move the cell selector to the upper-left corner of the area in which you want the table to appear (if you have not already done so). Press Enter and the table will appear on the spreadsheet. Note, however, that this table will overwrite any data that were already in those cells, so be sure that you first move the cell selector to an area that has two columns of blank rows beneath it. Figure 7.10 shows both the Names menu and the table of block names created by Quattro Pro.

In this chapter, you've been introduced to some useful techniques for managing blocks of data on the spreadsheet. In the next chapter, you'll learn some advanced techniques for formatting the spreadsheet.

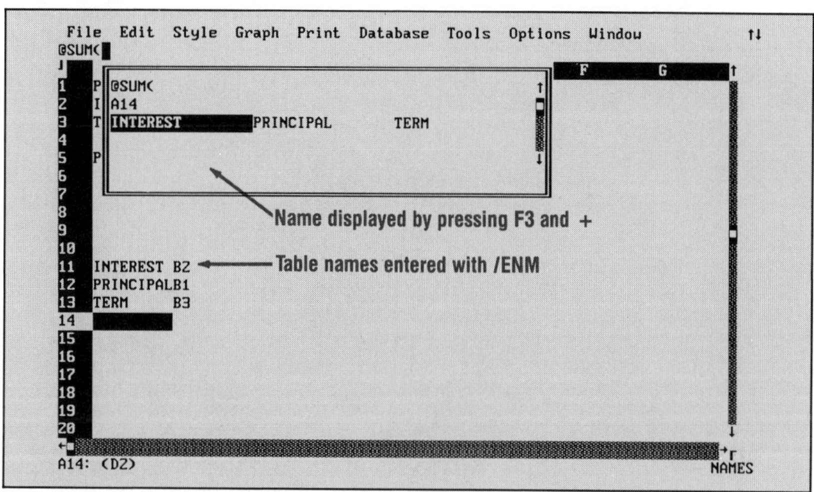

Figure 7.10: Block names and coordinates displayed on the screen

8

MAKING MORE PRODUCTIVE USE OF YOUR SPREADSHEET

FEATURING

Spreadsheet Protection from Accidental Changes

Searching the Spreadsheet for Particular Entries

Transposing Rows and Columns

Viewing Two Spreadsheet Areas Simultaneously

Formatting Cells to Emphasize Special Data

Until now, you've learned many basic skills for creating spreadsheets and handling data within them. In this chapter, you'll learn some slightly advanced, though simple and ultimately essential, techniques for managing your spreadsheet more effectively.

Protecting a Spreadsheet

Suppose that your work requires you to build many spreadsheets and let other people use them to enter data and perform calculations. It's quite possible, then, that less experienced people will make a mess of your work by accidentally replacing formulas with numbers or inadvertently erasing large blocks of text.

To protect against such catastrophes, you can place the entire spreadsheet in a protected mode, while leaving specific cells open for later changes.

To set up a protection scheme for your spreadsheet, first access the Protection option from the Style menu to specify which cells you want to make unprotected. Then select the Protection option from the Options menu to initiate the global protection feature, which will allow you to modify only those cells that have been made unprotected.

Consider the simple loan-payment spreadsheet you developed in the last chapter. Any person using this spreadsheet to calculate loan payments only needs to change the loan parameters in cells B1, B2, and B3. For example, increase the principal to $50,000 so the spreadsheet resembles Figure 8.1. The labels in column A and the function to calculate the payment in cell B5 do not need to be changed. We'll discuss how to protect cells in the following sections.

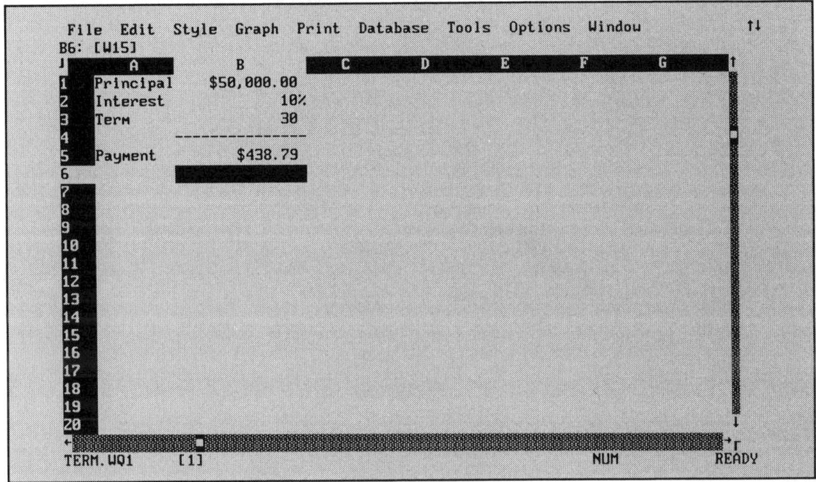

Figure 8.1: Simple loan payment spreadsheet

Unprotecting Designated Cells

The Style menu includes the Protection option which allows you to specify individual cells or a block of cells to protect or make unprotected. In the following steps, we'll use this option to unprotect cells in block B1..B3:

1. Move the cell selector to the cell or upper-left corner of the block to unprotect (in this example, cell B1).
2. Type /**SP** to select the Style menu and the Protection option from the menu. From the submenu select the Unprotect option and press Enter.
3. When Quattro Pro displays the prompt **Block to be modified,** press ↓ twice to extend the cell selector over cells B2 and B3, as shown in Figure 8.2.

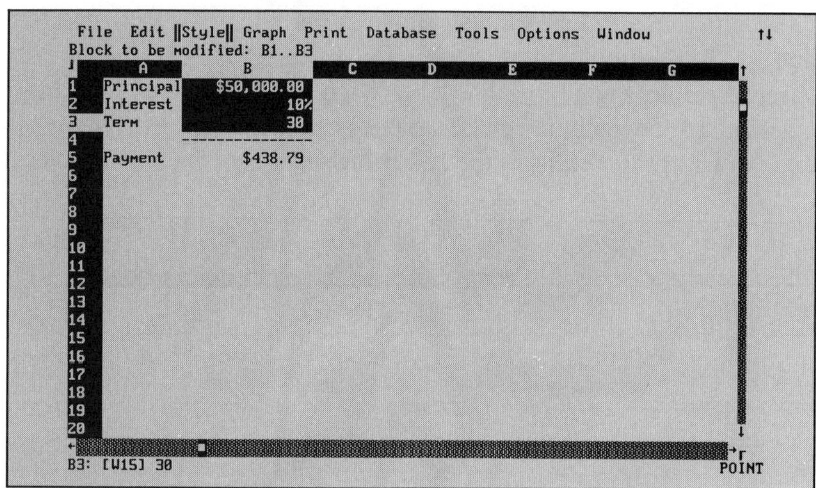

Figure 8.2: Cells to unprotect, highlighted on the screen

4. Press Enter to complete the job.

Turning On Global Protection

At this point, you've unprotected cells B1 through B3; but you have not yet turned the global protection feature on, so it is still possible to change or delete the contents of any cell on the spreadsheet. To turn on global protection, type /**OPE** to select the Protection and Enable options from the Options menu. (Hit Escape to clear the menu from the screen.)

To test the degree of protection, try changing any of the values in B1, B2, or B3. You'll see that Quattro Pro accepts the new data and recalculates the function accordingly. But try changing the contents of any other cell on the spreadsheet, and Quattro Pro will reject the action, beep, and display the error message shown in Figure 8.3. Press Enter or Escape to resume your work.

As you move the cell selector about the spreadsheet, you'll notice that the input line at the top of the screen displays **PR** when a protected cell is highlighted, and **U** when an unprotected cell is highlighted (along with other codes that show how the cell is formatted).

Note that after setting up a protection scheme, you should type /**FS** to save the spreadsheet so that the new protection scheme is saved as well.

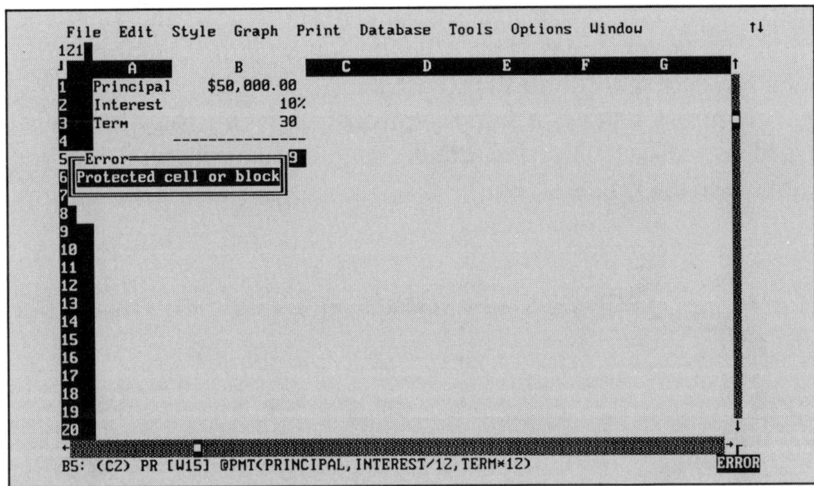

Figure 8.3: The error message for protected cells

Turning Off Global Protection

Of course, you may later decide to make changes to parts of the spreadsheet that are currently protected. To do so, just call up the Options menu, then the Protection and Disable options (keystrokes /**OPD**). Once again, you'll be able to move the cell selector to any cell and add, change, or delete data, functions, or formulas. (Press Escape first to clear the menu from the screen.)

Reprotecting Individual Cells

If you use the Style menu and the Protect option to unprotect a cell or group of cells, then later change your mind and decide to protect those cells, simply type /**SPP** to select the Protection option from the Style menu.

Remember to save the spreadsheet with its new protection scheme (keystrokes /**FS**).

Reformatting Long Labels

Quattro Pro includes a text-formatting feature, similar to something you might find in a word-processing system, that changes the margin width of long text labels, and neatly adjusts the long label within the new margins. This is handy for entering memos or other long passages of text into a spreadsheet.

Figure 8.4 shows a sample spreadsheet with a very long label typed into cell A1. The label actually spills over to column R, but you cannot see this on the screen.

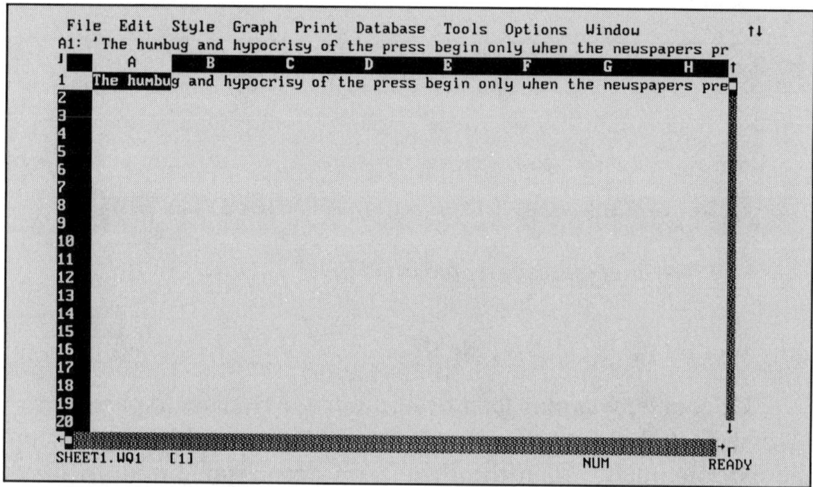

Figure 8.4: Sample spreadsheet with a long label in cell A1

Now suppose you wish to display the long label so that it can be read without having to scroll over to column R. Call up the Tools menu and the Reformat option to do so:

1. Move the cell selector to the beginning of the label (cell A1 in this example).
2. Type /**TR** to select the Reformat option from the Tools menu.
3. When the input line reads **Block to be modified: A1..A1**, specify the number of columns that you want the reformatted label to fit into. For example, if you want to adjust the current label to fit into columns A, B, and C, press → twice to specify the block A1..C1.
4. Press Enter to complete the operation.

Figure 8.5 shows the same label after reformatting. Notice that the label is neatly *word-wrapped*—that is, lines are broken between words rather than within words.

If you reformat a label, any data and formulas beneath it in the same column will be pushed down to make room for the reformatted text.

However, data or labels in other columns will not be pushed down, and existing data to the right of the reformatted cell may block the display of the reformatted text. If this occurs, move the existing data and formulas to a new location on the spreadsheet (keystrokes **/EM** to start). The reformatted labels will then appear on the screen after you complete the move operation.

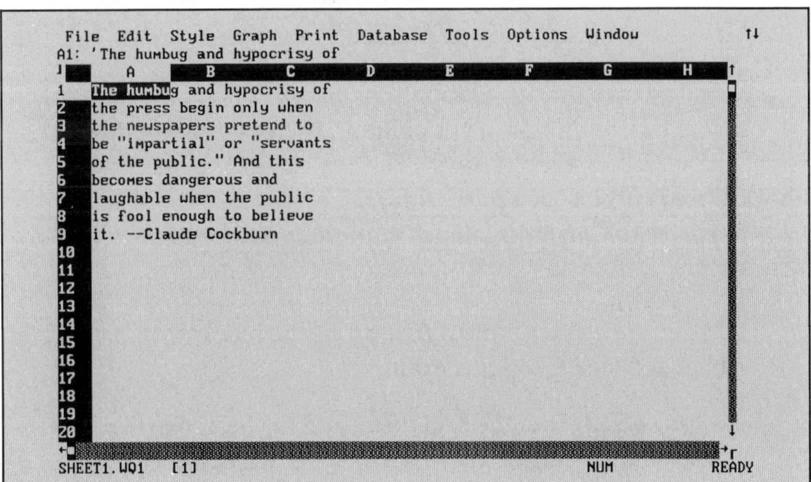

Figure 8.5: Long label reformatted to fit within three columns

Searching a Spreadsheet for a Specific Entry

Another handy technique for managing text that Quattro Pro offers is its global find-and-replace capability, which can be used to change all occurrences of text or numbers to some new value. An example will best demonstrate this powerful feature.

Figure 8.6 shows a sample spreadsheet with transactions for the month of December—that is, only the first 20 rows of the month's

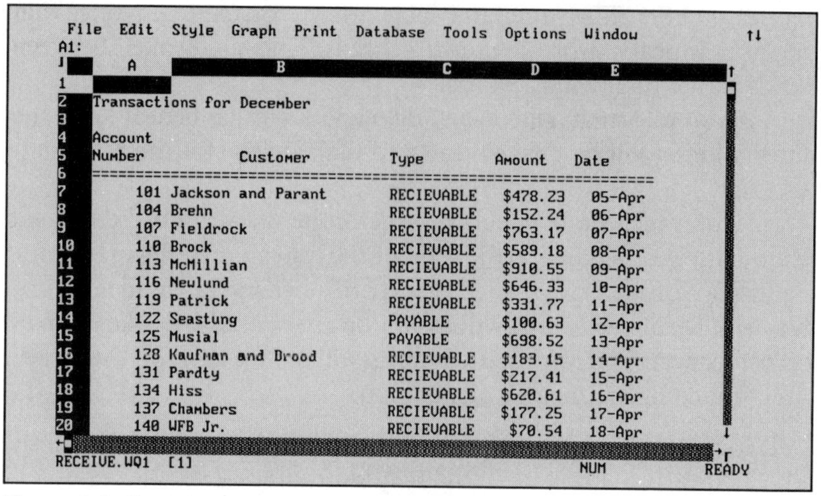

```
File  Edit  Style  Graph  Print  Database  Tools  Options  Window
A1:
     A              B                      C              D          E
1
2   Transactions for December
3
4   Account
5   Number         Customer             Type         Amount    Date
6   ================================================================
7        101 Jackson and Parant      RECIEVABLE    $478.23   05-Apr
8        104 Brehn                   RECIEVABLE    $152.24   06-Apr
9        107 Fieldrock               RECIEVABLE    $763.17   07-Apr
10       110 Brock                   RECIEVABLE    $589.18   08-Apr
11       113 McMillian               RECIEVABLE    $910.55   09-Apr
12       116 Newlund                 RECIEVABLE    $646.33   10-Apr
13       119 Patrick                 RECIEVABLE    $331.77   11-Apr
14       122 Seastung                PAYABLE       $100.63   12-Apr
15       125 Musial                  PAYABLE       $698.52   13-Apr
16       128 Kaufman and Drood       RECIEVABLE    $183.15   14-Apr
17       131 Pardty                  RECIEVABLE    $217.41   15-Apr
18       134 Hiss                    RECIEVABLE    $620.61   16-Apr
19       137 Chambers                RECIEVABLE    $177.25   17-Apr
20       140 WFB Jr.                 RECIEVABLE     $70.54   18-Apr
RECEIVE.WQ1  [1]                                     NUM        READY
```

Figure 8.6: Sample spreadsheet with misspellings

ledger. Note that within the Type column, the word *receivable* is consistently misspelled as *recievable.* The search-and-replace capability allows you to correct such misspellings.

To correct all the misspellings in the sample spreadsheet, follow these steps:

1. Move the cell selector to the top of the block with data to be changed (cell C7 in this example).

2. Type /**ES** to select the Edit menu and the Search & Replace option from the menu. You will see the Search & Replace menu, as in Figure 8.7.

3. Select Block (type **B**). The input line reads:

   Enter search block: C7

   Specify the block you want to search. In this example, press the period key to anchor the cell selector, then press End and ↓ to highlight all of column C. Press Enter.

4. Select Search String (type **S**). The screen displays a box with the prompt

   Find what:

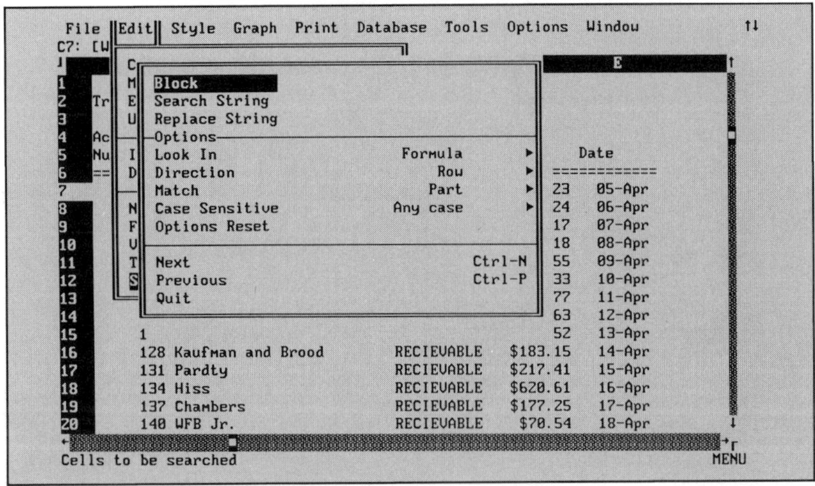

Figure 8.7: The Search & Replace menu

Type in the string to search for—**RECIEVABLE**—and press Enter.

5 Select Replace String from the menu (type **R**). The screen displays the prompt

Replace with:

Type in the replacement string—**RECEIVABLE**—and press Enter.

6 Select Next (type **N**) to begin the search-and-replace procedure.

The first time that Quattro Pro finds a string that matches the search string, it will display the contents of the cell, along with the menu in Figure 8.8. The replacement options are:

Yes	Replaces the current text, continues to the next matching string, and asks again
No	Does not replace the current string but moves on to the next matching string anyway and asks again
All	Changes all occurrences of the matching string without asking anymore

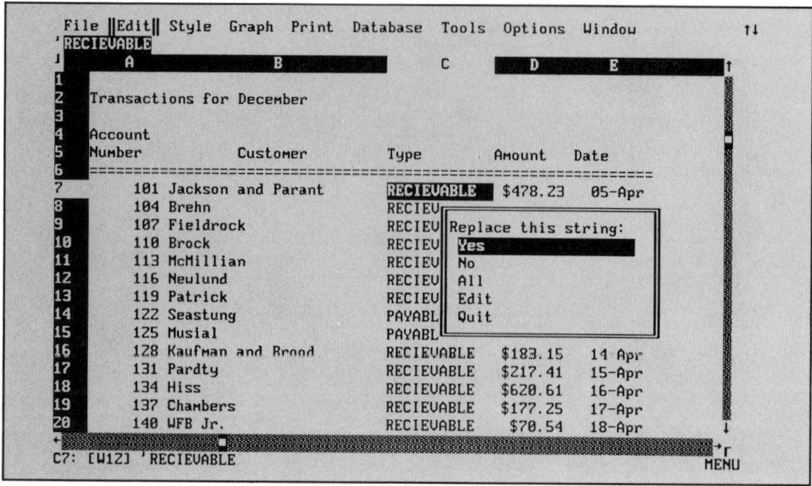

***Figure 8.8:** The Search & Replace confirmation menu*

Edit	Allows you to edit the cell entry; pressing Enter restarts the Search & Replace program
Quit	Stops the Search & Replace procedure

In this example, select All to replace all occurrences of the word *recievable.* Quattro Pro will instantly perform the entire search-and-replace operation. Figure 8.9 shows the sample spreadsheet after Quattro Pro has globally corrected all occurrences of *recievable.*

There are several other options presented on the Search & Replace menu:

Look In	Determines how a formula will be examined in the search process. The Formula choice searches for a formula only. The Values choice searches only for the results generated by a formula. The Condition choice allows you to include operators in your search. (For example, one conditional search might be **?>200**, which instructs Quattro Pro to look for all values greater than 200.)
Direction	Specifies whether to search row by row or column by column

```
File  Edit  Style  Graph  Print  Database  Tools  Options  Window
C7: [W12] 'RECEIVABLE
        A            B              C          D         E
1
2  Transactions for December
3
4  Account
5  Number       Customer          Type        Amount    Date
6  ==========================================================
7       101 Jackson and Parant    RECEIVABLE  $478.23   05-Apr
8       104 Brehn                 RECEIVABLE  $152.24   06-Apr
9       107 Fieldrock             RECEIVABLE  $763.17   07-Apr
10      110 Brock                 RECEIVABLE  $589.18   08-Apr
11      113 McMillian             RECEIVABLE  $910.55   09-Apr
12      116 Neulund               RECEIVABLE  $646.33   10-Apr
13      119 Patrick               RECEIVABLE  $331.77   11-Apr
14      122 Seastung              PAYABLE     $100.63   12-Apr
15      125 Musial                PAYABLE     $698.52   13-Apr
16      128 Kaufman and Brood     RECEIVABLE  $183.15   14-Apr
17      131 Pardty                RECEIVABLE  $217.41   15-Apr
18      134 Hiss                  RECEIVABLE  $620.61   16-Apr
19      137 Chambers              RECEIVABLE  $177.25   17-Apr
20      140 WFB Jr.               RECEIVABLE   $70.54   18-Apr
RECEIVE.WQ1  [1]                                   NUM         READY
```

Figure 8.9: Sample spreadsheet after globally changing RECIEVABLE to RECEIVABLE

Match	Specifies whether the search must match the entire cell entry or only a portion of the entry
Case Sensitive	Specifies whether the search should distinguish between upper and lower case, or treat all letters equally
Options Reset	Resets the search conditions, including block and string entries, to the default settings

If you just want to search for a particular item, without replacing it, you can select No from the replacement option in the search-and-replace procedure.

You can also use the Search & Replace option to change numbers in a spreadsheet. For example, suppose that the account number for Brock in the sample spreadsheet should be 110 rather than 103. You can then specify column A (i.e., block A7..A11) as the block to search and replace, 103 as the search string, and 110 as the replace string. Then select Next and proceed as discussed previously.

Use this technique with caution. Suppose that you were changing a receivable amount from $500 to $550. Quattro Pro will blindly change *all* occurrences of $500, disregarding whose invoice it may actually be. Keep this in mind when you use the Search & Replace command to make global changes to the price of an item or similar value in a spreadsheet. Sometimes you *want* the computer to go about changing things indiscriminately—as when you corrected the spelling of *receivable.*

Transposing Blocks

Typically, a spreadsheet consists of rows and columns of data, with headings in the top row and left-most column. How you arrange the rows and columns is a matter of your own choosing. But just in case you change your mind about the way you've laid out the rows and columns in a spreadsheet, Quattro Pro offers a quick and easy method for changing the row headings into column headings, and vice versa.

Figure 8.10 lists probable voting turnouts by state in a hypothetical (?) election. The columns are headed by state names, and the rows by politicians. Since there are only two candidates, but 50 states, this table would be more easy to read if the states were listed by rows and the two contenders by columns. Typing the entries again would be pointless drudgery; *transposing* the columns and rows would be a better way.

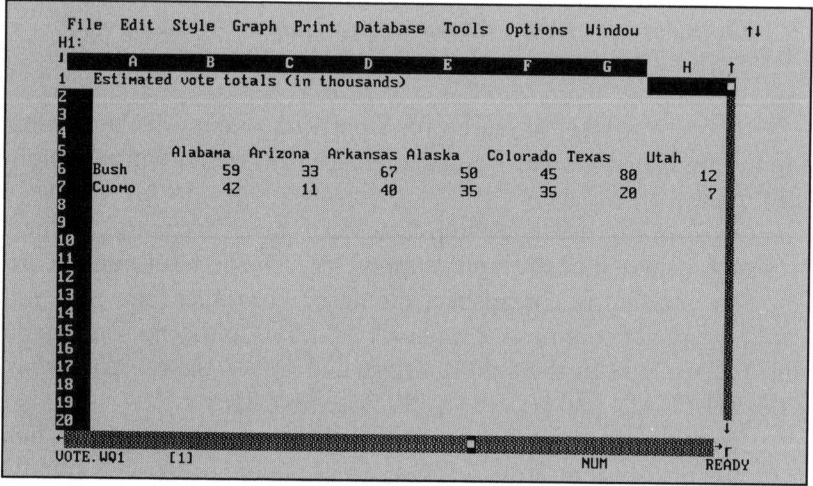

Figure 8.10: Voting turnouts by state for Bush and Cuomo

To rearrange the spreadsheet, follow these steps:

1. Move the cell selector to the upper-left corner of the block you wish to transpose (A5 in this example).
2. Type /**ET** to select the Transpose option from the Edit menu.
3. When you see the prompt **Source block of cells: A5..A5**, highlight the entire block that you wish to transpose (A5..H7 in this example), using the usual pointing method. Then press Enter.
4. When you see the prompt **Destination for cells:**, move the cell selector to the cell you wish to use as the upper-left corner of the transposed block. For this example, move the cell selector to cell A12.
5. Press Enter to complete the transposition.

Figure 8.11 shows the transposed block, starting in cell A12.

In the future, you should be aware of two important points when using the Transpose option. First of all, chances are that formulas (both with absolute and relative references) will become inaccurate

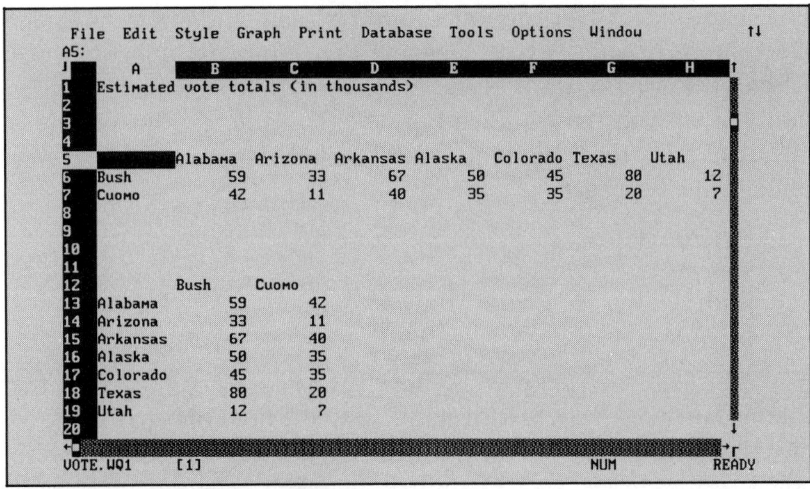

Figure 8.11: The vote totals transposed

after a transposition takes place, because Quattro Pro cannot alter a formula's variables to account for the change. That is, a formula that refers to, say, cell D4 in its calculation will continue to do so, even if a transposition has relocated the contents of cell D4 to cell A7.

Second, if the block into which you transpose data already contains data, the transposed data will overwrite (replace) the data originally in the block. When that happens you can immediately press Alt–F5 to undo the command, unless you don't care about it.

To play it safe, then, type **/FS** to save a spreadsheet *before* transposing data. If you find that the transposition created problems, just type **/FR** to retrieve the original, unchanged spreadsheet.

Freezing Titles

With any spreadsheet that is too large to fit on a single screen, you need to scroll around to locate particular data. As you do so, column titles and other pertinent data may move off the screen, so that you see only rows and columns of numbers. To avoid sinking in this sea of digits, you can freeze column and/or row headings at the edges of the screen. In this way, you can scroll deep within the spreadsheet and still know what the rows and columns are called.

This Locked Titles option is found on the Windows menu under the Options option. Before engaging this command, place the cell selector below a row of titles and/or to the right of a column of titles that you wish to freeze. Then type **/WOL** to access the Windows menu and select the Options and Locked Titles options. The following submenu will appear:

Horizontal
Vertical
Both
Clear

To freeze only those titles above the cell selector (i.e., only the column headings), select Horizontal. To freeze titles only to the left of the cell selector (i.e., only the row headings), select Vertical. To freeze both headings, select Both. (To unfreeze previously frozen titles, select Clear.) When you return to the spreadsheet and scroll far to the right or downwards, the titles will remain on the screen.

Figure 8.12 shows a sample spreadsheet that displays a political campaign budget. Though not currently visible on the screen, the months extend to the right, out to the month of December. There are also a few rows beneath row 20.

File Edit Style Graph Print Database Tools Options Window

B5: 7856

	A	B	C	D	E	F
1	1992 Campaign Budget (in thousands)					
2						
3		Jan	Feb	Mar	April	May
4	Funds raised					
5	Individuals	7856	9908	3454	2245	9385
6	PAC'S	15000	20000	25000	20000	30000
7	-------------------------	----------	----------	----------	----------	----------
8	Total Income	$22,856	$29,908	$28,454	$22,245	$39,385
9						
10						
11	Cost of Fund Raising	13713.6	17944.8	17072.4	13347	23631
12	TV	500	600	700	800	900
13	Radio	100	150	200	250	300
14	Print	200	300	400	500	600
15	Direct Mail	250	350	450	550	650
16	Phone Bank	500	500	500	500	500
17	Consultant	50	50	50	50	50
18	Rent for HQ	5	5	5	5	5
19	Phones	5	5	5	5	5
20	Salaries	50	50	50	50	50

CAMPAIGN.WQ1 [1] NUM READY

Figure 8.12: *Sample campaign spreadsheet, top-left corner*

Figure 8.13 shows how the large spreadsheet looks if you scroll to the lower-right corner. Because all row and column titles have since scrolled off the screen, it is difficult to tell what the various numbers refer to. But you want to know what's what. So, assuming you've already created the sample spreadsheet:

1. Move the cell selector to cell B4, which is the first row beneath the titles that you want to freeze. Figure 8.12 shows the the cell selector positioned accordingly.

2. Type /**W** to select the Windows menu. From the menu, choose Options. Select the Locked Titles option, and from the submenu, Both.

Nothing appears to happen at first. If you scroll down to the lower-right corner of the spreadsheet, however, the column and row titles will remain on the screen, as shown in Figure 8.14.

```
 File  Edit  Style  Graph  Print  Database  Tools  Options  Window            ↑↓
M28: (C0) +M8-M26
        G         H         I         J         K         L         M        N
11  274589.4     32004   43438.8   44718.6  393325.8   17398.2   12405.6
12      1000      1100      1200      1300      1400      1400      1400
13       350       400       450       500       550       550       550
14       700       800       900      1000      1100      1100      1100
15       750       850       950      1050      1150      1150      1150
16       500       500       500       500       500       500       500
17        50        50        50        50        50        50        50
18         5         5         5         5         5         5         5
19         5         5         5         5         5         5         5
20        50        50        50        50        50        50        50
21        20        20        20        20        20        20        20
22         1         1         1         1         1         1         1
23         5         5         5         5         5         5         5
24         5         5         5         5         5         5         5
25
26  278030.4     35795   47579.8   49209.6  398166.8   22239.2   17246.6
27  ======================================================================
28  $179,619   $17,545   $24,818   $25,321  $257,376    $6,758    $3,429
29
30
CAMPAIGN.WQ1 [1]                                              NUM        READY
```

Figure 8.13: Sample campaign spreadsheet when scrolled to bottom-right corner

```
 File  Edit  Style  Graph  Print  Database  Tools  Options  Window            ↑↓
M30:
        A                     I         J         K         L         M
1   1992 Campaign Budget
2
3                           Aug      Sept       Oct       Nov       Dec
4   Funds raised
15  Direct Mail             950      1050      1150      1150      1150
16  Phone Bank              500       500       500       500       500
17  Consultant               50        50        50        50        50
18  Rent for HQ               5         5         5         5         5
19  Phones                    5         5         5         5         5
20  Salaries                 50        50        50        50        50
21  Travel                   20        20        20        20        20
22  Entertainment             1         1         1         1         1
23  Contributions             5         5         5         5         5
24  Other                     5         5         5         5         5
25
26  Total Costs         47579.8   49209.6  398166.8   22239.2   17246.6
27  ==================================================================
28  Net                 $24,818   $25,321  $257,376    $6,758    $3,429
29
30
CAMPAIGN.WQ1 [1]                                              NUM        READY
```

Figure 8.14: Sample campaign spreadsheet scrolled with frozen titles

There is one small disadvantage to freezing sections of the spreadsheet: after you freeze an area, you can no longer use the arrow keys to move the cell selector into that area to make changes. If you need to make changes within the area, type **/WOLC** (accessing the Windows menu and the Options, Locked Titles, and Clear options) to unfreeze the area. Then press the Home key to bring you to the part of the spreadsheet where the titles are.

Viewing Two Spreadsheet Areas Simultaneously

Very often you'll find yourself having to scroll back and forth between two areas of a large spreadsheet. Rather than pressing the arrow and Page Up–Page Down keys incessantly, you can divide the screen in half, either horizontally or vertically, and scroll through the two separate sections independently.

Using the campaign budget spreadsheet shown earlier, you would follow these steps to split the screen into two horizontal windowpanes.

1. If frozen titles are in effect, type /**WOLC**. (Frozen titles are not necessary if you are using windowpanes).
2. Move the cell selector to the row at which you want to split the screen (we'll use row 9 in this example).
3. Type /**W** to select the Window menu, then choose Options.
4. Select Horizontal to split the screen horizontally.

At this point, the screen is split in half, and a new horizontal border appears between rows 8 and 9, as in Figure 8.15.

Switching between Two Panes

The cell selector will operate in only one window at a time. To switch it from one pane to the other, press the F6 key. If you move the cell selector to the bottom window, and hold down the ↓ key for a while, you'll be able to scroll through the expenses items without affecting the upper window. Figure 8.15 shows the sample spreadsheet with the cell selector scrolled down to row 29.

Synchronizing the Scrolling of Two Panes

While the campaign spreadsheet is split in half horizontally, take a moment to experiment with synchronized scrolling. Type /**WOS**. If

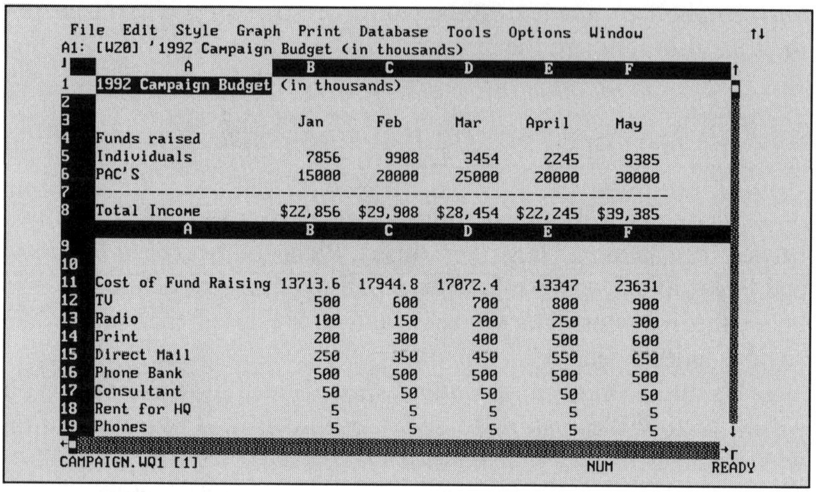

```
File  Edit  Style  Graph  Print  Database  Tools  Options  Window              ↑↓
A1: [W20] '1992 Campaign Budget (in thousands)
          A                B         C         D         E         F
1  1992 Campaign Budget (in thousands)
2
3                          Jan       Feb       Mar       April     May
4  Funds raised
5  Individuals             7856      9908      3454      2245      9385
6  PAC'S                  15000     20000     25000     20000     30000
7  ---------------------------------------------------------------------
8  Total Income          $22,856   $29,908   $28,454   $22,245   $39,385
          A                B         C         D         E         F
9
10
11 Cost of Fund Raising 13713.6   17944.8   17072.4     13347     23631
12 TV                       500       600       700       800       900
13 Radio                    100       150       200       250       300
14 Print                    200       300       400       500       600
15 Direct Mail              250       350       450       550       650
16 Phone Bank               500       500       500       500       500
17 Consultant                50        50        50        50        50
18 Rent for HQ                5         5         5         5         5
19 Phones                     5         5         5         5         5
CAMPAIGN.WQ1 [1]                                          NUM          READY
```

Figure 8.15: Campaign spreadsheet divided into two windowpanes

you hold down the → key for a few seconds to scroll to the right, then ← to scroll to the left, you'll notice that both windows scroll in synchronization—regardless of which window the cell selector is in. Note, though, that this joint scrolling holds for only one direction of motion: horizontal scrolling (← and → keys) for a horizontally split screen and vertical scrolling (↑ and ↓ keys) for a vertically split screen—described next.

You can unsynchronize the windows if you want, by typing **/WOU** to select the Options and Unsync options. Notice that the windows no longer scroll together; instead, only the selected window scrolls. To return to synchronized scrolling, type **/WOS**.

You cannot split the screen both horizontally and vertically at the same time. If you attempt to do so, Quattro Pro will beep at you. Before switching from a horizontal split to a vertical split, then, you must first clear the existing window split.

Clearing the Second Windowpane

To join the screen back into a single windowpane, simply type **/WOC** to access the Clear option from the Options and Windows menus. The bottom windowpane will disappear, and the cell selector will be returned to its last position in the top window.

Creating a Vertical Windowpane

The example above demonstrated a horizontal window break. To split the screen vertically instead, move the cell selector to the column at which you want to split the screen, and type /**WOV**. Remember, synchronized scrolling will *now* work only in the vertical direction.

The Effect an Open Pane Has on Spreadsheet Changes

While the spreadsheet is split into two panes, any changes you make to numbers used in calculations will be reflected immediately in both windows. They are, after all, just two views of the same spreadsheet.

Some cosmetic changes will not be automatically reflected in both panes, however. These include frozen titles, column widths, and display formats assigned with the Formats option under the Options menu, rather than the Numeric Format option under the Style menu. Think of the supplementary lower (or right) window as superimposing the upper (or left) one. Any cosmetic changes made to the second windowpane will disappear when you go back to the single-window mode; any made to the first will remain.

Emphasizing Special Cells

When you format cells for data entry, Quattro Pro automatically adds commas, currency symbols, or the appropriate number of decimals. To add even more emphasis to certain areas or cells of the spreadsheet (so that, say, negative numbers or unusual profits stand out), Quattro Pro offers several options that are found on the Style menu.

If you are running Quattro Pro in WYSIWYG mode (available only in version 3.0), you have the option of turning the grid lines that outline all of the cell borders off or on. The default setting is on. To turn the grid off, use the Window, Options, Grid commands (/**WOG**).

Line Drawing

Select the Line Drawing option in the Style menu to invoke a variety of techniques for emphasizing a block of cells. Quattro Pro will prompt you to enter a block. After the block is chosen, using the usual pointing method or typing in the block address, the Placement submenu will appear as in Figure 8.16.

The options on the Placement menu are as follows:

All	Puts a box around the block of cells you have specified and draws vertical and horizontal lines between the cells to produce a grid effect; an example is shown in Figure 8.17
Outside	Draws a box around the specified block of cells (but no grid)
Top	Draws a horizontal line across the top of the first row of the specified block
Bottom	Draws a horizontal line below the last row in the block
Left	Draws a vertical line along the left border of the specified block
Right	Draws a vertical line along the right border of the specified block
Inside	Draws lines vertically and horizontally between the cells, but does not draw a line around the

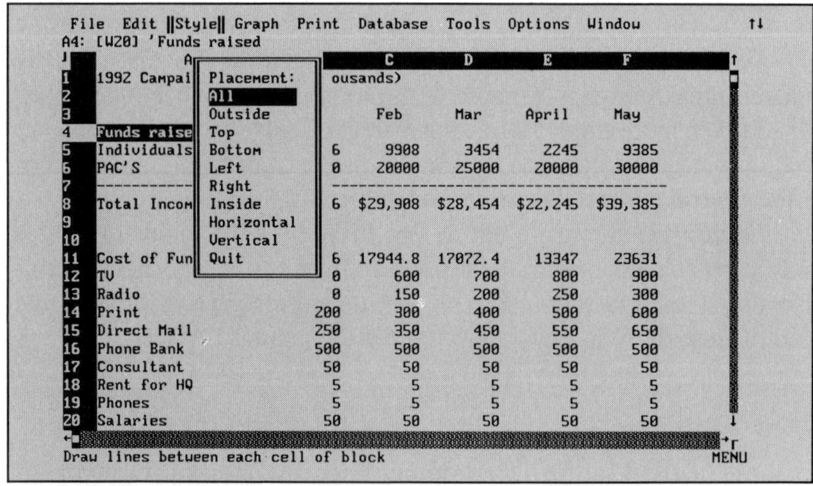

Figure 8.16: The Placement submenu

```
 File  Edit ||Style|| Graph  Print  Database  Tools  Options  Window          ↑↓
Enter block to draw lines: A4..A4
           A                B         C         D         E         F
1  1992 Campaign Budget (in thousands)
2
3                           Jan       Feb       Mar       April     May
4  Funds raised
5  Individuals              7856      9908      3454      2245      9385
6  PAC'S                    15000     20000     25000     20000     30000
7  ------------------       --------  --------  --------  --------  --------
8  Total Income             $22,856   $29,908   $28,454   $22,245   $39,385
9
10
11 Cost of Fund Raising  13713.6   17944.8   17072.4   13347     23631
12 TV                       500       600       700       800       900
13 Radio                    100       150       200       250       300
14 Print                    200       300       400       500       600
A4: [W20] 'Funds raised                                                  POINT
```

Figure 8.17: Spreadsheet with the All option

	perimeter of the block—i.e., draws a grid without a box
Horizontal	Draws horizontal lines between the rows in the selected block
Vertical	Draws vertical lines between the columns in the selected block

Choosing the Line Thickness

After selecting the line you want to add to the block of specified cells, a submenu will appear with four options. Select the type of line you want—Single, Double, or Thick Line—and press Enter. The line(s) will appear and the Placement menu will remain open, so you can modify your choice.

Removing Lines

If you decide that the lines you have added to the spreadsheet are not appropriate and you are still in the Placement menu, you can remove them by selecting All, and then choosing None from the Line Types submenu. The lines will be removed from the spreadsheet.

Not only can you add a line or box to a spreadsheet, but you can choose combinations of lines such as a double line around the outside of a block *and* horizontal lines between the rows.

Shading a Block of Cells

You can add black or gray shading to a block of cells with the Style menu and the Shading option. This will shade the white space in each cell—that is, the area not occupied by text.

Shading will appear in bold on a monochrome monitor, and in black or gray on a color monitor. On the latter you can change the shading's color with the Options menu and the Colors, Spreadsheet, and Shading Options.

When you print the shaded cells on paper, they will appear in reverse, the cells darkened and the characters in white. (Unless you have a color printer.)

Turning Shading Off

To turn shading off, follow these steps:

1. Type /**S** to select the Style menu.
2. Choose the Shading option. From the submenu select None.
3. When prompted, enter the block of cells that you do not want shaded, and press Enter.

Selecting Fonts

A *type font* determines the size of the printed character, the style, and the typeface. In addition, on a color printer, you can select the color to be printed. The number of fonts is quite large. In this example, though, we will modify a single font, but keep in mind that every font can be modified, and that you can add fonts.

To specify a font for a block of cells:

1. Type /**S** to select the Style menu.
2. Select the Font option. The font submenu appears as in Figure 8.18.
3. Highlight the font that you want to use and press Enter. Quattro Pro will return you to the spreadsheet.

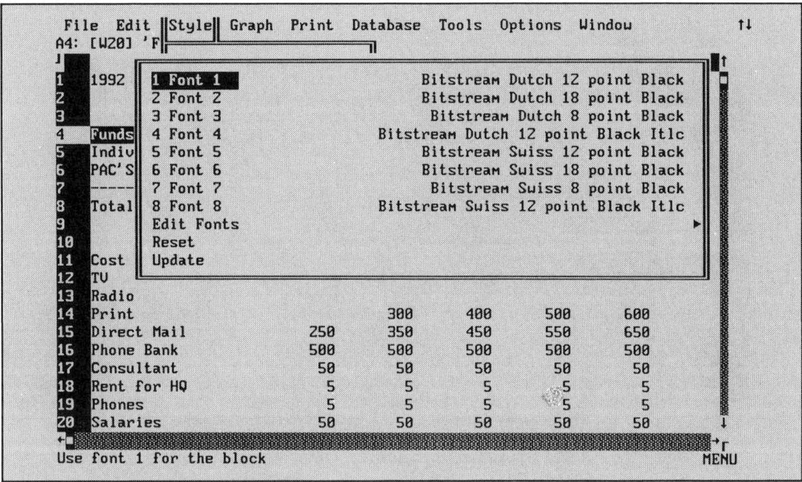

Figure 8.18: The font submenu

4. At the prompt, enter the block of cells that you want to modify with the selected font. Use the pointing method or type in the block address.

5. Press Enter.

No character changes will be apparent on-screen. However, on the input line the font will be noted by its number—e.g., F7 for font seven (Bitstream Swiss 8-point Black in default set-up). Here are the standard Quattro Pro (Hershey) typefaces: Roman, Roman Light, Roman Italic, Sans Serif, Sans Serif Light, Script, Monospace, Old English, and EuroStyle. Quattro Pro also uses Bitstream fonts: Dutch (similar to Times Roman), Swiss (similar to Helvetica), and Courier.

Changing a Font

If none of these *default fonts* meets your needs, you can modify it. To make the change follow these steps:

1. Type /**S** to select the Style menu.

2. Choose the Font option.

3. Select the Edit Fonts option. A second font submenu appears as in Figure 8.19.

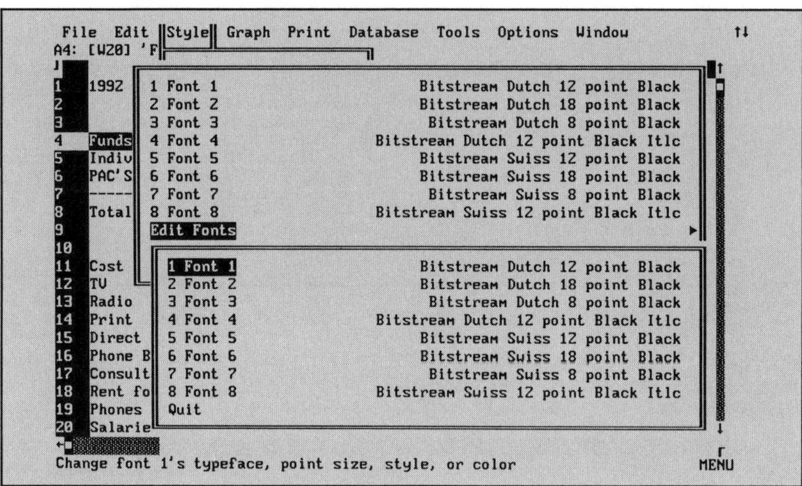

Figure 8.19: The second font submenu

4. Choose any one of the fonts listed and press Enter.

Another submenu appears with the following options:

Typeface	A further submenu listing all fonts. Select the appropriate typeface.
Point Size	The point size submenu. You can scale a font from 6 to 72 points. The larger the number, the larger the character.
Style	A submenu with the options Bold, Italic, Underlined, and Reset. The Reset option clears all style attributes.
Color	A submenu of available colors that can be used with color printers. A color change will not be seen in the screen preview.

The key to mixing font styles is to try a variety of them to see how they look. With the Screen Preview feature (described in Chapter 10), you can take a look at the spreadsheet before you waste time and paper actually printing it out.

Adding Bullets

A *bullet* is a leading or following character that you can have printed next to information that needs emphasis. Bullets are not found on any menu, but are an embedded command that you type into a cell. The bullet is not visible until the spreadsheet is viewed with Screen Preview or printed to a graphics printer (more on these in Chapter 10).

To insert a bullet in a cell:

1. Move the cell selector to the cell in which you want the bullet printed.
2. Type '**bullet** #\

You must use a label prefix (') or Quattro Pro will assume that you are inserting a repeating character. The #-sign stands for a number that you choose from the following list of eight distinct bullet designs:

#	**Prints:**
0	box
1	filled box
2	check-marked box
3	check mark
4	shadowed box
5	shadowed, check-marked box
6	filled circle

Three things are important to consider when choosing a font for your spreadsheet. First, if you select a Bitstream font that you didn't initially install with the software, Quattro Pro will have to create it anew when you use the Screen Preview feature or print the spreadsheet. Since this takes time, you may wish to set the Graphics Quality option (under the Options menu) to Draft until you are finished working on the spreadsheet. (In Draft mode, Quattro Pro substitutes your chosen Bitstream font with a Hershey font.) Then when you want to print (or preview) the final version, set Graphics Quality to Final.

Second, creating new fonts decreases disk space because new font files are created. Third, you must have a minimum of 125K of RAM available for each font file. This is a major amount of memory, so unless your system is equipped with extra RAM, you will not want to make more than one or two modifications.

WORKING WITH MULTIPLE SPREADSHEETS

FEATURING

Opening Multiple Spreadsheets

Stacking and Tiling Spreadsheet Windows

Repositioning and Resizing Windows

The File Manager

In the last chapter you learned how to view two different segments of a spreadsheet simultaneously. This is helpful if you are working on a large spreadsheet and don't want to scroll back and forth constantly between the two areas. Quattro Pro extends this ability to "be two places at once" by allowing you to call up several *distinct* spreadsheets at the same time.

Opening a Second File Window

When you start Quattro Pro, the *default name* of the opened, blank spreadsheet is SHEET1.WQ1. After entering information, you will probably want to open another spreadsheet while keeping the first one still on the screen, perhaps to compare data. To do so:

1. Type **/F** to access the File menu.
2. Press the ↓ key once to highlight the Open option. The status line now reads:

   Load a file into a new spreadsheet window

3. Press Enter to select Open. (If you were to select Retrieve, Quattro Pro would load the new spreadsheet into the *current* window, defeating the purpose of opening a *second* window.)

4. The file-directory window appears. Select the DORF spreadsheet that you saved in Chapter 4 and press Enter.

5. The spreadsheet appears, and on the status line, just to the right of the file name DORF.WQ1, is the code **[2]**, which indicates that DORF.WQ1 is being displayed in a *second* window.

Whenever you open a new spreadsheet, Quattro Pro will place it directly over the previous window. So if you were to open three different spreadsheets, only the third one would be visible on top. (You'll see that shortly.) To change this configuration to suit your needs better, you'll want to call up the Window menu, described below.

The Window Menu

The Window Menu (shown in Figure 9.1) lists the different ways you can format the layout of spreadsheet windows on the screen. To call it up, type **/W.** (Don't try any of the options just yet.)

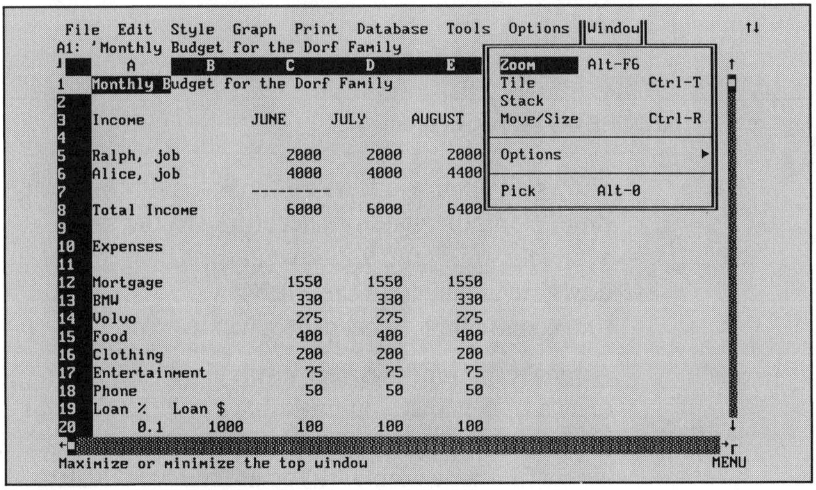

Figure 9.1: *The Window menu*

They are as follows:

Zoom — Shrinks a full-sized window to either half-screen size or to the size that you had previously shrunk the window. If you start with a window that you shrank with the Move/Size command (below), the Zoom option will resize it to cover the entire screen. In Figure 9.2, the DORF spreadsheet window has been zoomed.

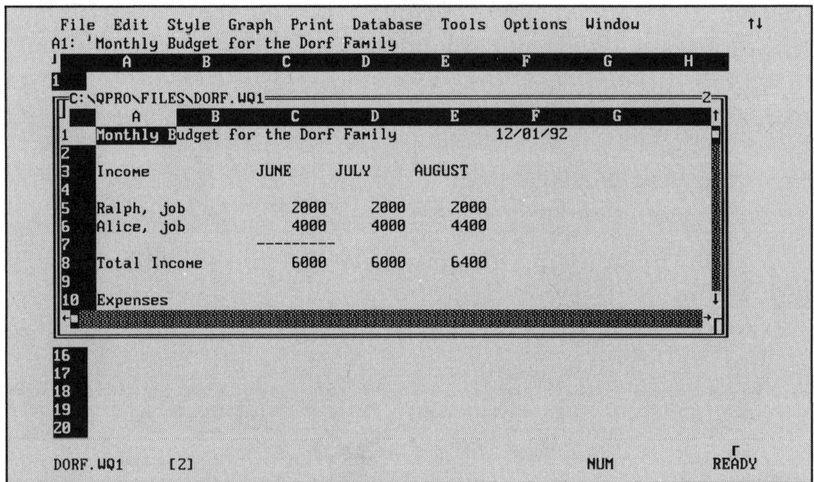

Figure 9.2: The DORF.WQ1 window zoomed

Tile — Shows all open windows on the screen at the same time, sizing the windows according to the space available. In Figure 9.3, several spreadsheet windows are arranged in the Tile view. (You'll create the second empty spreadsheet window soon.)

Stack — Arranges the windows very much like a series of manila folders that you might have on your desk, as in Figure 9.4. The top of each spreadsheet window has its file name visible. If you are running Quattro Pro in WYSIWYG display mode (version 3.0 only), the Stack option is not available.

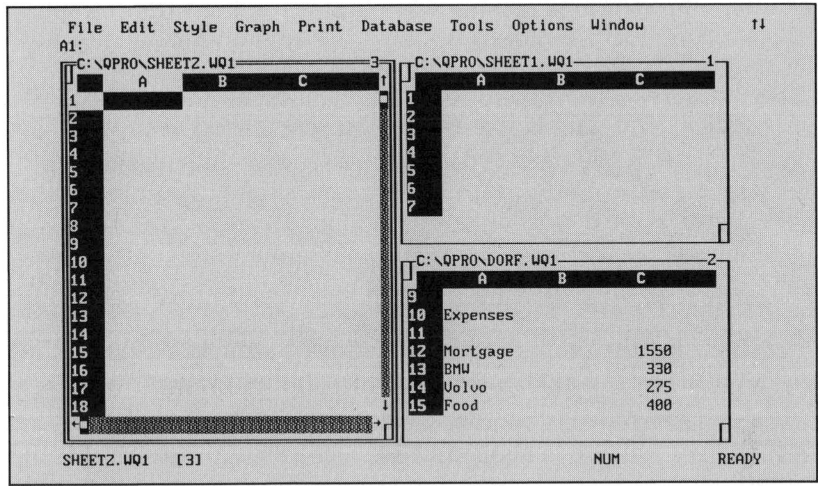

Figure 9.3: A Tile view of open windows

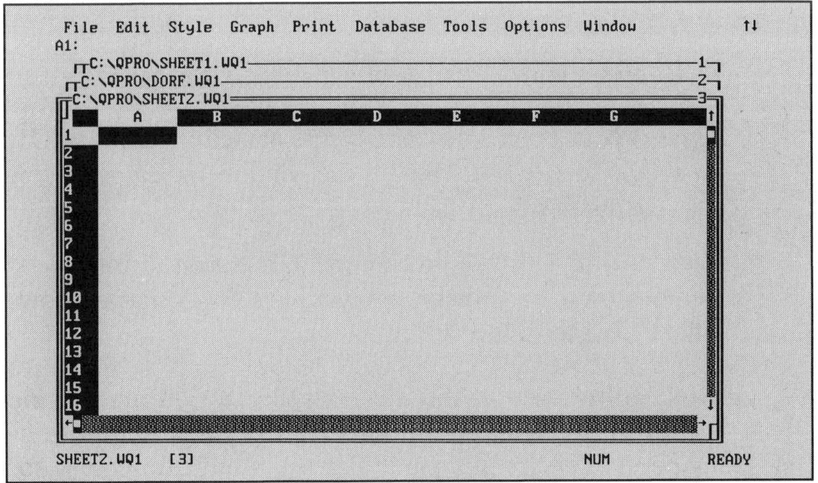

Figure 9.4: The spreadsheet windows stacked

Move/Size — Moves a window on the screen to a different position and changes the size of the *active window*—i.e., the window that is currently receptive to inputs, changes, etc. If you are running Quattro Pro in WYSIWYG display mode (version 3.0 only), the Move/Size options are not available.

Options	First mentioned in Chapter 8, these options split a *single* spreadsheet into separate panes and lock on-screen titles.
Pick	Displays a list of open spreadsheet windows, allowing you to pick a window to make active.

Let's go into these options in more detail now.

Zooming a Window

Zooming the active (current) window is straightforward. With the Window menu still on-screen (called up by typing /W), press Enter or type **Z** to access the Zoom option. The DORF window shrinks from full-size to about a half-screen in size. Press Alt–F6; the DORF window is Zoomed to full-size on the screen. (Alt–F6 is a shortcut for typing /WZ.)

Tiling Several Windows

Now let's open a third file and display the windows in a tiled format.

1. Type /**FN** to open a new empty file named SHEET2.WQ1. At the bottom of the screen is the window indicator; in this case the number 3 appears.

2. Press Ctrl–T. This will execute the Tile option directly from the Window menu (otherwise keystrokes /WT). The windows will be sized to fit the screen.

As you can see, two of the windows fill the right half of the screen while the third takes up the left half. Now you can move or change the position or size of a particular window. Before doing so, however, you have to be able to designate which window you want to change.

Making a Window Active

Although you can work in only one window at a time, there are three quick ways to make the window you want to work in the active window—i.e., to make it open to changes. The first is to use the Next

Window key combination, which is Shift–F6. In the Tile format, pressing Shift–F6 moves the active window in clockwise fashion:

1. Press Shift–F6. The active window becomes the one containing the SHEET1 spreadsheet.
2. Press Shift–F6 again. The DORF spreadsheet is now the active window.
3. Press Shift–F6 and SHEET2 becomes active again. Make DORF.WQ1 active before reading on.

Look in the border at the upper-right corner of the windows. In each, there appears a number corresponding to the order in which the spreadsheet was opened. The SHEET1 window is enumerated with a 1, the DORF window with the number 2, and the SHEET2 window with 3. At the bottom left of the screen, Quattro Pro indicates that the active window contains the DORF spreadsheet, which is window 2.

A second way to activate a window is to use the Alt key. Pressing the Alt key and a window number together causes that window to become active. Press Alt–1 and window 1 will become the active window. Try this with the other window. Another way to pick an open window is to press Alt–0 (zero). Quattro Pro will display a list of the open windows, as shown in Figure 9.5. Depending on which window is active at the moment you press Alt–0, the box will appear in either window 1, 2, or 3. (It may not list the names in the same order as the figure shows.) Move the highlight to the DORF [2] listing and press Enter. The DORF window will become the active window.

Finally, you can also press Shift–F5 to display the list of open windows and make your selection.

Changing the Size of a Window

Make the DORF spreadsheet the active window. Now suppose that you want to resize the window:

1. Type /**WM** to activate the Move/Size option from the Window menu. The word MOVE appears in a box in the upper-left corner of the active window.

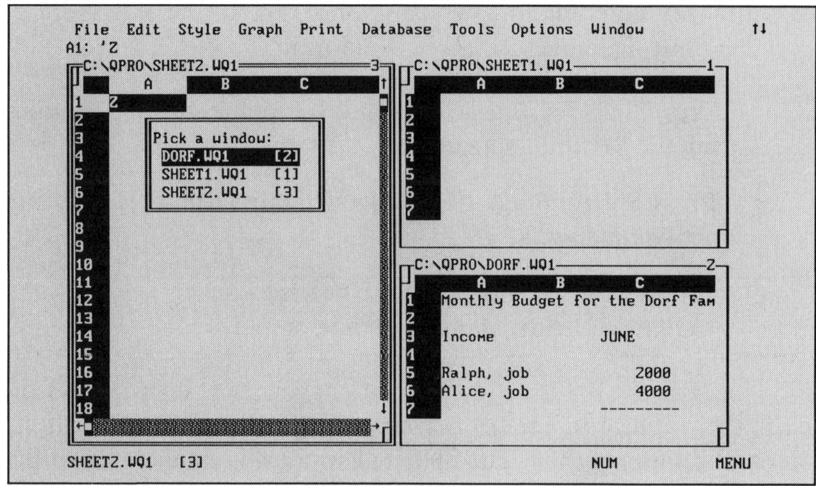

Figure 9.5: *The list of open windows*

2. Press the Scroll Lock key, then press the arrow keys: ↑ makes the window shorter, ↓ makes it taller, ← makes it thinner, and → makes it fatter. As you resize the window, the word MOVE in the box will change to SIZE.

3. Press Enter to see the change become permanent.

Moving a Window

To move a window, type /**WM** to select the Move/Size option from the Window menu. This time, just hit the arrow keys to position the window where you want it and press Enter. (Remember, you cannot use the Move/Size options if you are in WYSIWYG display mode.)

When moving or resizing a window, you can use several other keys to accelerate the process. Be sure you've already typed /WM (or shortcut Ctrl–R) to use them:

T	Moves/resizes the active window to fill the top half of the screen
B	Moves/resizes the active window to fill the bottom half of the screen

L Moves/resizes the active window to fill the left half of the screen

R Moves/resizes the active window to fill the right half of the screen

Z Enlarges the active window to fill the entire screen

If you are using a mouse, click any portion of a window to make it active. To move a window, click and drag any border to the position where you want it and release. To resize a window, click and drag the small box in the lower-right corner of the window to size the window as you like.

Stacking Windows

Stacking is a useful way to view a nearly full-sized active window, while keeping tabs on how many other windows you currently have open and what their names are. (Remember, if you are running Quattro Pro in WYSIWYG display mode, the Stack option is not available.) Type /**WS** to arrange your windows in a stacked format. Notice that the active window appears on top. To make another window active, press either Alt–0 (zero) or Shift–F5. Quattro Pro will display a list of the open spreadsheet names in a box. Highlight the window you want to make active and press Enter to see it appear on top of the stack.

There is a new command available on the Quattro Pro 3.0 File menu: Save All. When Save All is invoked, Quattro Pro begins to save all open worksheets. If a worksheet has been modified during the work session, Quattro Pro asks if you want to Replace or Backup the worksheet, or Cancel the Save operation. Selecting Replace copies the new changes to the file. Selecting Backup saves the file with the changes with the new extension .BAK.

The File Manager

The File Manager makes it easy to work with many spreadsheet files. If you have some experience with DOS, you know that it can be tedious to copy, find, or rename files. Quattro Pro simplifies this task.

The File Manager works within a window, in the same manner that you worked with spreadsheet files in the previous section, and displays the file names and subdirectories. To open a File Manager window, follow these steps:

① Type **/FU** to access the Utilities option from the File menu. A submenu will appear as in Figure 9.6.

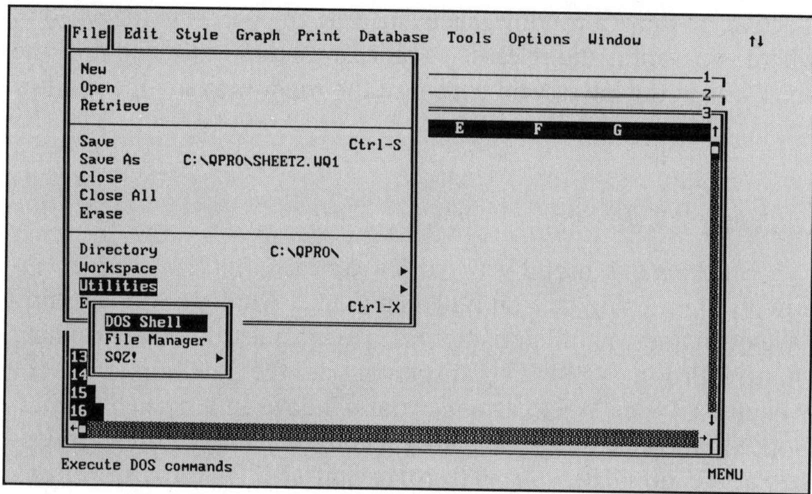

Figure 9.6: The Utilities submenu

② Choose File Manager from the three options and press Enter. If you still have the three windows open from the previous example, the new window will show up on the left half of the screen and become window number 4, as in Figure 9.7.

This window consists of two distinct areas. The bottom half lists all the files in the QPRO directory and is called the *file-list pane.* The top half is called the *control pane* and contains the following disk and file information:

- **Drive**: The default drive is C, if that is where you installed Quattro Pro. (If you installed Quattro Pro on a different drive, that drive will appear as the default.) If you want to see files on a particular floppy disk, move the highlighted cursor

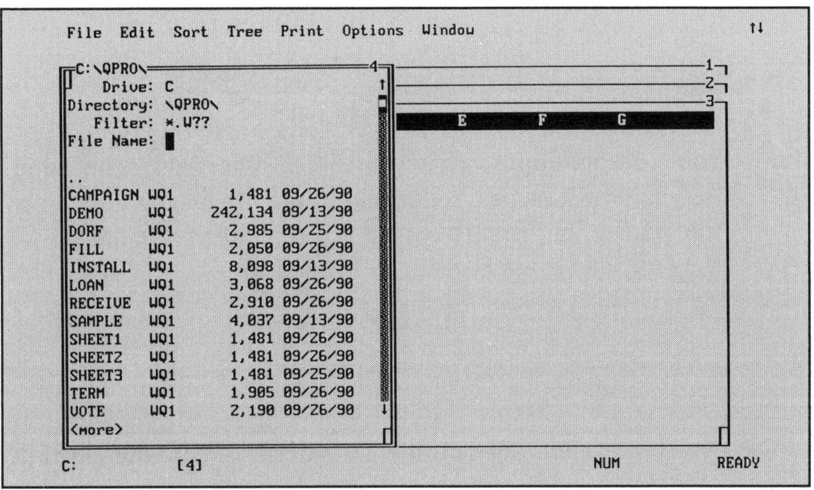

Figure 9.7: The File Manager window

to the space after the **Drive:** label and type in the drive letter—**A**, for example, if your files are on a floppy disk in the A drive. Press Enter.

- **Directory**: Quattro Pro is normally installed in a directory named QPRO, in which the files created by Quattro Pro are saved. To display a different directory, move the highlight to the space after **Directory:** and enter its name. If you highlight the double period (..) entry at the top of the file-list pane, Quattro Pro will display the *root directory* of the current drive—i.e., the master directory that lists all files and subdirectories stored on the disk. Moving the highlight to another directory name and pressing Enter will display that directory and its files in the file-list pane.
- **Filter**: This entry determines which files will be displayed in the file-list pane. The default setting is ***.W??**, which causes Quattro Pro to display all files that carry the extension .W and two other characters. For example, all files with the extension .WQ1 (i.e., Quattro Pro files) or the extensions .WKS or .WK1 will be displayed. The filter can be modified as you like. To display all files in a directory, type ***.***. The * symbol stands for one

or several characters, whereas the ? symbol takes the place of only a single character.

- **File name:** This entry can be used to open a spreadsheet file, or to look for a file that is stored somewhere on your disk. If you are searching for a particular file, simply enter the name. As you type it in, you'll notice that the file-list pane scrolls to that name. Hit Enter to see it. Or just highlight the name with the ↓ key and press Enter.

The File Manager Menus

A new set of menus appears at the top of the screen when the File Manager window is open and active.

The File Menu

This File menu looks similar to the File menu in the speadsheet window:

New	Opens a new window and a new (blank) spreadsheet file
Open	Opens a new window and allows you to load an existing file
Close	Closes the File Manager window
Close All	Closes all open files and windows, including the File Manager window
Read Dir	Reads the disk that is currently selected in the **Drive:** setting
Make Dir	Allows you to create new directories
Workspace	Saves the current setup as a file
Utilities	Allows you to go directly to DOS, open another File Manager window or set SQZ! utility options
Exit	Closes all windows and exits Quattro Pro

The Edit Menu

The Edit menu has several options that are unique to the File Manager.

Select File	Allows you to select the file or files that you want to copy, move, or erase. By repeatedly selecting this option, you can affect many files with a single command. The fastest way to select a file is by moving the highlight to the file name and pressing Shift–F7.
All Select	Selects all of the files listed in the file-list pane for moving, copying, or deleting. The fastest way to select all files in the list is to press Alt–F7. (Pressing Alt–F7 again will *deselect* the files.)
Copy	Used after you have selected the file or files for copying. The files are stored temporarily in the *paste buffer* and can then be copied to a different disk or directory. Pressing Shift–F9 also executes a file copy.
Move	Used after you have selected the file or files for moving. The files are stored temporarily in the paste buffer and can then be moved to a different disk or directory. Pressing Shift–F8 also executes a file move.
Erase	Permanently erases the selected files. Use this option with extreme caution. It is a good idea first to copy any files you plan to delete to a floppy disk and then erase them from the hard disk. That way, if you mistakenly erase a file, it can be resurrected from the floppy disk.
Duplicate	Allows you to copy a file and rename it at the same time.
Rename	Allows you to change the name of an existing file. The option can also be executed by pressing the F2 key.

The Sort Menu

After creating many spreadsheet files, you may want to list them in a different order. The default sort is Name, which lists files in alphabetical order. Files not starting with a letter will be positioned first in the list. The other sorting options work as follows:

Timestamp	When you save a file, DOS records the time and date of its creation and subsequent changes. Using this method, the oldest files will be listed first.
Extension	Sorts files in alphabetical order by extension, and then by file name as a secondary sort.
Size	Displays the smallest files first, and any subdirectories last.
DOS Order	Sorts the files in the same order that DOS does with the DIR command (i.e., alphabetical by file name, numbers first).

The Tree Menu

When you want to delete, copy, or move files, the Tree menu provides a concise, visual map of the files that are on either your hard disk or floppy disk. Using a filter (described above in the section on the File Manager), you can make changes to multiple files with a single command, rather than working with each file individually.

The Tree menu becomes part of the File Manager window, or else can be seen in a separate window. The best way to see the Tree menu is to zoom the File Manager window and then open the Tree menu:

1. With the File Manager window activated, type /**WZ**. The File Manager will fill the screen, as in Figure 9.8.

2. Type /**TO** to open the Tree menu. The menu tree will appear as in Figure 9.9.

At the top of the tree, on the right side of the window, is the name of the disk drive—in this case, **C:**—followed by the directories

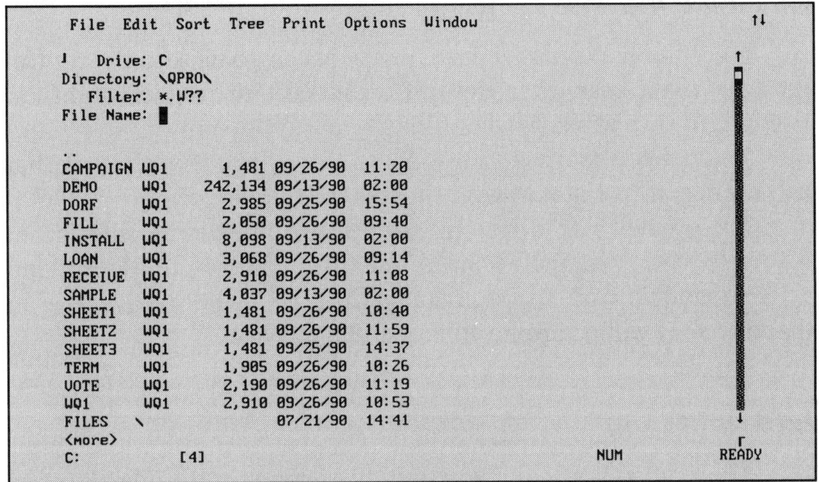

Figure 9.8: The File Manager window zoomed

```
File  Edit  Sort  Tree  Print  Options  Window

   Drive: C
Directory: \QPRO\                                     C:
   Filter: *.W??                                      ├─CLOCKPRO
File Name:                                            ├─DOS
                                                      ├─HSG
..                                                    ├─IMCAP
CAMPAIGN WQ1      1,481 09/26/90  11:20               ├─INSET
DEMO     WQ1    242,134 09/13/90  02:00               ├─MEMO
DORF     WQ1      2,985 09/25/90  15:54               ├─MODEM
FILL     WQ1      2,050 09/26/90  09:40               ├─NC
INSTALL  WQ1      8,098 09/13/90  02:00               ├─PIX
LOAN     WQ1      3,068 09/26/90  09:14               ├─QPRO
RECEIVE  WQ1      2,910 09/26/90  11:08               │ ├─FILES
SAMPLE   WQ1      4,037 09/13/90  02:00               │ └─FONTS
SHEET1   WQ1      1,481 09/26/90  10:40               ├─QUICKEN3
SHEET2   WQ1      1,481 09/26/90  11:59               ├─SPRINT
SHEET3   WQ1      1,481 09/25/90  14:37               │ └─123B
TERM     WQ1      1,905 09/26/90  10:26               └─ZAP
VOTE     WQ1      2,190 09/26/90  11:19
WQ1      WQ1      2,910 09/26/90  10:53
FILES    \              07/21/90  14:41
<more>
C:          [4]                                  NUM        READY
```

Figure 9.9: The File Manager window tree

and subdirectories on that disk. QPRO is highlighted because it was the directory you were in when you activated the Tree menu.

If you move the highlight with the ↑ or ↓ keys to a different directory, no files will appear unless the filter setting is modified, or unless you have some .W?? files stored there. (The default filter, *.W??, is designed to find files relating to Quattro Pro.)

Changing the Tree Contents

Once the Tree menu is displayed, you can go back to the control pane and make changes to view different disks, directories, and files. Press F6 (or the Tab key) to do this.

To change the drive you want to view, type the letter of that drive. Then press Enter to read the tree for that drive.

To see files with different extensions, change the filter from *.W?? to *.*. Press the F6 key a few times to make the Tree menu active again. Now when you highlight different directories, *all* files in that directory will be displayed in the file-list pane.

The Print Menu

The Print menu allows you to print portions of the File Manager window and its contents as described below:

Block	Has a submenu that allows you to pick what you want to print. You can print the list of files, the Tree menu, or both.
Destination	You can direct the matter to go to a printer or to a disk file for printing at a later time. If you select a file as the destination, you will have to enter a file name.
Page Layout	Used to add a header or footer, page breaks, page margins, and any setup strings needed to output to your printer. The default margin settings are for standard $8^1/_2 \times 11$ paper.
Reset	Resets the page-layout settings to their default values
Adjust Printer	Moves the paper in the printer to the top of the next page
Go	Begins printing
Quit	Closes the menu

The Options Menu

The Options menu here contains some of the same settings as the Option menu in the spreadsheet window. Two of the options, though, are specific to the File Manager:

Startup	Lets you determine the menu tree that will be loaded when Quattro Pro is started, and which directory is going to be the default when you first open the File Manager window. For example, if the default setting is drive C and you want it to be drive D, use this option to make that change.
File List	Changes the way in which the files in the file-list pane are displayed, either one per line with detailed file information, or in several columns with only the file name and its extension.

The Window Menu

The Window menu contains the same options as the Window menu in the spreadsheet window. You can view the windows in tile or stack format, and move or size the individual windows as desired. The Pick option is also available to make a window active.

PRINTING YOUR SPREADSHEET

FEATURING

Setting the Page Layout
Adjusting the Printer
Printing to a Disk File
Previewing a Spreadsheet
Special Print Features

Overview of Printing Options

All the options for printing a spreadsheet are on the Print menu, which you can access by typing /**P**. Figure 10.1 shows how the print menu looks on the screen. The various options on this menu are briefly summarized below (we will discuss them in more detail throughout this chapter).

Block	Specifies a block of cells for printing
Headings	Specifies the row and/or column heading that will be printed on each page
Destination	Decides whether to print the spreadsheet or store the printed copy on disk
Layout	Specifies a general format for the printed page(s)
Format	Chooses between printing the spreadsheet as it appears on the screen and printing the actual contents of the cells—functions, formulas, cell addresses, format codes, etc.
Adjust Printer	Adjusts your printer to prepare for the printout

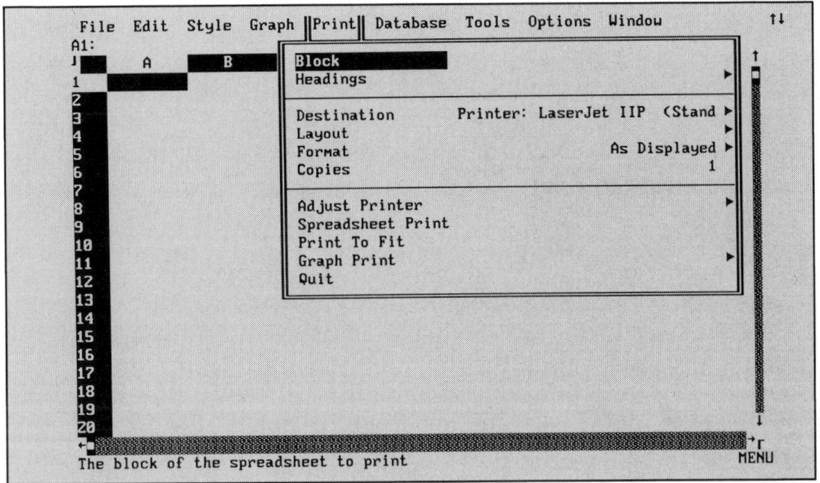

Figure 10.1: The Quattro Pro print menu

Spreadsheet Print	Starts the spreadsheet printing process
Print to Fit	Automatically sizes the data in the print block to print on a single page (available only in version 3.0)
Graph Print	Starts the graph printing process
Quit	Leaves the Print menu and returns to the Ready mode

Before turning on your printer, be sure that a page perforation appears just above the printer head. That way, Quattro Pro will know where the top of each page is.

The General Printing Technique

Printing a spreadsheet is an easy task. Quattro Pro assumes that you are printing on standard $8^{1/2} \times 11$-inch paper and formats the spreadsheet accordingly. If the spreadsheet that you are printing is wider or longer than a single page, Quattro Pro will automatically divide the spreadsheet among two or more pages.

To print any spreadsheet, follow the basic steps below:

1. Enter **/FR** or **/FO** to call up the spreadsheet that you want to print, if it is not already on-screen.
2. Position the cell selector in the upper-left corner of the area that you want to print.
3. Type **/P** to access the Print menu.
4. Select the Block option and extend the cell selector (with the usual pointing method) to highlight the area of the spreadsheet you want to print. Press Enter after the block is highlighted.
5. Select other parameters (discussed in this chapter) to format the printed page.
6. If necessary, select the Adjust Printer option to line up the paper in the printer. Press Escape to return to the Print menu.
7. Select Spreadsheet Print from the Print menu to begin printing.
8. When printing is complete, select the Adjust Printer and Form Feed options, if necessary, to eject the last page from the printer.
9. Select Quit from the Print menu to return to the spreadsheet's Ready mode.

The sections below discuss the various steps and printing options in more detail.

Defining the Block to Print

Before you print a spreadsheet, you need to type **/PB** and specify the cells to be printed. You can use the usual pointing method to anchor the cell selector and highlight the area to print, or you can simply type in the block's coordinates (e.g., A1..G27). Only the cells that you specify will be printed.

If a spreadsheet contains long labels, you need to highlight the *entire* label if you want it printed. For example, if cell A1 contains a long label that spills over into column D, you will want to include columns A, B, C, and D in the block to print. Otherwise, the long label will be cut off to fit within the block you specify.

As soon as you've finished highlighting the block, select Spreadsheet Print from the Print menu to print the spreadsheet. You can also add headings, change margins, and choose other features to create a fancier display.

Printing with Headings

If your spreadsheet is too wide to fit across a single page, Quattro Pro will automatically divide the spreadsheet among two or more pages that you can splice together into one wide spreadsheet (or handle separately). For example, Figure 10.2 shows the campaign spreadsheet divided into two pages.

As you can see in the sample printout, the row headings are not repeated on the second page. Unless you tape the pages together, it will be difficult to determine what the various numbers on the second page refer to. As with frozen titles, discussed in Chapter 8, you can repeat row and/or column headings on consecutive printed pages by defining a left and/or top heading.

Defining a Left Heading

The Headings option on the Print menu allows you to repeat row headings on each printed page of a spreadsheet. To use this option:

1. Select the Block option from the Print menu to specify the block to print (keystrokes **/PB**).
2. Highlight the area to print, *excluding* the columns that you want repeated on each page. Press Enter.
3. Select the Headings option from the Print menu and, from that, the Left Heading option. The status line will read

   Row headings to print on the left of each page:

   followed by the address of the currently selected cell, and wait for you to specify a block.
4. With the usual pointing method, specify the columns to be repeated on the left side of each page. In Figure 10.3 the left headings are highlighted. Press Enter.

1992 Campaign Budget (in thousands)

	Jan	Feb	Mar	April	May
Funds raised					
Individuals	7856	9908	3454	2245	9385
PAC'S	15000	20000	25000	20000	30000
Total Income	$22,856	$29,908	$28,454	$22,245	$39,385
Cost of Fund Raising	13713.6	17944.8	17072.4	13347	23631
TV	500	600	700	800	900
Radio	100	150	200	250	300
Print	200	300	400	500	600
Direct Mail	250	350	450	550	650
Phone Bank	500	500	500	500	500
Consultant	50	50	50	50	50
Rent for HQ	5	5	5	5	5
Phones	5	5	5	5	5
Salaries	50	50	50	50	50
Travel	20	20	20	20	20
Entertainment	1	1	1	1	1
Contributions	5	5	5	5	5
Other	5	5	5	5	5
Total Costs	15404.6	19985.8	19463.4	16088	26722
Net	$7,451	$9,922	$8,991	$6,157	$12,663

First printed page

June	July	Aug	Sept	Oct	Nov	Dec
7649	3340	2398	4531	5543	8997	5676
450000	50000	70000	70000	650000	20000	15000
$457,649	$53,340	$72,398	$74,531	$655,543	$28,997	$20,676
274589.4	32004	43438.8	44718.6	393325.8	17398.2	12405.6
1000	1100	1200	1300	1400	1400	1400
350	400	450	500	550	550	550
700	800	900	1000	1100	1100	1100
750	850	950	1050	1150	1150	1150
500	500	500	500	500	500	500
50	50	50	50	50	50	50
5	5	5	5	5	5	5
5	5	5	5	5	5	5
50	50	50	50	50	50	50
20	20	20	20	20	20	20
1	1	1	1	1	1	1
5	5	5	5	5	5	5
5	5	5	5	5	5	5
278030.4	35795	47579.8	49209.6	398166.8	22239.2	17246.6
$179,619	$17,545	$24,818	$25,321	$257,376	$6,758	$3,429

Second printed page

Figure 10.2: Printed campaign spreadsheet on two pages

⑤ Select Spreadsheet Print from the Print menu and press Enter (or just type **S**).

Figure 10.4 shows the printed copy of the campaign spreadsheet. Notice that the row titles are repeated on the second page.

```
File  Edit  Style  Graph ||Print|| Database  Tools  Options  Window
Row headings to print on the left of each page: A1..A28
      A                         B        C        D        E        F
10
11  Cost of Fund Raising  13713.6  17944.8  17072.4    13347    23631
12  TV                        500      600      700      800      900
13  Radio                     100      150      200      250      300
14  Print                     200      300      400      500      600
15  Direct Mail               250      350      450      550      650
16  Phone Bank                500      500      500      500      500
17  Consultant                 50       50       50       50       50
18  Rent for HQ                 5        5        5        5        5
19  Phones                      5        5        5        5        5
20  Salaries                   50       50       50       50       50
21  Travel                     20       20       20       20       20
22  Entertainment               1        1        1        1        1
23  Contributions               5        5        5        5        5
24  Other                       5        5        5        5        5
25
26  Total Costs           15404.6  19985.8  19463.4    16088    26722
27  =====================================================================
28  Net                    $7,451   $9,922   $8,991   $6,157  $12,663
29
A28: [W20] 'Net                                                  POINT
```

Figure 10.3: Left heading highlighted for printed spreadsheet

Defining a Top Heading

Just as the Left Heading option allows you to specify spreadsheet columns that you want to repeat on each printed page, the Top Heading option lets you specify spreadsheet rows to repeat on each page. The general technique used with top headings is the same as that used with left headings: position the cell selector at the upper-left corner of the block of cells you wish to repeat, type **/PHT**, and highlight the rows that should be included in the top heading.

As with the Left Heading option, the block that you specify to print should exclude the block that you specify as the top heading. For example, if the spreadsheet that you wish to print has column headings in the block A1..C4, and data beneath those headings extending to row 100, you would specify A1..C4 as the top heading and A5..C100 as the block for printing.

1992 Campaign Budget (in thousands)

	Jan	Feb	Mar	April	May
Funds raised					
Individuals	7856	9908	3454	2245	9385
PAC'S	15000	20000	25000	20000	30000
Total Income	$22,856	$29,908	$28,454	$22,245	$39,385
Cost of Fund Raising	13713.6	17944.8	17072.4	13347	23631
TV	500	600	700	800	900
Radio	100	150	200	250	300
Print	200	300	400	500	600
Direct Mail	250	350	450	550	650
Phone Bank	500	500	500	500	500
Consultant	50	50	50	50	50
Rent for HQ	5	5	5	5	5
Phones	5	5	5	5	5
Salaries	50	50	50	50	50
Travel	20	20	20	20	20
Entertainment	1	1	1	1	1
Contributions	5	5	5	5	5
Other	5	5	5	5	5
Total Costs	15404.6	19985.8	19463.4	16088	26722
Net	$7,451	$9,922	$8,991	$6,157	$12,663

First printed page

1992 Campaign Budget

	June	July	Aug	Sept	Oct
Funds raised					
Individuals	7649	3340	2398	4531	5543
PAC'S	450000	50000	70000	70000	650000
Total Income	$457,649	$53,340	$72,398	$74,531	$655,543
Cost of Fund Raising	274589.4	32004	43438.8	44718.6	393325.8
TV	1000	1100	1200	1300	1400
Radio	350	400	450	500	550
Print	700	800	900	1000	1100
Direct Mail	750	850	950	1050	1150
Phone Bank	500	500	500	500	500
Consultant	50	50	50	50	50
Rent for HQ	5	5	5	5	5
Phones	5	5	5	5	5
Salaries	50	50	50	50	50
Travel	20	20	20	20	20
Entertainment	1	1	1	1	1
Contributions	5	5	5	5	5
Other	5	5	5	5	5
Total Costs	278030.4	35795	47579.8	49209.6	398166.8
Net	$179,619	$17,545	$24,818	$25,321	$257,376

Second printed page

Figure 10.4: Campaign spreadsheet printed with left headings

Setting the Page Layout

As mentioned earlier, Quattro Pro automatically assumes that the paper in the printer is the standard $8^1/_2 \times 11$-inch size and formats the printed spreadsheet accordingly. The Page Layout option under the Print menu lets you change the way Quattro Pro formats the printed page. When selected, the Page Layout option presents the following submenu, as in Figure 10.5.

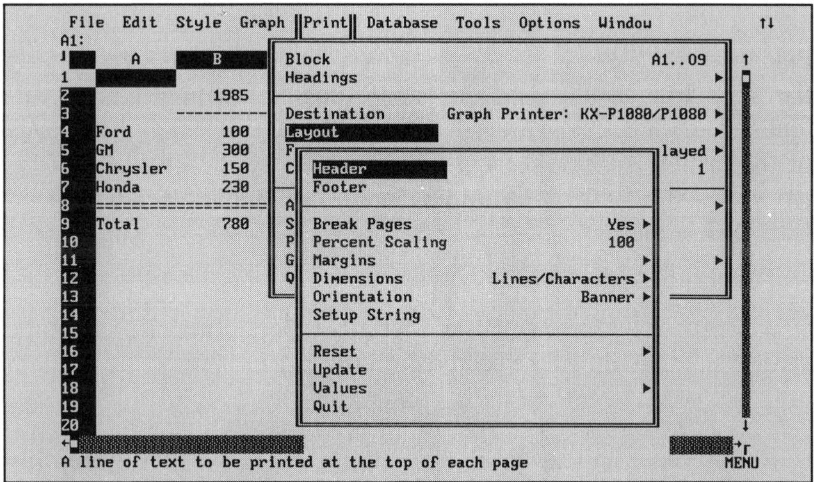

Figure 10.5: The Page Layout menu

Each of these options is discussed in the following sections. When you finish making selections from this menu, just press the Escape key to return to the Print menu.

Adding Headers and Footers to Your Spreadsheet

The Header and Footer options on the Page Layout submenu let you specify text that is to be printed above and beneath the spreadsheet on each printed page. Unlike the Top Heading and Left Heading options, which repeat spreadsheet rows and columns on each page, the Header and Footer options repeat any text that you enter above and beneath the overall spreadsheet. (Two blank lines separate the header or footer from the spreadsheet data.) This text can be up to 254 characters long.

You can use special characters in headers and footers:

@	Displays the current (system) date
#	Displays the page number
¦	Centers the header or footer
¦¦	Right-justifies the header or footer

Below are some examples of various headers or footers and the way they would be displayed on the printed page (assuming that the current system date is November 1, 1991, and that this is the fourth page of the printed spreadsheet). If you do not use the vertical bar (¦) anywhere—i.e., just type **Monthly Sales**—then the text will be aligned with the left margin:

Monthly Sales

If you precede *Monthly Sales* with a single ¦ symbol—i.e., type ¦**Monthly Sales**—it will be centered on the page:

Monthly Sales

If you precede the text with two ¦ characters—i.e., type ¦¦**Monthly Sales**—it will be aligned with the right margin of the page:

Monthly Sales

Of course, you can align the other codes as well. Typing ¦# will center the page number on the page:

4

Typing @¦¦# yields:

1–Nov–91 **4**

And reversing the code gives:

4 **1–Nov–91**

Finally, sandwiching *Monthly Sales* between the two—as in @¦**Monthly Sales**¦**page #**—yields:

1–Nov–91 **Monthly Sales** **page 4**

To create a header or footer for a printed spreadsheet, follow these steps:

1. Type **/PL** to access the Page Layout submenu.
2. From the submenu, select either Header or Footer.
3. Type in the text of the header or footer, including special characters, when prompted. Use the usual Backspace or arrow keys to make corrections if necessary.
4. Press Enter.

Note that the header or footer is not displayed on-screen; it appears only on the *printed* spreadsheet.

Changing the Percent Scaling

The Percent Scaling options are available only in version 3.0, and they allow you to shrink or enlarge the print block by the percentage you specify. The default setting is 100%. Quattro Pro can print as small as 1 point and as large as 72 points. Using the Percent Scaling in conjunction with the Landscape printing orientation, you can accurately adjust the way a spreadsheet looks on a piece of paper.

The Percent Scaling options do not work on graphs when printed alone. They do work when a graph is inserted into a spreadsheet and is then printed. When you save the spreadsheet, the percentage is saved also.

Setting the Page Length and Margins

By default, Quattro Pro leaves a half-inch margin at the left and right side of each printed page (assuming the standard 8½ × 11-inch page size and 10 printed characters to the inch). The Margins submenu from the Page Layout menu lets you change these margins. When you select this option, it displays the submenu shown in Figure 10.6.

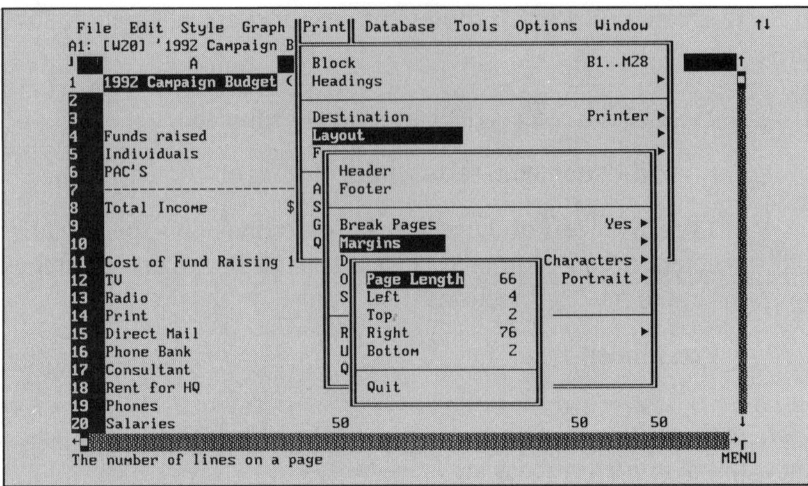

Figure 10.6: The Margins submenu

Setting the Left and Right Margins

The Left and Right options from the Margins submenu let you specify margins for the printed page. When you select Left, the screen prompts you to enter a new left-margin setting, ranging from 0 to 254 characters, and displays the current setting (4 by default). The margin you set is measured in terms of characters, not inches. Most printers print 10 characters to the inch, so entering 10 would leave a one-inch margin at the left side of the printed page.

Of course, if you adjust your printer to print more or fewer characters to the inch, you'll need to make these same adjustments when defining the margin. For example, if your printer displays 12 characters to the inch, a left margin of 6 will leave a half-inch margin.

The right margin is measured as the number of characters from the left edge of the page to the right-most printed column. Hence, the default setting of 76 prints 7.6 inches of text across one line on the page (again assuming 10 printed characters to the inch). When you select Right from the Margins submenu, you'll be prompted to enter a new right-margin setting, within the range of 0 to 511 characters. Quattro Pro version 2.0 allows a range of 0 to 254 characters.

If you are printing more than 10 characters to the inch, or are using very wide paper, you'll probably want to increase the right margin accordingly. For example, if you are using compressed print with $8^1/_2 \times 11$-inch paper, a right margin-setting of 120 is usually preferred. If you are using wide green-bar paper, and the standard 10 characters-to-the-inch setting, you could set a right margin of 140.

Adjusting Top and Bottom Margins

The Top and Bottom options from the Margins submenu determine the number of blank lines to leave at the top and bottom of each printed page. Both options allow from 0 to 32 blank lines. Most printers print six lines to the inch, so you can calculate the number of inches accordingly. For example, a top or bottom margin of 6 will leave a one-inch margin.

If you create a header for the printed spreadsheet, it will be printed just below the top-margin setting, followed by two blank lines. Footers are printed just above the bottom margin, with two blank lines separating them from the spreadsheet data.

Setting the Page Length

The Page Length option from the Margins submenu determines the number of lines printed on each page. Most printers display six lines to the inch, so the default setting for an 11-inch long page is 66. If your printer prints more lines to the inch, or you use longer or shorter pages, adjust this setting accordingly.

To calculate the correct page length, multiply the page length, in inches, by the number of lines printed per inch. You need not concern yourself with top or bottom margins in this calculation, as these are determined by the Top and Bottom margin settings.

How to Leave the Margins and Length Submenu

When you finish setting the new page margins and length, select Quit and you'll be returned to the Page Layout submenu. If you save the entire spreadsheet after changing margins or page length, these new settings will be saved as well. Unless you change the saved settings, the spreadsheet will always print with these page margins and this length. But they apply only to *this* spreadsheet, not all. Selecting Update will make them the default settings for all spreadsheets.

Adding Page Breaks

Quattro Pro automatically divides a spreadsheet into separate pages based on the length of the page and top and bottom margins. You can also insert hard page breaks into a spreadsheet to force Quattro Pro to start printing on a new page at a particular row in the spreadsheet. Type /**EIR** to insert a blank row (if one does not already exist) where you want the next printed page to begin. Then move the cell selector to column A of the blank row and type /**SI**. You can also insert a hard page break simply by typing ¦:: (a vertical line followed by two colons) into the cell.

Whichever technique you use to enter the hard page break, it will be displayed in the cell as two colons; the vertical line will not be displayed. Furthermore, any data that are in the same row as the hard-page-break symbol will not be printed. Therefore, be sure to place ¦:: in a row that is completely blank (or one that you do not want to appear on the printed spreadsheet).

Figure 10.7 shows a sample spreadsheet with a hard page break inserted in row 10 (cell A10). When printed, the Income section (rows 1 through 9) will be displayed on one page, and the rest of the spreadsheet, from row 11 onward, will be displayed on the next page. A single spreadsheet can contain any number of hard page breaks, as long as each is stored in its own row.

Printing without Page Breaks

You can also have Quattro Pro print your spreadsheet as a single, long continuous stream of information. This format is often preferred when printing spreadsheets to a disk file (discussed later in this chapter) rather than to a printer, or when you want to print in Landscape mode. To prevent Quattro Pro from inserting page breaks, select the Break Pages option from the Layout submenu and choose

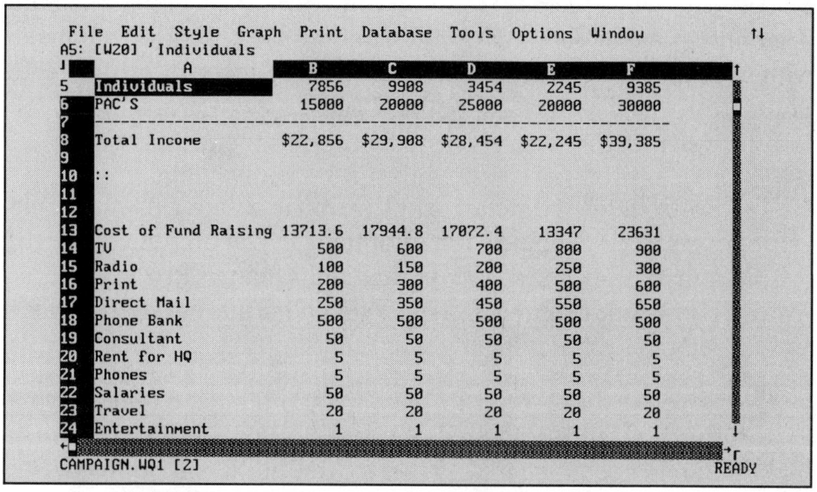

```
File  Edit  Style  Graph  Print  Database  Tools  Options  Window        ↑↓
A5: [W20] 'Individuals
     A                        B         C         D         E         F
5   Individuals             7856      9908      3454      2245      9385
6   PAC'S                  15000     20000     25000     20000     30000
7   ------------------------------------------------------------------
8   Total Income         $22,856   $29,908   $28,454   $22,245   $39,385
9
10  ::
11
12
13  Cost of Fund Raising 13713.6   17944.8   17072.4     13347     23631
14  TV                       500       600       700       800       900
15  Radio                    100       150       200       250       300
16  Print                    200       300       400       500       600
17  Direct Mail              250       350       450       550       650
18  Phone Bank               500       500       500       500       500
19  Consultant                50        50        50        50        50
20  Rent for HQ                5         5         5         5         5
21  Phones                     5         5         5         5         5
22  Salaries                  50        50        50        50        50
23  Travel                    20        20        20        20        20
24  Entertainment              1         1         1         1         1
CAMPAIGN.WQ1 [2]                                                      READY
```

Figure 10.7: Sample spreadsheet with hard page break in row 10

No. The setting is a toggle; selecting Break Pages again will change the setting back to Yes.

Note that this technique only prevents natural page breaks from occurring. Hard page breaks inserted as the ¦:: code will still occur. To prevent these hard page breaks from taking effect, you'll need to delete them from the spreadsheet itself. If you select Banner as the print orientation under the Layout submenu, Quattro Pro version 3.0 ignores all page breaks, hard and soft.

If you save the spreadsheet after setting the Break Pages option to No, this setting will be saved as well, and future printouts of this spreadsheet will not be printed with page breaks.

Choosing the Printer Orientation

Quattro Pro will print your spreadsheets in any of three ways: Portrait mode (text running across width of page), Landscape mode (text running along length of page), or Banner mode (text running along length of page with no page breaks). (Banner mode is available only in Quattro Pro version 3.0.) Landscape mode is particularly useful for printing spreadsheets because more columns can be printed on a single page. As a further extension of Landscape printing, the Banner printing mode continues printing along the length of the paper with no regard to page breaks. Banner printing can only be used with dot-matrix printers. To print in either Landscape or Banner mode, follow these steps:

1. From the Print menu, select Destination and, from *its* submenu, the Graphics printer option. If you do not choose the graphics printer as the destination, Quattro Pro ignores the Landscape or Banner orientation and prints in Portrait mode only.
2. If you want to print in Landscape mode, enter the Layout submenu and set Break Pages to No. Quattro Pro will print in Landscape mode if this is set to Yes, but it will not recognize soft page breaks, only hard page breaks. (This step is not necessary if you plan to print in Banner mode, as Quattro Pro ignores all soft and hard page breaks.)
3. Select the Spreadsheet Print from the Print menu and press Enter.

Adjusting the Printer

There are two very common problems that occur when printing spreadsheets. One is improper vertical alignment, where a spreadsheet starts printing in the middle of one sheet of paper, spills over onto the next sheet, and then begins printing the next page in the middle of the next sheet of paper. The second problem is when the last printed page is not ejected from the printer (this occurs mostly with laser printers). Both of these problems are easily solved with the Adjust Printer option on the Print menu.

How to Align the Paper

Whether you are printing on continuous form-feed paper or single sheets, Quattro Pro assumes that the top of the first page to print is positioned just above the print head. Furthermore, Quattro

Pro assumes that you will never manually crank the paper out of this position while the printer is turned on. If you are not sure that both of these assumptions are correct, here's what you can do.

First type **/P** to select the Print menu. Then select the Adjust Printer option. From the Adjust Printer submenu, select the Skip Line option until a page perforation is positioned just above the print head in the printer. Then select the Align option from the Adjust Printer submenu. This tells Quattro Pro that the paper in the printer is now properly aligned, and that all page breaks should take place in relation to the current print-head position.

How to Eject the Final Page

The second common problem can be resolved by using the Form Feed option on the Adjust Printer submenu. Many printers will not eject the last printed page until that page is filled or a special code is sent telling the printer to eject the partially filled page. Selecting the Form Feed option sends the appropriate code so that the last printed page is indeed ejected from the printer. (This option also solves the first common problem because it automatically positions the next blank page correctly in the printer.)

Alternatively, you can place a hard page break in column A of the first blank row beneath the bottom of your spreadsheet to ensure that the last printed page is ejected from the printer, and that the next printout is properly aligned at the top of the next blank page—but only if that row is included in the block that you print.

Whichever method you choose, avoid cranking the paper manually in the printer; you'll keep the pages aligned better.

How to Start and Stop Printing

When you are certain that the paper in the printer is properly aligned for your printout, and you've selected all the other options to define and format the block to print, simply select the Spreadsheet Print option from the Print menu. If you want to print multiple copies of the spreadsheet, select the Copies option before selecting Spreadsheet Print, and enter the number of copies you want. (This option is available only in Quattro Pro 3.0.)

If you intentionally want to abort the printing job, press Ctrl–Break. (On many keyboards, Break is the same as the Scroll Lock or Pause key.) If your printer has a large buffer (that is, the printer itself stores data to be printed), it may take awhile for the printer to stop. After printing stops, do a form feed and then select the Adjust Printer option on the Print menu to realign the paper before printing again.

If an error occurs before or during the printing process, such as the printer is not turned on, not on-line, or is out of paper or ribbon, Quattro Pro will display the message:

Printer Error
Abort
Continue

If the problem is one that you can correct immediately, then do so and select the Continue option. Otherwise, select Abort to terminate the printing. After you resolve the problem, realign the paper in the printer and select Spreadsheet Print once again to start over.

Fit to Print

In either WYSIWYG (available only in version 3.0) or Text mode, Quattro Pro can shrink the block you selected to print so that it prints as small as possible on a single page or on as few pages as possible. The determining factor is the resolution of the graphics printer you are using. The higher the dots-per-inch capability of the printer, the smaller the type.

Printing a Spreadsheet to a Disk File

If you would like to incorporate a printed spreadsheet into a document you've prepared with your word processor, or would prefer to use a print spooler or word-processing program to print your spreadsheet, you can tell Quattro Pro to store the printed spreadsheet in an ASCII file on a disk rather than sending it directly to a printer. (ASCII stands for the American Standard Code for Information Interchange and is the accepted standard for translating the first 128 alphabetic and numeric characters, symbols, and control instructions into 7-bit binary code.) This ASCII file can be easily imported into most other types of programs, including word processors, and can also be accessed by the DOS commands TYPE, SORT, and FIND. (The file in which Quattro Pro stores the spreadsheet, with the .WQ1 file name extension, can only be accessed by Quattro Pro.)

Sending a printed spreadsheet to an ASCII file is an easy process. To begin with, type **/PB** and specify the block to print in the usual manner.

If you plan to incorporate the printed spreadsheet into a word-processed document, or want to use your word processor to format the printed spreadsheet, you might want to ensure that no page break characters are inserted into the disk file (keystrokes **PBN**). You should also set the left margin to zero if your word processor already puts the appropriate left margin into its printouts. Also, you should remove any printer-setup strings that you have defined or embedded in the spreadsheet (mentioned later); these codes might have unpredictable effects when you run the disk file with another program.

After you've defined the spreadsheet block to print and the format for the printed spreadsheet, select the Destination option from the Print menu. You will be given five alternatives, two draft-quality modes and three final-quality modes, as described below:

Printer	Sends the spreadsheet to a printer
File	Sends the spreadsheet to an ASCII file
Binary File	Sends the spreadsheet to a disk formatted to take advantage of the graphics printer you have installed (for example, if you have installed a PostScript-capable printer, a PostScript file will be created)
Graphics Printer	Sends the spreadsheet to a graphics printer you have installed. This option makes Quattro Pro add any special formatting to a file when it is printed, including an inserted graph. (See Chapter 11 on inserting a graph into a spreadsheet.)
Screen Preview	Displays the spreadsheet on-screen as it will look when printed

To print to an ASCII file, select File. Quattro Pro will display a window that lists files with the .PRN extension. You'll see the prompt

Enter print file name:

as well as the current disk drive and directory, and a list of all existing disk files (if any) in the current directory. For example, if Quattro Pro is stored in a directory named QPRO on drive C of your computer, the window will display **C:\QPRO*.PRN** underneath the prompt.

At this point, you can enter a drive, directory, and file name for the ASCII version of the spreadsheet file. If you simply type in a file name, such as PROJECT, Quattro Pro will print the spreadsheet to a file in the current directory, adding the extension .PRN to the name you provide. (In this example, the file would be stored in the directory named QPRO on drive C with the name PROJECT.PRN.) If you specify your own file-name extension, Quattro Pro will use that extension. For example, if you type in **FIG7.8** as the name for the spreadsheet file, Quattro Pro will print it to a file in the directory named QPRO on drive C under the name FIG7.8.

Now, if you press the Escape key *before* typing in a file name, Quattro Pro will allow you to choose a different drive and directory name. For example, if you press Escape and enter **B:PROJECT**, the ASCII version of the spreadsheet will be printed to a file on the disk in drive B called PROJECT.PRN. Suppose WordPerfect is your word processor and you keep it in a directory named WP on drive C of your computer. Press Escape, and enter **C:\WP\PROJECT.DAT**. Quattro Pro will print the ASCII version of the spreadsheet to a file in the WP directory on drive C called PROJECT.DAT.

If you happen to specify the name of an existing file to which to print the spreadsheet, Quattro Pro will display the message below:

File already exists:
Cancel
Replace
Backup
Append

Select Cancel to cancel the whole operation. Select Replace to replace the existing file with the one currently being saved. If you select Backup,

Quattro Pro will store the existing file under its current file name, but with the extension .BAK instead of .WQ1. It will then store the current file under the name you specified. If you select Append, the current ASCII file will be appended to the end of the already existing ASCII file.

After you specify the appropriate drive, directory, and file name for your spreadsheet, you must still select Spreadsheet Print from the Print menu to print it. The Wait indicator will flash in the bottom-right corner of the screen while the spreadsheet is being printed to the file. Then you'll be returned to the Print menu. Select Quit to return to the spreadsheet-ready mode (or hit Escape).

Importing an ASCII File into a Word-Processing Document

Suppose you have a spreadsheet that you would like to insert in a word-processed report. The ideal situation would be to have the numbers appear beside the relevant text in the report—i.e., make them *part* of the document. You can do this by printing the numbers in Quattro Pro to an ASCII file (mentioned above) and then inserting that file into your text at any point.

To import (insert) an ASCII file into a word-processed document, first exit Quattro Pro to return to the DOS prompt, and then run your word-processing program in the usual manner. Position the cursor where you want the imported spreadsheet to appear. Use the appropriate command for your word processor to merge or read-in an external file. When prompted, enter the full name of the file to import, including the .PRN extension or any other extension you gave the spreadsheet's file name. (Make sure it's the ASCII-printed file, not a proper Quattro Pro file!)

If the ASCII file is not in the same directory as your word processor, be sure to provide the appropriate directory path in the file name. For example, to import an ASCII file that you named PROJECT and stored in the \QPRO directory of drive C, you would specify C:\QPRO\PROJECT.PRN as the name of the file to import. (Remember to save your word-processing document after importing the spreadsheet file.)

Previewing a Spreadsheet

If you want to know how a spreadsheet will appear on paper without actually printing a hard copy of it, select Screen Preview from the Destination submenu on the Print menu (keystrokes /**PDS**). This will tell Quattro Pro to "print" to the screen. Now to see the result, select Spreadsheet Print from the Print menu.

When you do so, Screen Preview will display the spreadsheet, along with its own set of menu commands at the top of the screen:

Help	Accesses the Help section
Quit	Exits Preview mode and returns to the spreadsheet
Color	Changes the screen display colors (on a monochrome monitor, the screen will either be displayed in normal or reverse mode)
Previous	Moves to the previously displayed screen, if you are previewing several pages
Next	Moves to the next screen, if you are previewing several pages
Ruler	Overlays a grid on the previewed page in one-inch-square divisions. The command is a toggle; selecting it again will turn off the grid lines.
Guide	When in Zoom mode, displays a window in the upper-right corner of the screen to show what area of the page is enlarged. (Guide is a toggle; the default is to display the guide, and selecting the menu command will turn it off.) To view a different portion of the page, reposition the little box in the window with the arrow keys and press Enter.
Unzoom	Restores page to full-size if you are in Zoom mode
Zoom	Enlarges page on the screen by 200 percent (and another 200 percent when selected again)

Screen Preview is best used when you have inserted special fonts or added annotation to a graph, because then you can see exactly what will be printed before actually printing.

Handling Printer-Setup Strings

Many printers allow you to use setup strings to invoke certain features, such as compressed, expanded, underlined, boldfaced, or italicized print. A setup string is a special series of characters that is not actually displayed by the printer. Instead, the printer uses this string as an instruction for defining a print style.

Determining the Codes for Your Printer

Unfortunately, different printers use different setup strings, so we can't tell you the specific codes to use with your particular printer. However, Table 10.1 lists some setup strings for the popular Epson FX, IBM, and Hewlett-Packard LaserJet printers.

It is *essential* to respect upper- and lowercase letters in these strings, because the ASCII code distinguishes between the two. (Thus \027p1 is *not* the same as \027P1.) And, of course, do not confuse l (el) with *1* (one), or O (oh) with 0 (zero).

Table 10.1: Examples of Printer-Setup Strings

PRINTER	FORMAT	SETUP STRING
Epson FX and IBM	Start compressed print	\015
	End compressed print	\018
	Start expanded print	\027W1
	End expanded print	\027W0
	Start expanded print (one line)	\014
	End expanded print (one line)	\020
	Start boldface print	\027E
	End boldface print	\027F

Table 10.1: Examples of Printer-Setup Strings (continued)

PRINTER	FORMAT	SETUP STRING
	Start underlined print	\027-1
	End underlined print	\027-1
	Start superscript	\027S0
	Start subscript	\027S1
	End super/subscript	\027T
	Start double-strike print	\027G
	End double-strike print	\027H
Epson only	Start italic print	\0274
	End italic print	\0275
	Start proportional print	\027p1
	End proportional print	\027p0
	End underlined print	\027-0
Hewlett-Packard LaserJet	Portrait print	\027E\027&*l*0O
	Portrait compressed print	\027E\027&*l*0O\027&k2S
	Landscape print	\027E\027&*l*1O
	Landscape compressed print	\027E\027&*l*1O\027&k2S

For more detailed information about any of these or other printer-setup strings, consult your printer's manual.

Many printer manuals will display setup strings as a multicode sequence, where the first character sent is a press on the Escape key, and the other characters are either printable or nonprintable characters. Others will use only a single nonprintable character or two. If a multicode sequence begins with an Escape character, convert it to \027 in your setup string. For example, if your printer uses Escape–G to start compressed print, the printer-setup string for this feature should be \027G. (See the appendix in the *Quattro Pro User's Guide* that lists printer-setup strings.)

If your printer uses a Ctrl-key combination, use the appropriate ASCII value in your setup string. This can be determined by the alphabetical position of the character used. For example, the setup string for Ctrl–A is \001, the setup string for Ctrl–B is \002, and so forth to Ctrl–Z, which is \026.

Still other printer manuals may list setup strings as ASCII character numbers. These can usually be converted to three-digit numbers for use as setup strings. For example, if your printer uses ASCII code 9 to invoke a special feature, the setup string for use with Quattro Pro would be \009; an ASCII value of 15 would be converted to \015; and so on.

Inserting a Setup String into a Spreadsheet

After you've determined the setup string you want to use, there are two ways to place them into a Quattro Pro spreadsheet for printing. The first method is to type /**PLS** to select the Setup String option. Type in the appropriate setup string and press Enter. It will be sent to the printer first; the entire printed spreadsheet will then use the print feature determined by the setup string. Note that after you send a setup string to a printer, the printer remains in that mode until you either send another setup string to use another mode, or turn the printer off and back on again.

A second technique is to place the setup strings directly in the spreadsheet. They should be placed in a blank row, or to the right of any data being printed. (Any data to the right of a setup string will not be displayed on the printed spreadsheet.) This technique lets you combine various printer features in a single spreadsheet.

When entering setup strings directly into a cell, precede the string with the ¦ character. For example, to print a spreadsheet in compressed print on an Epson FX or IBM printer, enter the code ¦\015 into column A of a blank row on the spreadsheet. (The ¦ character will not be displayed in the cell, but it will show up on the input line. You can also enter multiple codes, as long as your printer can accept them; just don't insert spaces between them.)

Figure 10.8 shows a sample spreadsheet with setup strings to print the spreadsheet header in expanded print and the body of the spreadsheet in compressed print on an Epson FX or IBM printer.

```
 File  Edit  Style  Graph  Print  Database  Tools  Options  Window
A5: [W20]
             A             B         C         D         E         F
1   \014
2   1992 Campaign Budget (in thousands)
3   \020
4   \015
5
6                         Jan       Feb       Mar     April       May
7   Funds raised
8   Individuals           7856      9908      3454      2245      9385
9   PAC'S                15000     20000     25000     20000     30000
10  ------------------------------------------------------------------
11  Total Income       $22,856   $29,908   $28,454   $22,245   $39,385
12
13
14
15  Cost of Fund Raising 13713.6  17944.8  17072.4     13347     23631
16  TV                     500       600       700       800       900
17  Radio                  100       150       200       250       300
18  Print                  200       300       400       500       600
19  Direct Mail            250       350       450       550       650
20  Phone Bank             500       500       500       500       500
CAMPAIGN.WQ1 [2]                                                 READY
```

Figure 10.8: Spreadsheet with embedded setup strings

Because expanded print is rather wide, any text that you want centered on the printed spreadsheet should be offset to the left to compensate for the wider letters. Alternatively, when using compressed print, the printer can fit more characters across the printed page. Therefore, you might want to type /**PLMR** and extend the right margin to 120 or more.

Updating and Checking Values

After you have made the adjustments you want to the print layout of your spreadsheet, you can save the new settings so that they will be in effect each time you print. Embedded print commands are not saved as defaults but are only saved with the spreadsheet. To save the print settings:

1. Select Layout from the Print Menu.
2. Select Update.

The new settings are now the defaults. You can see what the new defaults are if you are using Quattro Pro 3.0. To see the new defaults:

1. Select Layout from the Print Menu.
2. Select Values.

The Values settings window is shown in Figure 10.9. You cannot modify any of the settings from this window; they are displayed as information only.

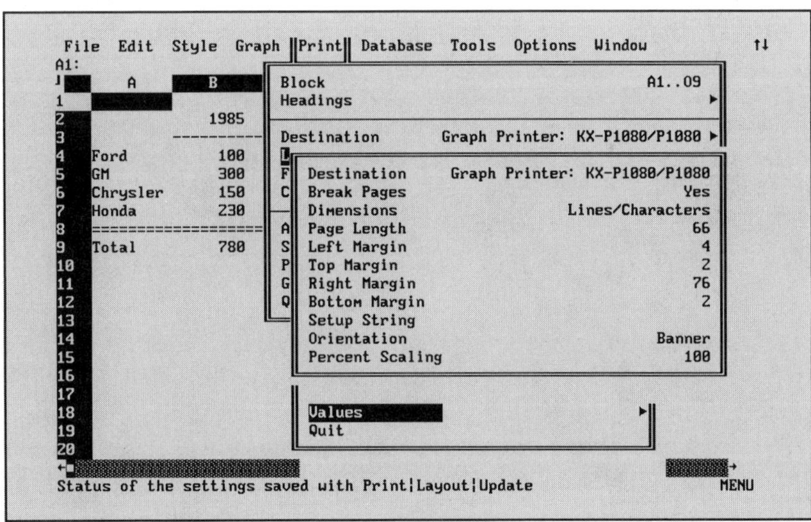

Figure 10.9: The Values settings window

CREATING QUALITY GRAPHS

FEATURING

- *Creating and Customizing Different Types of Graphs*
- *Graph Annotator*
- *Inserting a Graph in a Spreadsheet*
- *Creating a Fast Graph*
- *Combining Graph Types*

Quattro Pro offers many different types of graphs as well as combinations of graphs to help you present data visually. It also offers a variety of sophisticated techniques for customizing graphs to help you present information in exactly the format you wish. There is no limit to the number of professional-quality graphs you can create.

All the menu options for designing and displaying graphs are on the Graph menu, accessed by typing **/G**. Before getting into the specific how-tos of graphs, though, let's take a moment to discuss the different types of graphs that are available and the kinds of situations for which each is most suitable.

Types of Graphs

The Graph Type option on the Graph menu displays a submenu of the various types of graphs: line, bar, X–Y, stacked-bar, pie, area, rotated bar, column, high-low, text, and three-dimensional (3-D). Keep in mind that you can change a graph's type at any time. For example, if you design a complete bar graph and then decide it's not right, you can easily change it to some other type of graph—provided, of course, that the alternate is in a suitable format for graphing the same data. You don't have to redefine the plotted data, titles, or any other customization feature. This means that you can experiment to discover the graph type that best illustrates the information you want to convey.

You can also combine several graph types on a single graph—for instance, to highlight particular areas of interest. In the sections below, we'll discuss the various types of graphs and the most suitable use for each one.

The Line Graph

The most common graph used in business is the line graph. It lends itself well to the linear environment of business because it reflects trends over time. Sales, price movements, and shipping volumes are only a few of the kinds of data that are suitable for line graphs. Figure 11.1 shows a sample line graph that plots sales raised over a 6-month period.

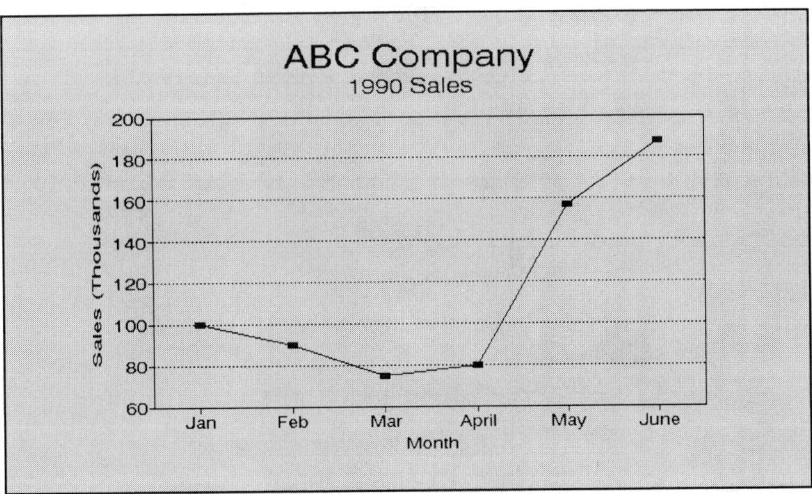

Figure 11.1: Sample line graph

The Bar Graph

Bar graphs are useful for comparing values at a particular point in time rather than for reflecting trends. For example, a marketing department might design a bar graph that compares the market shares of competitive products from one year to the next as a guide for planning marketing strategy, as in Figure 11.2. You may also display information in a rotated bar graph, as in Figure 11.3.

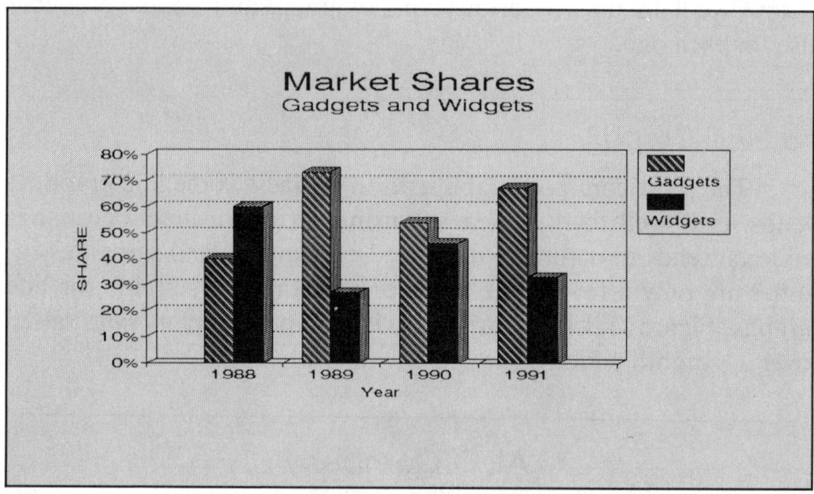

Figure 11.2: Sample bar graph

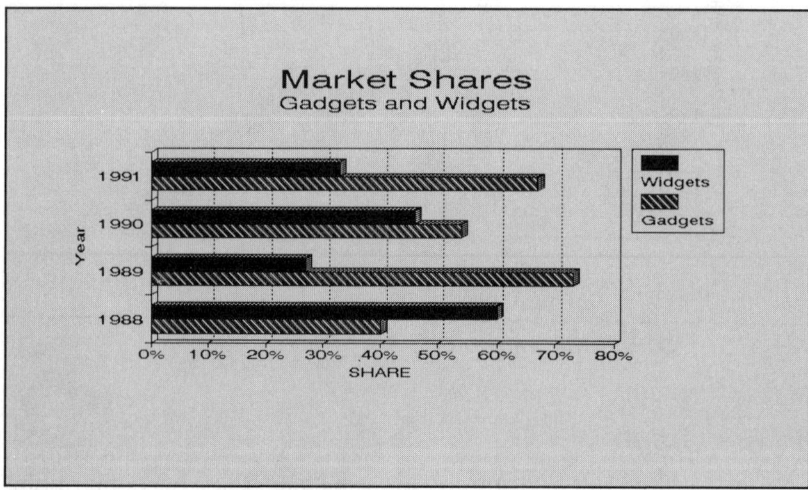

Figure 11.3: Sample rotated bar graph

The X–Y Graph

An X–Y graph shows the relationship between two values, which should be related so that as one goes up, the other goes up or down proportionally. For example, an X–Y graph could represent the relationship between educational level and annual income or between advertising investment and sales. Figure 11.4 shows a sample X–Y graph that shows sales increasing in proportion to the money spent on advertising.

The Stacked-Bar Graph

A stacked-bar graph shows the relative value of a series of numbers as they contribute to the whole. For example, a college might want to distinguish the breakdown of where its funds are raised. Figure 11.5 shows a sample stacked-bar graph that reflects the relative contributions of various sources of funds: business, foundation, individual, and grant contributions.

The Pie Chart

A pie chart is different from the rest of the graphs because it displays only one series of values at a time. For instance, graphing the

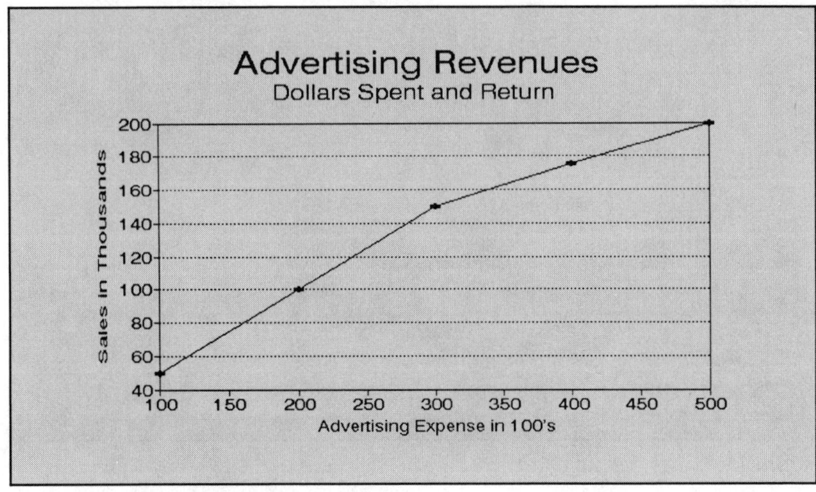

Figure 11.4: Sample X–Y graph

total sales of five products in a pie chart will show the relative contribution of each in a way that is much different than a bar graph. This graph is excellent for showing market shares and numeric components. Figure 11.6 shows a sample pie chart that exhibits the relative costs for living expenses in a family budget.

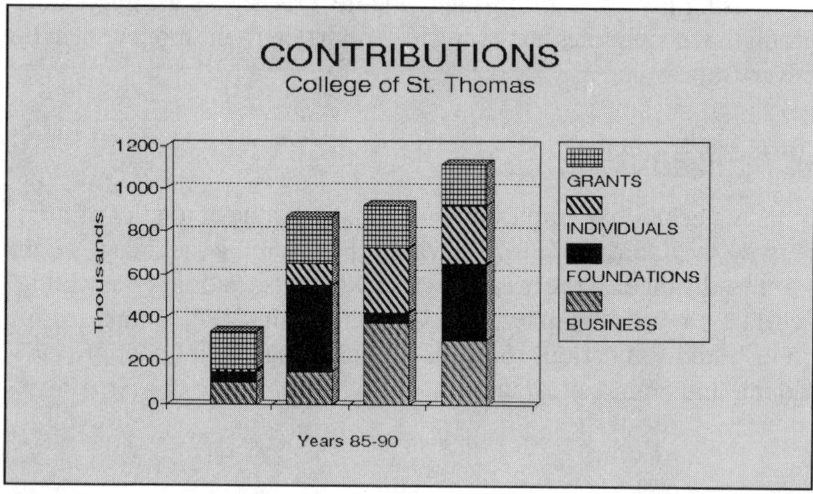

Figure 11.5: Sample stacked-bar graph

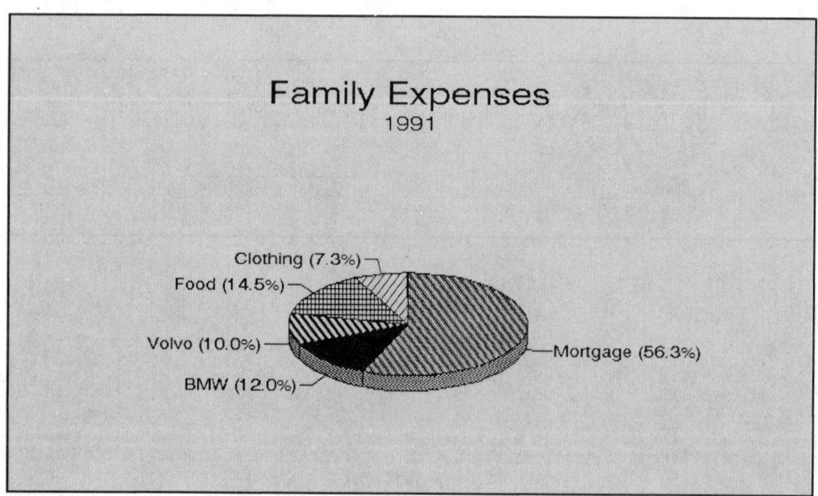

Figure 11.6: Sample pie chart

The Area Graph

An extension of the line graph, the area graph combines the best features of a stacked-bar graph and a line graph by making a continuum of the values from period to period. Each series is graphed separately and placed, like blocks, alongside the others. The interior of the graph shows the relative contributions of various products by averaging the values in each series.

Figure 11.7 shows a sample area graph that plots market shares over time, along with the names of the chip manufacturers. As the graph shows, market shares as a group have increased over time. However, the relative position of each manufacturer has changed.

The Column Graph

The column graph displays information from a single series in much the same way that a pie chart does. The information is stacked vertically on a rectangular column as in Figure 11.8.

The High-Low Graph

The high-low (open-close) graph is most often used for graphing the movement of stock prices. It can be also used for plotting

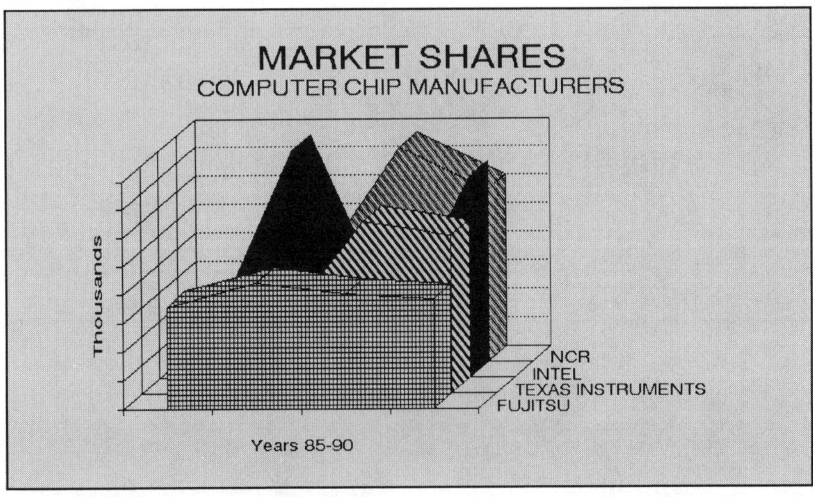

Figure 11.7: Sample area graph

experimental data, such as the concentrations of fluids at different times. Figure 11.9 is a typical example of using the high-low graph for stock prices.

The Text Graph

The text graph is not a defined graphical type. It is a drawing pad for you to create any type of graph you choose. Because of all the

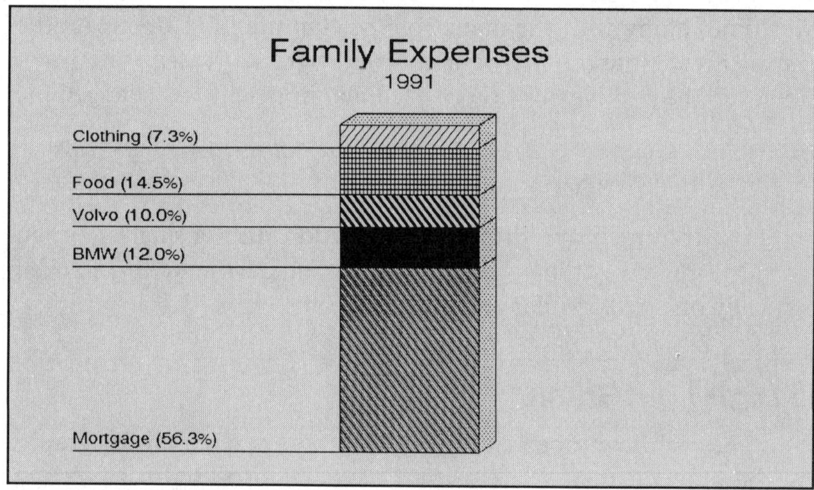

Figure 11.8: *Sample column graph*

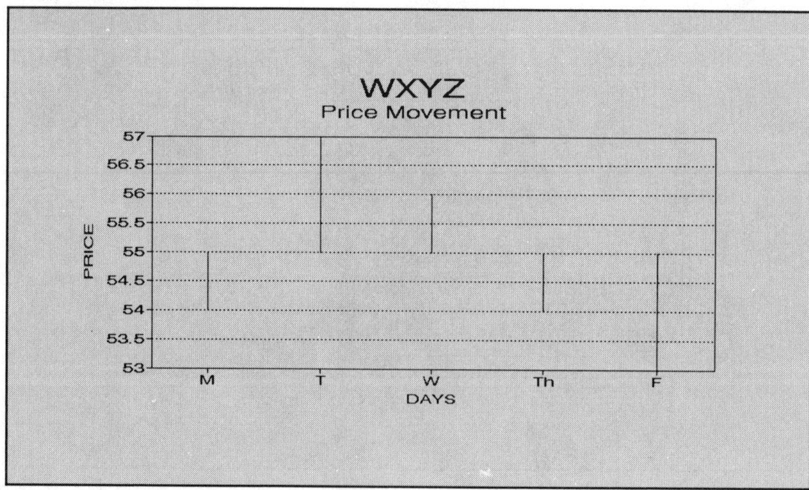

Figure 11.9: *Sample high-low graph*

many shapes, fonts, and text styles available to you in the Annotate option, you can create a multitude of graphical effects. Figure 11.10 shows an example of what can be produced.

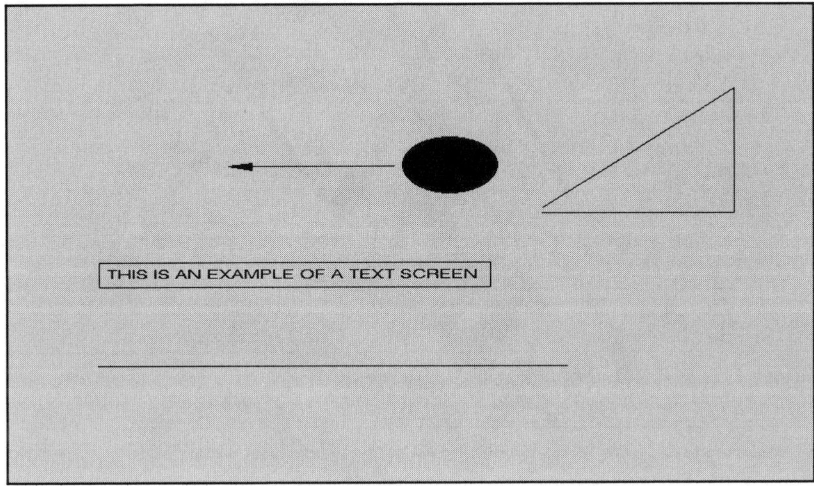

Figure 11.10: Sample text graph

The 3-D Graphs

There are four types of three-dimensional (3-D) graphs: bar, ribbon, step, and area. Except for the 3-D ribbon graph, it is best to use this graph type for data that can be arranged with the largest values plotted first. This is because the 3-D effect overlays values, and if the first set were the smallest, the remaining values might cover them. Figure 11.11 shows a sample 3-D ribbon graph.

Creating and Viewing a Graph

Before you can plot data on a graph, you need some data to work with (except for the text graph). The first few sample graphs you develop in this chapter will use the spreadsheet shown in Figure 11.12. This spreadsheet shows the sales, in arbitrary units, of four car manufacturers from 1985 to 1990. The totals at the bottom of the spreadsheet are calculated with the @SUM function, so that any changes in the sales figures above will be immediately reflected in the totals.

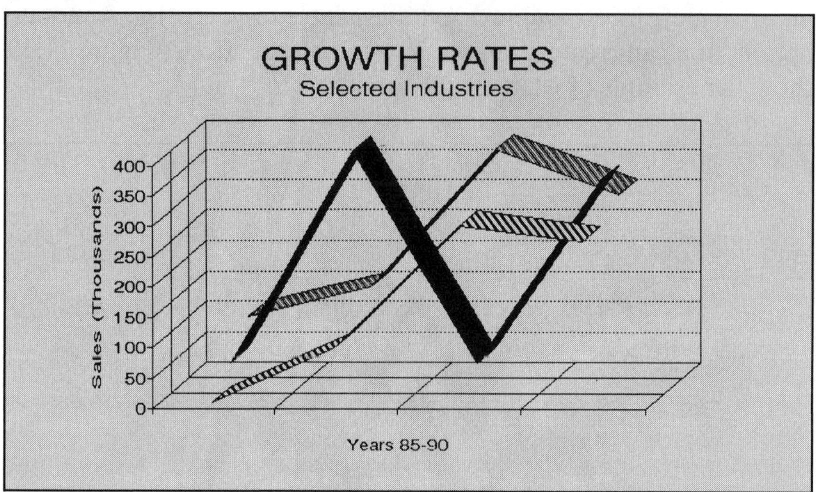

Figure 11.11: A 3-D ribbon graph

File Edit Style Graph Print Database Tools Options Window

A4: 'Ford

	A	B	C	D	E	F	G	H
1								
2		1985	1986	1987	1988	1989	1990	
3		-----	-----	-----	-----	-----	-----	
4	Ford	100	90	75	80	157	188	
5	GM	300	270	220	250	288	390	
6	Chrysler	150	145	123	160	166	302	
7	Honda	230	235	234	400	450	444	
8	-----	-----	-----	-----	-----	-----	-----	
9	Total	780	740	652	890	1061	1324	
10								
11								
12								
13								
14								
15								
16								
17								
18								
19								
20								

SHEET1.WQ1 [1] READY

Figure 11.12: Sample spreadsheet for developing graphs

To define the data you want to plot, select the Series option from the Graph menu (keystrokes /**GS**) and a series option, from 1 through 6. In this first graph, we'll plot only one block of data. Follow the steps below after you create the spreadsheet shown in Figure 11.12:

1. Type /**G** to access the Graph menu.
2. From the Graph menu, select Series.

3. Type **1** to select 1st Series. The input line displays the prompt

   Enter 1st series block:

   and a cell address.

4. To plot the totals on the spreadsheet, move the cell selector to cell B9 and press the period key to anchor the cell selector. Press the End key, then the → key to extend the cell selector to cell G9, so your spreadsheet looks like Figure 11.13. The input line now displays the selected block of values to plot, B9..G9. (As with all other menu options, you can also just type in the coordinates of the block to plot.)

5. Press Enter after specifying the block being plotted to return to the Series submenu.

6. Press Escape to return to the Graph menu.

7. From the Graph menu, select Graph Type.

8. From the submenu, select Bar.

At this point, you've defined the data to be plotted and the graph type. To see the graph, press the Graph key (F10), or select View from the Graph menu. The graph will appear on the screen, as shown in Figure 11.14.

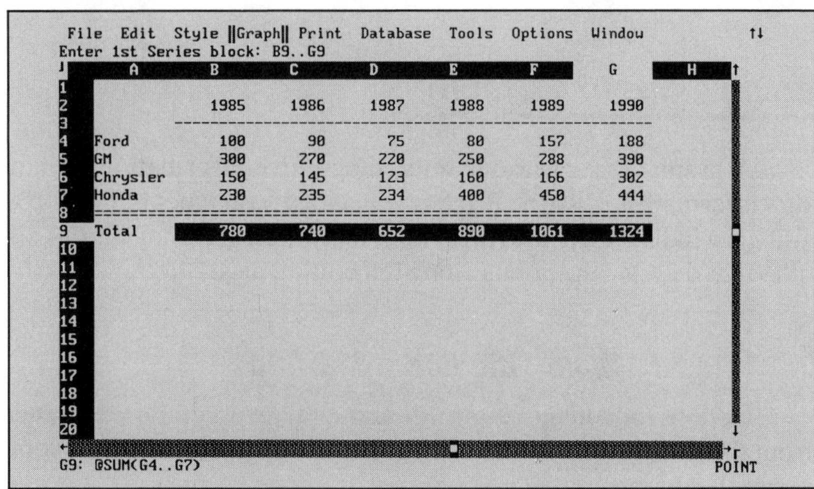

***Figure 11.13:** Block of cells to plot, highlighted*

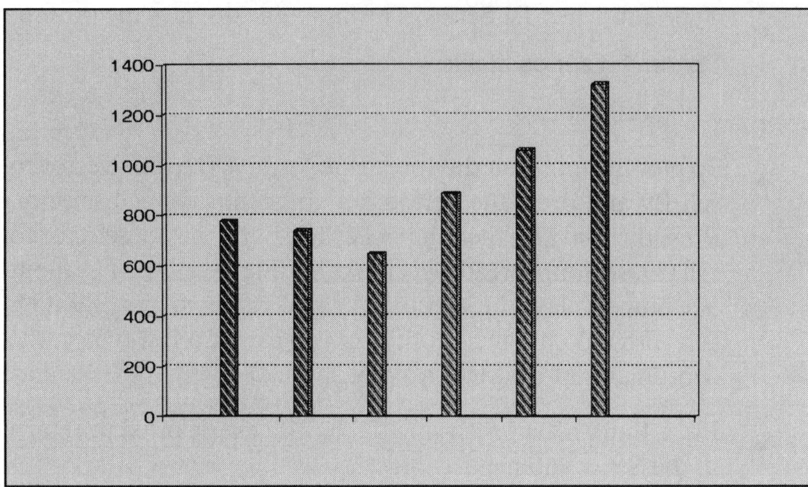

Figure 11.14: Bar graph created with car-sales data

When you are done viewing the graph on the screen, press any key to return to the spreadsheet and Graph menu.

If you would like to experiment with other graph types at this point, select the Graph Type option from the Graph menu, pick another type of graph from the submenu, and then select View to see it. Of course, not all types are suitable for these data. Select High-Low, X–Y, or Text and you'll see why. Press any key to leave the graph and return to the Graph menu (or a Graph submenu).

Adding Titles to a Graph

A graph alone, without some descriptive information, is not very informative. Quattro Pro lets you add several types of titles to a graph, including main title (first line), subtitle (second line), and *x*-axis titles that describe the points along the bottom axis.

How to Add a Main Title and a Subtitle

Options for adding a main title and subtitle to a graph are chosen from the Text option on the Graph menu. Add a main title to your sample bar graph.

1. From the Graph menu, select the Text option. A submenu of title options will appear.
2. From the submenu, select the 1st Line option.
3. When prompted, type in **CAR SALES** and press Enter.
4. Select the 2nd Line option from the Text submenu.
5. When prompted for a title, type **1985–1990** and press Enter.

If you would like to see the graph now with these two titles added, press F10. You'll see the same graph with the new titles on top. Press any key after viewing the graph to return to the spreadsheet and the Text submenu.

How to Add X-Axis Values

The *x*-axis values appear along the *x* axis (bottom line) of the graph. These values come from column or row cells that are already on the spreadsheet, rather than from labels you enter as text. In your sample spreadsheet, you can use the column labels in row 2 as the *x*-axis titles:

1. Select Series from the Graph menu.
2. Select the X-Axis Series option.
3. Move the cell selector to cell B2, press the period key to anchor the cell selector, and press the End and → keys to extend the cell selector over the block B2..G2. Press Enter.

To view the graph once again with all the titles added, press F10. The graph will appear as shown in Figure 11.15. Note that the titles at the top of the graph are centered. When you are done viewing the graph, press any key to return to the spreadsheet and Graph menu.

Adding X- and Y-Axis Titles

You can add titles beneath the *x* axis and to the left of the *y* axis with the Text option. When you select one of the options from the Text

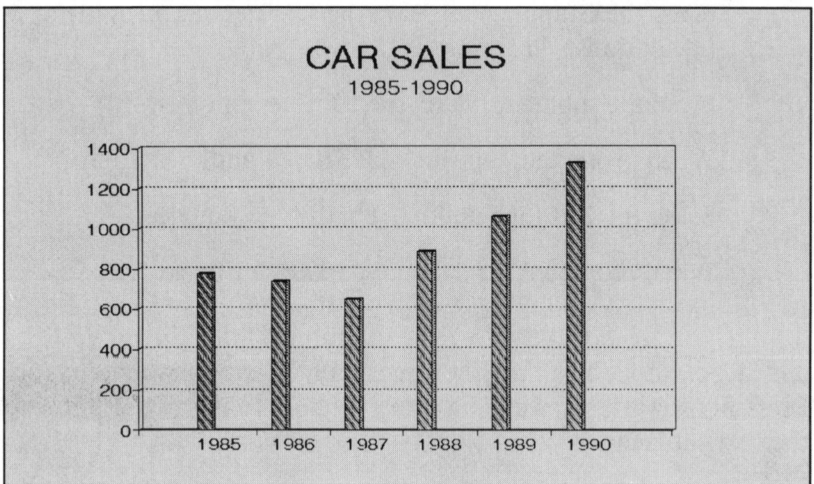

Figure 11.15: *Sample bar graph with titles added*

submenu, Quattro Pro will prompt you to enter a title. The *x*-axis title will be centered beneath the *x*-axis values and the *y*-axis titles will be displayed vertically to the left of the *y* axis.

Try this by adding the title *Years* beneath the *x* axis and *Units* to the left of the *y* axis. Here are the steps:

1. Select Text from the Graph menu.
2. Select X-Title.
3. When Quattro Pro displays the prompt

   X-axis Title Line:

   type **Years** and press Enter.
4. Select Y-Title.
5. When Quattro Pro displays the prompt

   Y-axis Title Line:

   type **Units** and press Enter.
6. Press F10 to view the graph.

Saving a Graph

In many situations, you'll want to create several graphs from a single spreadsheet. In order to do so, you must assign a name to each graph associated with the spreadsheet. Assign the name right after you've designed the graph, before making a new one. The menu options for naming graphs and managing named graphs are accessed from the Name option on the Graph menu.

To assign the name TOTALS to your sample car-sales–totals bar graph, follow these steps:

1. From the Graph menu, select the Name option.
2. Select the Create option from the submenu.
3. Type in **TOTALS** and press Enter. The graph is now saved under the graph name TOTALS, but only in memory (RAM) at the moment.
4. To make this graph a permanent addition to the spreadsheet, select Quit (or press Escape) to return to the spreadsheet-ready mode.
5. Type /**FS** to access the File menu and Save options.
6. Type in the name **CARSALES** and press Enter.

Now the entire CARSALES spreadsheet and the TOTALS graph are stored together on disk. Of course, even though everything is saved, you can change any data on the spreadsheet. When you press F10 or select View from the Graph menu, all graphs associated with that spreadsheet will automatically reflect your changes. The Autosave Edits option is available only in Quattro Pro 3.0. Quattro Pro automatically saves the current graph before displaying another if you set /Graph, Name, Autosave Edits to Yes.

Retrieving a Graph

Whenever you want to retrieve a previously saved graph, choose Display from the Name submenu. A box of graph names will appear. Highlight the graph you want to open and press Enter. It will then appear on-screen. When you press any key to return to the spreadsheet, that graph's layout settings will become the new default settings for any new graphs you create.

Erasing a Graph

The Erase option on the Name submenu lets you delete any previously named graph. When you select it, the screen will display a menu of all named graphs. Highlight the graph you want to delete and press Enter. After you have erased it, you will not be able to recall it unless you type **/FR** or **/FO** to retrieve or open the previously saved spreadsheet. (Note that this won't work if you already saved the spreadsheet after erasing the graph.)

Erasing All Graphs

The Reset option on the Name submenu lets you delete all named graphs permanently from the current spreadsheet. When you select it, Quattro Pro will double-check your intentions by displaying the prompt:

Delete all named graphs?
No
Yes

Select Yes to delete all graphs from that spreadsheet. Remember, if you change your mind—and have wisely enabled Undo before making the deletion—you can get the graphs back by pressing Alt–F5. Or, if you haven't saved the spreadsheet yet, you can open or retrieve the previously saved version.

Plotting Multiple Data Groups

The first graph you created displays only a single block of data: the total car sales for the years 1985 through 1990. But you can also combine several blocks of data into a single graph (except a pie chart or a column graph), as we'll demonstrate in this section.

Plot four blocks of data, each representing the sales for a single car manufacturer. Here are the steps:

1. Type **/GS1** to access the 1st Series option from the Series submenu on the Graph menu.
2. At this point, Quattro Pro remembers the first series defined for the previous graph. However, we do not want to use this series on the new graph, so press the Backspace or Escape key to unanchor the cell selector.
3. Move the cell selector to cell B4, press the period key, and then press the End and → keys to specify B4..G4 as the new first series to plot. Press Enter.
4. Select 2nd Series and specify B5..G5 as the second series.
5. Select 3rd Series and specify B6..G6 as the third series.
6. Select 4th Series and specify B7..G7 as the fourth series.
7. To check the results, press F10.

Your graph should now appear as shown in Figure 11.16. Note that Quattro Pro still remembers the graph type (bar), titles, and *x*-axis settings from the previous graph.

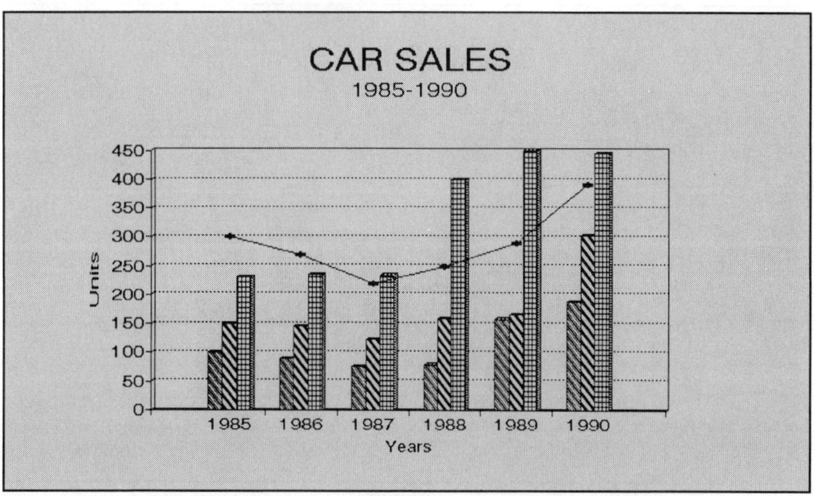

***Figure 11.16:** Sample bar graph plotted from four blocks of data*

Perhaps these data would actually be better displayed in a stacked-bar graph, which would show the relative contributions of various manufacturers to the total sales for each year. To change the bar graph to a stacked-bar graph, follow these steps:

1. Press any key to leave the graph display.
2. Press Escape to leave the Series submenu and return to the Graph menu.
3. Select the Graph Type option, then the Stacked Bar option.

Now if you press F10, you'll see these same data plotted on stacked bars, as shown in Figure 11.17. The relationship of one company's sales to the entire market is much more distinct with this graph than with a standard bar graph. Press any key when you are done viewing the graph.

Saving the New Graph

Take a moment now to save this new graph. Follow the same steps that you did to save the TOTALS graph. That is:

1. Select Name from the Graph menu.

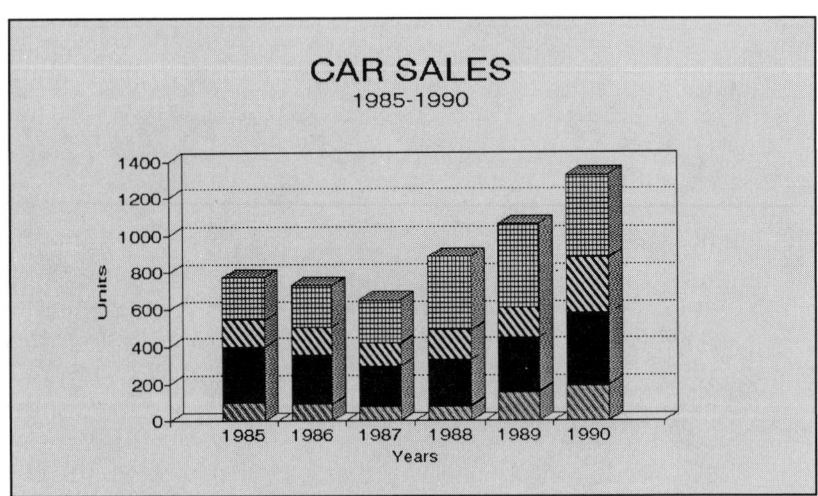

Figure 11.17: Stacked-bar graph of car sales

2. Select Create from the submenu.
3. Type in the graph name **STACKED.**
4. Press Enter.

Adding Legends to a Graph

Adding legends makes a graph easier to understand. To do so, select Text from the Graph menu, then Legends from the submenu. To demonstrate, we'll show you how to add legend titles to the stacked-bar graph:

1. Type /**G** to call up the Graph menu, if you are not already in it.
2. Select the Name and Display options from the submenu. When prompted, highlight the name STACKED and press Enter to make the stacked-bar graph the current graph.
3. Press any key after viewing the graph.
4. From the Graph menu, select the Text option.
5. Select Legends from the submenu, and then choose 1st Series. Type in the title **Ford** and press Enter.
6. Select 2nd Series, type in **GM**, and press Enter.
7. Select 3rd Series, type in **Chrysler**, and press Enter.
8. Select 4th Series, type in **Honda**, and press Enter.
9. Select Position from the submenu and then choose Bottom.
10. Press Escape twice to bring you back the Graph menu and select View to see the graph.

Figure 11.18 shows the graph with the customized legends. Press any key after viewing the graph.

As usual, to save the graph with these new legends, you must type **NC** (to select the Create option from the Name submenu) to re-save the graph under the original name STACKED. This will erase the

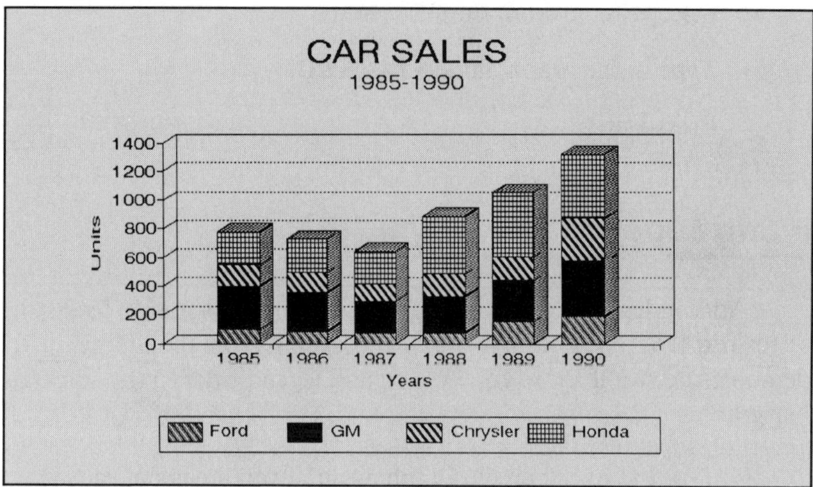

Figure 11.18 : Sample stacked-bar graph with customized legends

old version of STACKED. Furthermore, you'll need to type /**FS** from the main menu eventually to save the entire CARSALES spreadsheet. After you've saved CARSALES, TOTALS and STACKED will be part of CARSALES.WQ1. (The backup file, CARSALES.BAK will include only the TOTALS graph.)

How to Remove a Legend

To remove a legend from a graph:

1. Display the graph you want to modify (keystrokes /**GND**)—in this case, STACKED.
2. Press any key after viewing the graph.
3. Select the Text option.
4. Select the Legends option, then Position, and None.
5. Press F10 to view the graph. The legend will be gone.

Put the legend back on STACKED before continuing, or else save the legend-less version under a different name.

From Bar Graph to Pie Chart

At the beginning of this chapter, we said that it is quite easy to replot data in another format, as long as the new format is suitable for the same data. You've already changed a simple bar graph (TOTALS) into a stacked-bar graph. Let's try something else. Change TOTALS into a pie chart:

1. Type /**GND** and choose TOTALS. The graph will appear on the screen.
2. Press any key after viewing TOTALS to get back to the Graph menu.
3. Type **G** to select the Graph Type option.
4. Type **P** to select Pie.
5. Press F10.

The TOTALS pie chart automatically calculates the percentage of each value in the charted range. Rather than keep these percentages, which have only a trivial meaning in this graph, you can modify the chart to display the numbers themselves:

1. Press any key to go back to the Graph menu.
2. Select Customize Series, Pies, and Label Format (keystrokes **CPL**).
3. Highlight the Value option and press Enter.
4. Press the Graph key (F10) to see the graph shown in Figure 11.19.

Notice that the pieces of the pie are not distinguished from each other—i.e., you don't know who sold how much—because Quattro Pro interpreted the charted numbers as though they came from the same data set. In the following example, you'll choose a different set of data to yield distinct pie slices.

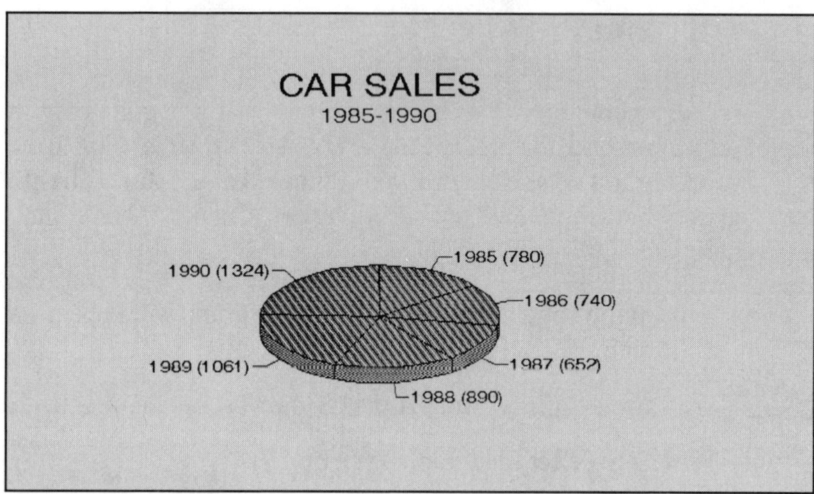

Figure 11.19: The pie chart with numbers

Exploding the Pie Chart

To distinguish better between the different car manufacturers, you'll need to graph a new set of numbers. It would also be a good idea to explode a segment for emphasis:

1. Go into the spreadsheet-ready mode. Then press Ctrl–G to activate the Fast Graph feature.
2. Highlight the block of cells A4..B7 and press Enter. Quattro Pro will graph the data as a pie chart, since that was the last format you selected. Hit any key to go back to the spreadsheet-ready mode.
3. Type **/GCP** to start modifying the pie chart's appearance.
4. Type **L%** to select Label Format and change it to Percentage (%).
5. Type **E** to select Explode.
6. Type **2E** to select the 2nd Slice and, from the submenu, Explode. Hit Escape three times.

7. Now type **T2** to select the Text option from the Graph menu and 2nd Line from the submenu. Use the Backspace key to delete part of the title, **-1990**, so it reads just **1985**.

8. Hit Enter once and Escape twice, then press F10 to see the new pie chart. It should appear as in Figure 11.20.

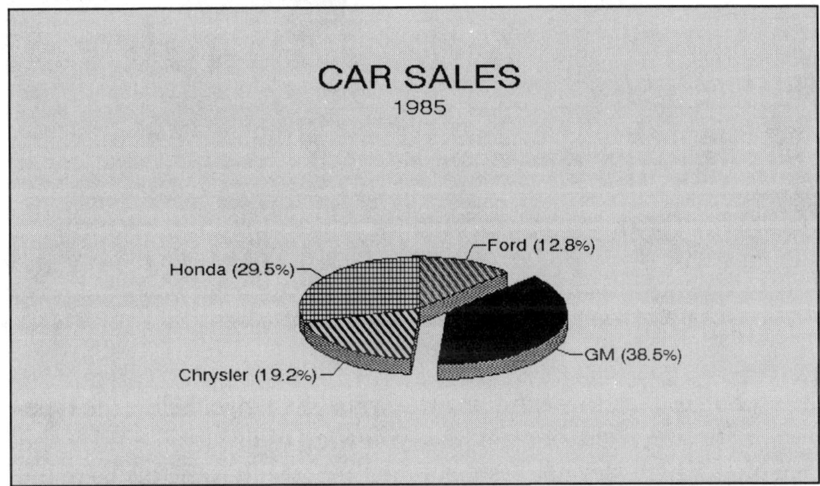

Figure 11.20: The pie chart with distinct pie slices

Save the new chart as PIE85 and save the spreadsheet. Now type /**GND** to see that TOTALS, STACKED, and PIE85 are all part of the CARSALES spreadsheet.

Customizing Titles

Quattro Pro offers several options for customizing titles on a graph, which mainly involve changing the title's font. By default, Quattro Pro displays titles above the graph in a plain block font. If you don't like it, you can select from among 11 fonts for these titles. Figure 11.21 shows the names of the available fonts in the type styles they display.

To change a font, select a named graph to make it current. Then select the Text option from the Graph menu and the Font option from

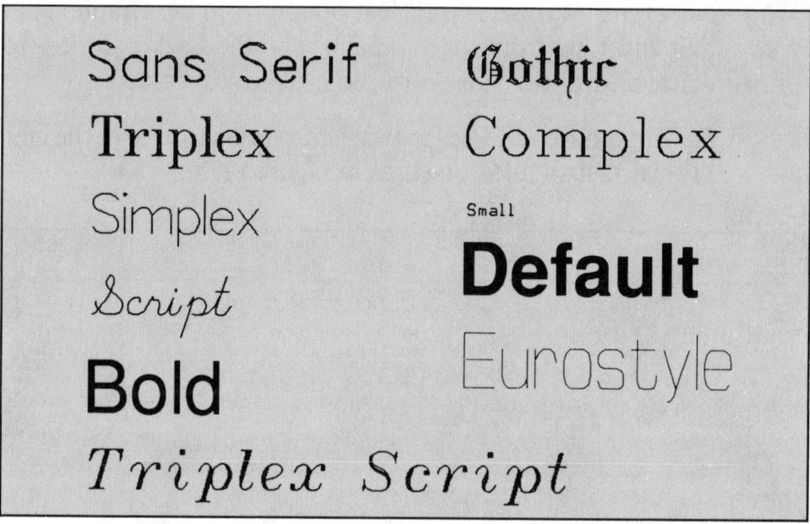

Figure 11.21: Examples of fonts for displaying graph titles

the submenu. Pick the text items you want to change. Select the typeface, point size, style, or color that you want to use for the titles and then press F10 to view the results. Experiment with some of the many varieties available.

Changing Markers and Fill Patterns

When you create a line graph, Quattro Pro automatically selects a symbol for each block of plotted data. Similarly, when you create a bar, stacked-bar, or area graph, Quattro Pro automatically selects a fill pattern for each plotted series. You can change the markers or fill patterns with the options on the Customize Series submenu.

To change marker symbols, first select Customize Series from the Graph menu, then select Markers & Lines from the submenu. When you select the option Markers, Quattro Pro will then display a submenu that describes the markers for each of six series. Highlight the series for which you wish to customize the marker and press Enter.

To change a fill pattern, select Fill Patterns from the Customize Series option. Select the series for which you want to change the fill pattern (type a number 1–6). From the subsequent submenu, select the fill pattern by typing the letter corresponding to the pattern, or by moving the highlight to the name of the pattern and pressing Enter. Press the Graph key (F10) to see the results. When you're through, hit Escape three times to return to the Graph menu.

Choosing Graph Colors

If you have a color monitor, Quattro Pro provides many features for coloring a graph. To see the available options, select Customize Series from the Graph menu, and Colors from the Customize Series submenu. Quattro Pro displays a submenu that lists each series and its respective color.

Select the series you want to customize by highlighting it and pressing Enter. Quattro Pro displays the list of 16 colors available. Highlight the color you desire and press Enter. Press F10 to see the result of the change.

Note that graph colors are affected by the resolution setting of your monitor. To see what it is, type **/OHSR.** Your color monitor might not display any colors if the resolution is set too high.

Remember to use the Name and Create options to store the new graph colors (keystrokes /**GNC**), and then type /**FS** from the main menu to save the spreadsheet with its new settings.

Annotating a Graph

The Annotation feature of Quattro Pro is a powerful means of producing graphs with features that could only be produced previously by specialized graphics programs. There are two ways to view the Annotator screen:

- Press the forward slash (/) while viewing a graph
- Select the Annotate option from the Graph menu

Figure 11.22 shows the Annotator screen.

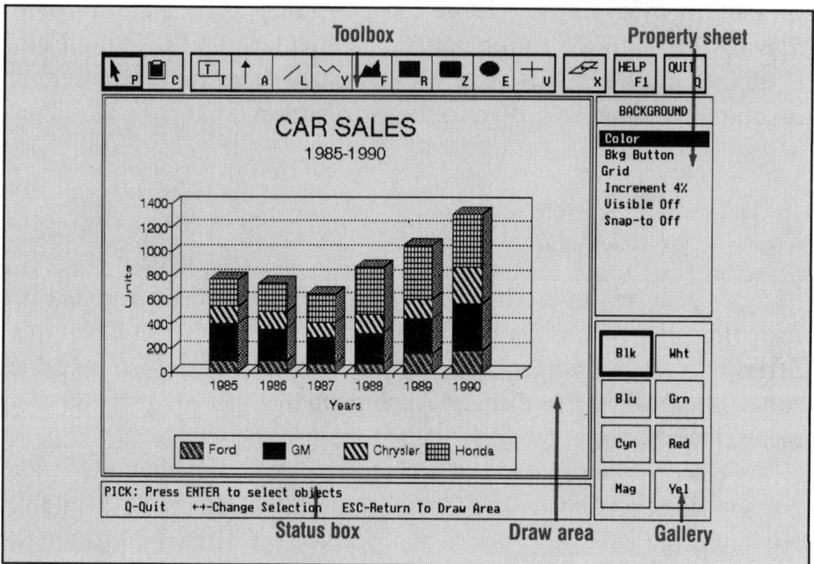

Figure 11.22: The Annotator screen

There are five distinct areas on the Annotator screen:

- The **Draw Area** is where the annotations are added.
- The **Toolbox** is the series of boxes across the top of the screen. Each one can be used to add an element to a graph.
- The **Property Sheet** adjusts the particular element that you add to a graph.
- The **Gallery** lists the options available for an element that is highlighted on the property sheet. If you are using a color monitor, the colors are visible in the Gallery.
- The **Status Box** contains instructions, shortcuts, and menu-command descriptions.

Special Keys

The use of the function keys and other special keys in the Annotator is completely different from their use in the spreadsheet mode. Table 11.1 lists each key and its application.

Table 11.1: Annotator Function Keys

KEY	WHAT IT DOES
F1	Help
F2	The Edit key when modifying a text element
F3	Activates the Property Sheet
F7	Activates the Proportional Resize mode when a group of elements is selected, so that you can adjust the size of the elements *and* the space between them simultaneously
Shift–F7	Retains current element selection, allowing you to select a second element with Tab or Shift–Tab
F10	Annotator draws only a skeleton of very complex graphs, to save editing time, so this redraws the graph in its entirety
Tab	Selects the next element in the Draw Area
Shift–Tab	Selects the previous element in the Draw Area
Shift	If you have a mouse, holding Shift down allows you to click multiple elements (if you are drawing a polygon or polyline, pressing Shift puts you in the Curve Draw mode)
Del	Deletes a selected element or group of elements
Period Key	After you select an element, anchors the selected area and lets you resize it
Home, End, Page Up, Page Down	Moves the corners of a selected area diagonally
Arrow keys	Move or resize a selected element or group of elements
Ctrl–Enter	Starts a new line when you're in Edit or Text mode
Backspace	In Edit mode, deletes the character to the left of the cursor; at the beginning of a line, joins it with the line above

Table 11.1: Annotator Function Keys (continued)

KEY	WHAT IT DOES
/	Activates the Toolbox
Esc	When drawing, cancels the current action; in a menu, exits the menu
Enter	Executes the desired action
Alt	With a mouse, hold down the Alt key while dragging a group of elements in a selection box to resize the elements proportionally
/Q	Quits the Annotator

Figure 11.23 shows the STACKED graph to which an arrow and text box has been added. The arrow emphasizes the direction of growth for the auto industry and the text box indicates the increasing sales of Japanese-built cars.

There are a few steps involved in adding these elements to the STACKED graph you saved earlier. They're easy, too. But first you should become familiar with the Annotator.

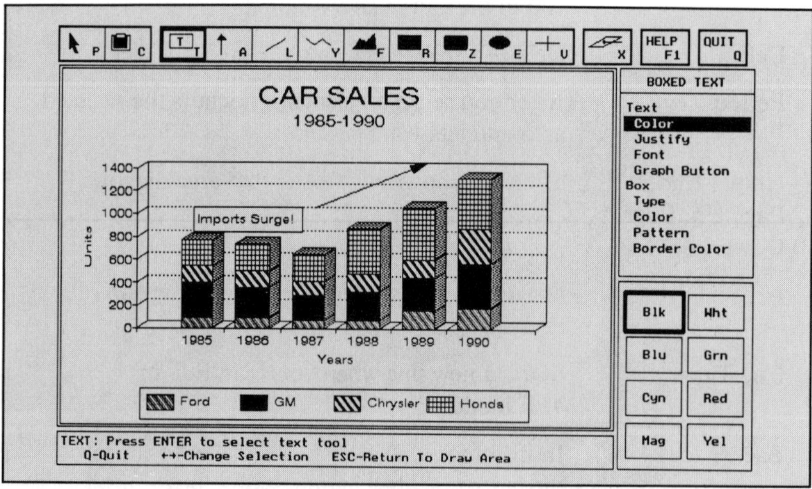

Figure 11.23: The STACKED graph with an arrow and text box

Retrieve the graph, if you don't already have it on-screen (select Display from the Name submenu). Once you have STACKED on-screen, press the / key to activate the Annotator. Once that's done, note that the first modifiable portion of the graph will be its background color. On a monochrome screen, though, this cannot be changed from black.

Right now, no element of the graph itself is currently selected: neither the title, nor the legend, nor the graph area. To start selecting these areas, press the Tab key once.

The legend is the first selected element. Quattro Pro alerts you to this by placing boxes (or handles) at eight border locations around the legend. The Property Sheet also lists the modifiable pieces of the legend: the text color and/or font, and the box color and/or type.

Press the Tab key again. The title is now surrounded by eight handles to indicate that it is the selected element. In the Property Sheet, Quattro Pro lists the pieces of the title that are modifiable. Under the Text part, the color of the text and the font of each line of the title can be modified. In addition, you can change the box type and color.

Press the Tab key again. The graph is now the selected element, as shown in Figure 11.24.

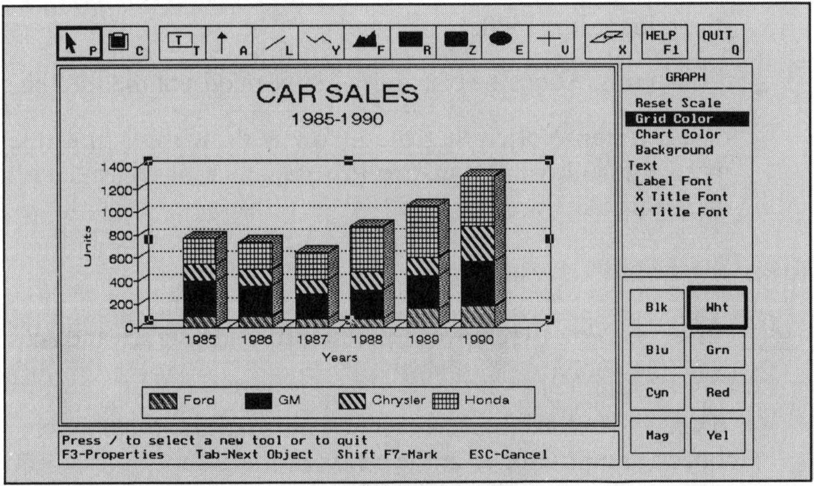

Figure 11.24: Graph as the selected element

Press F3 to activate the Property Sheet. Now you can highlight the element of the graph you want to change. For example, highlight the Label Font entry in the Property Sheet and press Enter.

Quattro Pro displays the options for selecting a new label font above the graph in the Draw Area. (The current settings are displayed.) If you want, you can change the typeface, point size, and style. Press Escape and Quattro Pro will redraw the graph.

Now you're ready to add the two elements. To add the arrow:

1. Press Escape again. In the Status Box, the message **Press / to select a new tool or to quit** appears.
2. Press the / key. The Toolbox is now activated. Press → three times or type **A**. This action selects the arrow tool.
3. Press Enter. Quattro Pro inserts a large + sign in the middle of the graph. (If you are using a mouse, an arrow will be displayed.) This is the pointer for drawing the arrow.
4. Press ↑ to move the pointer to the 1000-units grid-line. Then press ← to move the plus sign over the middle of the 1987 bar.
5. Press the period key. This anchors the beginning of the arrow, opposite its tip. Press the ↑ key until the pointer is at the top of the grid, at line 1400.
6. Next, press → until the pointer is over the middle of the 1989 bar.
7. Press Enter. Notice that the arrow is drawn and that the pointer is still visible. Quattro Pro assumes that you still wish to use the Arrow tool.

To add the descriptive text:

1. Press the / key to remove the pointer from the screen and activate the Toolbox.
2. Type **T**. The boxed-text tool is now selected and the pointer is once again positioned at the center of the graph.
3. Press ↑ until the pointer is positioned on the 1000 grid-line.

4. Press ← until the pointer is positioned directly over the 1985 bar.
5. Type **Imports Surge!**
6. Press Enter. The text will be enclosed in a box.

Using the Annotator Clipboard

With the Annotator Clipboard you can cut, copy, paste, or delete elements from the Draw Area. To select one element, press the Tab key. To select a group of elements, first select one element with the Tab key and then press Shift–F7 to hold onto that element while you select additional elements with the Tab or Shift–Tab keys.

After selecting the element(s) you want to manipulate, press the / key to access the Toolbox. Use → or ← to move the highlight to the Clipboard tool, which is the second tool from the left. Press Enter to activate the Clipboard. Use the arrow keys to highlight the appropriate option described below. (The Status Box will reflect the currently selected option in the Property Sheet.)

Cut	Removes the selected elements(s) from the Draw Area onto the Clipboard. The cut element will remain there until you cut a different element or leave the Annotator
Copy	Creates a copy of the selected element(s) and stores the copy on the Clipboard for pasting or storing
Paste	Inserts the element(s) stored on the Clipboard at the same place from which they were cut or copied
Delete	Permanently removes element(s) from the Draw Area without first storing on the Clipboard. An element can also be deleted by selecting it and pressing the Del key
To Top	Moves the selected element to the front of the other elements. For example, if a text box is covered by a bar graph, it can be placed "on top" of the bar graph

To Bottom	Moves the selected element behind the other elements that it covers
Cut To	Removes the selected element(s) from the Draw Area and stores it in a Clipboard file. By storing elements in a file, you can always retrieve them as needed rather than create them again from scratch
Copy To	Makes a copy of the selected element and saves it to a Clipboard file
Paste From	Inserts a stored element into the Draw Area, in the same position and size it was when you saved it. You can then resize and reposition it

The graph itself cannot be cut, copied, or modified. Only the components you add later can be manipulated.

Moving an Element

To move an element, it must first be selected. For example, suppose you wanted to move the title from the top middle of the STACKED graph to the top left:

1. Press the Tab key until the titles element is selected.
2. Press any arrow key. This automatically selects the Edit mode from the Toolbox.
3. Press ← until the left edge of the titles box is positioned over the *y* axis (Shift-← will move it faster).
4. Press Enter. The graph will appear as in Figure 11.25.

Aligning Elements

When you have selected several elements in the graph, you may wish to align them along the sides, centers, tops, or bottoms. The Group Property sheet (in version 3.0 only) automatically appears when you have selected more than one element. Select the Align option, and a submenu displays the alignment options.

Using Grids

To aid in placing elements in the graph, Quattro Pro includes two styles of grids. These grids are available only in version 3.0 of Quattro Pro. The first grid, Visible, can be seen on the screen. With the Visible grid, you can move elements manually, positioning them as they correspond to the grid dots. The grid does not appear in the graph or printed versions.

The second type of grid is Snap-to. When Snap-to is on, elements are attracted to the grid's lines and objects are automatically aligned.

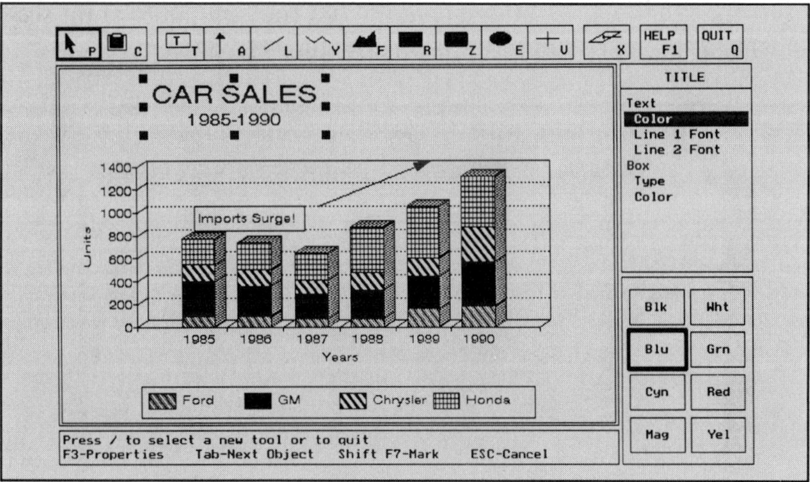

Figure 11.25: The Titles box moved to the left edge of the graph

Resizing an Element

To resize an element, select it with the Tab key and press the period key. Quattro Pro will highlight a corner of the selected element. Repeatedly pressing the period key will highlight a different corner or end of the element. Once it is at the corner you want, use the arrow keys to move it to a different position. The element will shrink when you move one corner toward another, and stretch when you move it away. Only the highlighted portion will move. Press Enter to resize the element.

As a precaution, before making any drastic changes to any part of the graph, save it and the spreadsheet. That way, if you really make a mistake, you can retrieve the graph as part of the saved spreadsheet.

Creating a Slide Show

After creating several graphs, you can display them in a slide-show fashion with each graph shown for a number of seconds (determined by you). To create a slide show, you must first create a series of named graphs—one for each slide. After creating the graphs, move the cell selector to an area of the spreadsheet where there is room to insert the graph names in one column and the time interval (in seconds) in a second column, as shown in Figure 11.26.

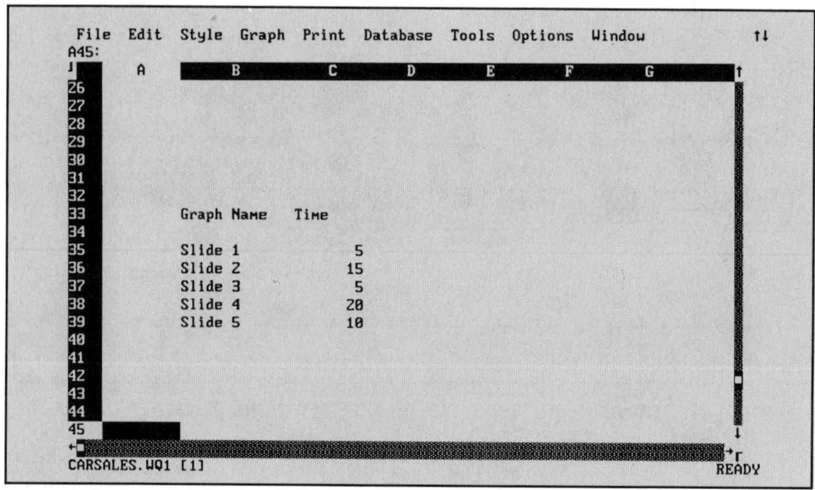

Figure 11.26: Columns with graph names and time intervals

The slide names here are arbitrary; you'll want to enter your actual graph names. If you do not specify a display time, Quattro Pro will assume it is 0 and wait until you press a key before continuing to the next graph.

To implement the slide-show feature, select Slide from the Name submenu (keystrokes **/GNS**). Quattro Pro will display the prompt

Enter block of graph names to show slides:

along with the current cell address. In this example the block is B35..C39. After entering the block of cells containing the names of the graphs and their display times, Quattro Pro will immediately begin the slide show, displaying each graph in succession. After the last graph has been shown, Quattro Pro will return you to the Graph menu.

Adding Visual and Sound Effects

After creating the graphs for your slide show, you have the option of adding visual and sound effects. This option is available only in Quattro Pro 3.0.

Visual effects are different methods of transition from one slide to the next. Normally, a slide disappears and is then replaced by the next. However, you can add up to 24 different effects such as Wipe left or Dissolve into 2 × 1 rectangles. You must be in EGA mode to create Visual effects.

To add Visual effects, add a third column to the right of the Time column and enter the Visual number as outlined in the Quattro Pro manual. The fourth column then holds the speed of the Visual effects.

To add Sound effects, you can add a fifth column that includes the sound file name. Sound effects come with Quattro Pro and are stored in files with a .SND extension. The names are indicative of the type of sound made. You may also use sound effects in macros, using the {play filename.snd} command.

Inserting a Graph in a Spreadsheet

Quattro Pro allows you to insert an *interactive graph* directly into an area of the spreadsheet. That way, as you change spreadsheet numbers, the graph will change accordingly. To do so, you must have the proper hardware; you need a VGA or EGA monitor. (Unless you have an old model or a low-end computer, you'll have the right hardware.)

Figure 11.27 shows the CARSALES spreadsheet. The TOTALS graph has been inserted in the block B16..E24. To insert this graph in the spreadsheet, type **/OD** to select Display Mode from the Options menu. Select Graphics Mode from the submenu.

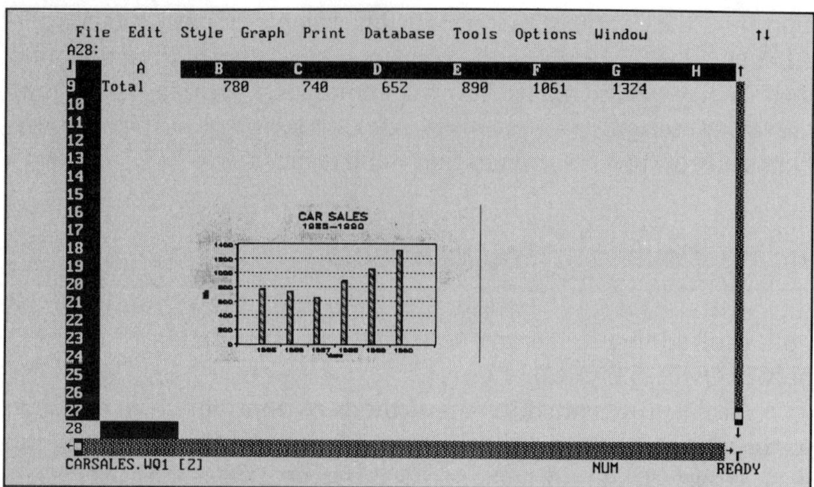

Figure 11.27: The TOTALS graph inserted in the CARSALES spreadsheet

Now you are ready to insert the graph:

1. Select Insert from the Graph menu.
2. From the list of graph names, select TOTALS.
3. Quattro Pro will ask you on the input line for a block in which to insert the graph. Enter the block B16..E24.

Quattro Pro inserts the graph and adjusts it in a 4:3 width-to-height ratio.

Note that if the graph you insert has too many points or elements to fit into the block you allot it, you'll get the error message, **Graph too complex**.

Printing an Inserted Graph

To print a spreadsheet with an inserted graph, simply include the entire block coordinates as part of the block to print, and set the Destination option under the Print menu to Graphics Printer (keystokes/**PDG**). Then type **S** for Spreadsheet Print. (Printing graphs alone is discussed in the next chapter.)

Removing an Inserted Graph

To remove an inserted graph, select the Hide option from the Graph menu (keystrokes /**GH**). Quattro Pro will display the list of graph names. Select the name of the graph that has been inserted and press Enter. The graph will disappear, leaving blank cells behind.

Creating a Fast Graph

If you want to graph a group of contiguous data in a hurry, without a lot of formatting, the Fast Graph feature will be of great help. With the CARSALES spreadsheet on the screen, select the Fast Graph option from the Graph menu (keystrokes /**GF**). Quattro Pro will respond with the prompt:

Enter Fast-Graph block:

Enter the block A2..B9 and press Enter to fast-graph the data in the block.

Notice that Quattro Pro picked the correct labels for the bars, but it also made a bar for 1985 instead of a label—and left a blank bar-space for blocks A3..B3 and A8..B8, which contain underlines (\- and \=, respectively). Cell B2 shouldn't have been included in the block to graph, since it contains a year, not a unit of cars. To get rid of that bar, hit any key to get back to the spreadsheet mode, then press Ctrl–G, the shortcut for Fast Graph. This time, select the block A4..B9 and press Enter. Your quick-and-dirty Fast Graph should resemble the one in Figure 11.28. Editing the Fast Graph is identical to editing any other graph, and by no means are you limited to bar graphs. When you save it, give it a unique name.

Combining Graph Types

To call attention to one particular series in a graph—say, Honda's sales—you may want to choose a different graph type in which to display it. First, you have to override the graph type in which that series is currently graphed and change it to something else. Only line, bar, and

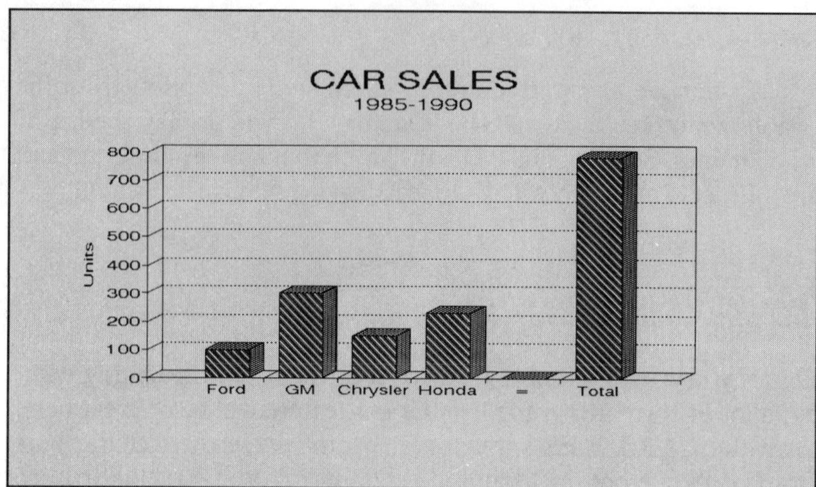

Figure 11.28: *The CARSALES Fast Graph*

X–Y graphs can be overriden in this manner. To do that, select Customize Series from the Graph menu (keystrokes /**GC**). From the submenu, select the Override Type option.

Quattro Pro will present the list of data series. Select the series you want to change. From the submenu, choose Bar if the rest of the graph is a line or X–Y graph; choose Line if the rest is a bar graph. Press F10 to view the new graph.

If you like it, save the graph under a new name and save the spreadsheet with the changes. If you don't, select Override Type and the particular series again; then choose Default to reset the series to how it was in the first place.

As you can see, Quattro Pro's extensive graphing capabilities are quite flexible. With the Fast Graph feature, experimenting with various graph types is downright fun. In the next chapter, you'll learn how to print the graphs you've just learned how to create.

PRINTING GRAPHS

F E A T U R I N G

Selecting a Graphics Printer
Formatting Printed Graphs
Printing a Graph to a File

Selecting a Graphics Printer

Before you actually start printing a graph, you need to select a printer on which to print it. Now, you may be thinking that you already did so when you installed Quattro Pro in the beginning—and you'd be right—however, what you chose might not be suitable for printing graphical output, or you might want to be able to choose between two printers in your office, depending on which is being used by someone else at the moment. In any case, you'll appreciate the fact that you don't have to reinstall the software just to make Quattro Pro's output go to a different printer.

To redefine a printer to which you want to direct your output, type **/OHP** to select the Printers option from the Hardware submenu on the Options menu. You'll see a submenu with the following options:

1st Printer	Lets you define the make, model, baud rate, etc., of one graph-printing device (either a printer or a plotter)
2nd Printer	Lets you define another printing device
Default Printer	Lets you tell Quattro Pro whether to print to the 1st or 2nd Printer

Plotter Speed	Lets you select a speed for printing graphs on a plotter. A setting of 0 specifies the fastest speed for your plotter and a setting of 9 the slowest. (A setting of 2 is the recommended speed for printer transparencies and for plotters with old, worn pens.)
Fonts	Lets you tell Quattro Pro which laser font cartridge you are installing in your printer and the fonts therein (if any). Also lets you choose whether or not to scale fonts. When you print a graph with several fonts, Quattro Pro scales the fonts to fit the graph's dimensions. If you set this to No, the fonts will be printed in their exact point size, regardless of the relative size of the graph
Auto LF	Determines whether a *line feed* should be sent to the printer, i.e., whether the paper should be advanced after each printed line. To see if your printer should be sent a line feed, test-print a spreadsheet: if the printer prints all of the text on a single line, set this to Yes; if the text is printed double-spaced, set this to No
Single Sheet	Lets you tell Quattro Pro whether you are sending single sheets of paper through the printer or a ream of form-feed sheets. Select Yes if you want the printer to pause after each page and wait for you to insert another sheet of paper

When you select 1st Printer or 2nd Printer from the submenu, you'll be presented with options for defining (choosing) that printer. There are hundreds of printers on the market today, each with its own quirks. Quattro Pro contains technical information about many printers, so the chances are good that you can select the appropriate options for your graphics printer or plotter. Note that if you selected a printer during Quattro Pro installation, it will already show up under 1st Printer.

To (re)define either 1st Printer or 2nd Printer, select the option called Type of Printer. Quattro Pro will display a list of makes. Scroll through the list until you find the make of your printer or plotter and press Enter.

Choose the model of your printer or plotter from the next box that appears—or a model that is most similar to what you have—and press Enter. What comes next depends on whether you are defining a printer or plotter as your printing device:

- If you are defining a *printer*, you'll see a box that lists different modes. Highlight one of several dots-per-inch (dpi) settings, usually broken down into low, medium, and high. Selecting a high dpi will produce crisper graphs but will slow down overall printing. You may want to experiment until you find the best setting for your particular needs.
- If you are defining a *plotter*, you'll have a choice of Auto, Manual, and Monochrome. The Auto option uses whatever pens are in the plotter to print the graph. The Monochrome option prints in one color and then gives you time to change the pen in the plotter to another color.

Most computers use parallel printers and do not require any additional settings. If, however, you are using a serial printer or an unusual port for your printer, you'll need to set some of the options described below to specify the printer more clearly:

Device	Specifies how your printer is connected to your computer; choose Serial 1 if it is connected to the first serial port
Baud Rate	Specifies the speed at which information is transferred to the printer from the computer
Parity	Specifies the manner in which information from the computer is sent; you can specify Odd, Even, or None
Stop Bits	Specifies the number of stop bits to expect at the end of an information byte; you can specify 1 or 2 bits

When you have finished, press Escape until the Options menu is displayed and select Update. Quattro Pro will store any changes as the new default settings.

Printing a Graph

Once you've defined the graphics printer hooked up to your computer, printing a graph is easy:

1. First view the graph you want to print, either by pressing the Graph key (F10) or by choosing the Name and Display options from the Graph menu. Press any key after viewing the graph on the screen.
2. Select the Print menu and choose the Destination option from the Graph Print submenu (keystrokes **/PGD**). Quattro Pro presents three options: you can print the graph to a disk file for printing at a later time; you can print the graph on a graphics printer; or you can print the graph on the computer screen so you know how it will look on paper.
3. Select the Graph Printer option, and then Go.

Depending on the complexity of the graph, you will have to stop working while **WAIT** is displayed in the lower-right corner of the screen. Quattro Pro may have to build some fonts first. (If you want to interrupt the printing process, press Ctrl–Break.) When the graph has been fully printed, you'll be returned to the Graph menu.

Formatting a Graph

When you print a graph, Quattro Pro automatically uses dimensions that best fill an $8^1/_2 \times 11$-inch page. You can, however, alter these dimensions to control the margins on the page. To do so, select the Graph Print option from the Print menu. From the submenu, select the Layout option. You'll be given the options summarized below:

Left Edge	Designates the number of inches or centimeters from the left edge of the paper to the graph
Top Edge	Designates the number of inches or centimeters from the top edge of the paper to the graph
Height	Designates the height of the printed graph
Width	Designates the width of the printed graph
Dimensions	Selects inches or centimeters as the unit of measurement
Orientation	Designates the graph to be printed along the width of the page (portrait) or along the length of the page (landscape)
4:3 Aspect	Adjusts the graph to print in a 4:3 aspect ratio, four units in width by 3 units in height. If you select No, you can adjust the proportions of the graph however you wish
Reset	Resets all printing options to their default settings
Update	Saves current settings as new defaults. (Watch out: after you do this, Reset will no longer change the values back to the default values originally supplied with Quattro Pro.)
Quit	Closes menu

Figure 12.1 shows how some of the layout options are affected by the orientation of a graph. The top half shows a graph printed in portrait mode. The bottom half shows the same graph in landscape mode. Note that the top-edge measurement in the top graph is different than the top-edge measurement in the bottom graph. The same applies to the left-edge, height, and width measurements. Make sure you know how you want to orient the graph on the page *before* you set the page-spacing dimensions!

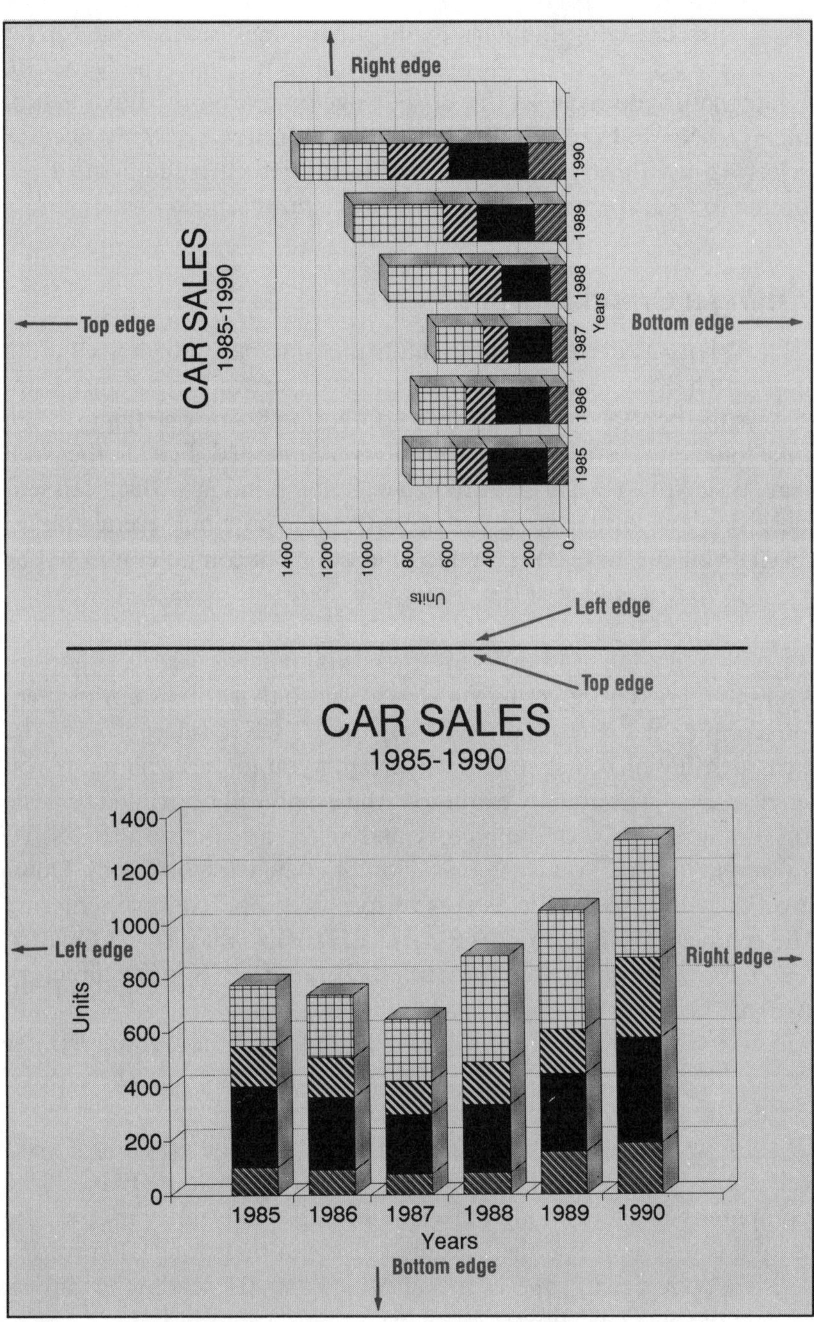

Figure 12.1: Vertical and horizontal orientation of a graph

After changing the various layout settings, select Quit (or hit Escape) to get back to the Graph Print submenu. Then type **G** for Go. (Note that if you have set the Break Page option on the Layout submenu to No and are printing with a laser printer, you may need to select Adjust Printer from the Print menu and then the Form Feed option to eject the printed graph from the printer.)

Printing a Graph to a File

This is an extremely handy feature that you may find yourself using quite often. Printing a graph while you have Quattro Pro running is not always the best (or handiest) way to do business. For one thing, it can take some time, especially if the graph is complicated. For another, you can't do anything else in Quattro Pro while it is printing—which can seriously bog you down in your work if you want to print out several graphs. Even if you only have one graph to print out, your computer may not be hooked up to a printer, or the printer you share with other users may not often be free for you to use.

To make the most efficient use of your time in such a situation, you should *first* print your graphs to a disk so that you can print them on a printer at a later time. To do so, type **/PDF** to select a file as the print destination. Quattro Pro will prompt you for a file name. If you enter a name without any extension, the graph will be printed to a file on the current drive and directory and given the extension .PRN. If, however, you add your own extension or change the directory, Quattro Pro will store the file as you've specified. For example, entering the complete file name **C:\WP\GRAPH1.BIN** will instruct Quattro Pro to print the graph to a file named GRAPH1.BIN in the directory WP on the C drive.

After you enter your file name, be sure to set the Default Printer option (keystrokes **/OHPD**) to the correct printer—i.e., the type of printer to which you'll be printing the disk file later on.

Now that you've told Quattro Pro to print the graph to a disk, select Go from the Graph Print submenu (keystrokes **/PGG**). The computer will act as though it were printing to a printer. Indeed, the output is the same whether it prints to a disk or a printer. By printing to a disk, you simply capture the outputted data for sending towards a printer at some later time.

Printing the Disk Copy to a Printer

When you finally get to print the disk file to a printer, you must use the DOS command called COPY. Enter the DOS shell and, at the prompt, type **COPY FILENAME.EXT /B LPT1,** where **FILENAME.EXT** is the name of the graph you printed to disk, including the extension (most likely .PRN). If your printer is connected to a port other than LPT1, such as COM1 or PRN, specify that port in the COPY command.

Note that the saved version of the graph is no longer connected to Quattro Pro in any way. There is no way, for instance, to bring this disk version of the graph back into Quattro Pro and update it with new data. Therefore, do not attempt to use this technique as a means of saving graphs for future use. Use it only to store graphs that you wish to print at a later time.

Storing a Graph in an EPS, PIC, or PCX File

You can store your graph in three other formats. The EPS format creates a PostScript-compatible file, which can be used to import graphs into some word-processing systems such as PageMaker (Aldus Corp.) and Sprint (Borland International, Inc.). The PIC format creates a file that is compatible with Lotus 1-2-3, Lotus Symphony, and WordPerfect. The PCX format creates a file that is compatible with PC Paintbrush (Z-Soft Corp.), a graphics program. The Slide EPS format creates a file that later can be made into a 35-mm slide. This format is similar to EPS, except that it correctly translates the on-screen colors and ensures proper proportions for the slide.

To store a graph in a file using one of these formats, select the Graph Print and Write Graph File options from the Print menu (keystrokes /**PGW**). Then select the format you need. When you do, Quattro Pro will prompt you for a file name. Be sure to enter a name without an extension—Quattro Pro will add its own. You can also specify a new disk drive and/or directory in front of the file name. For example, entering **C:\123\GRAPH1** will store the saved file in the directory 123 on drive C. Press Enter after typing in the file name; you'll be returned to the Graph Print submenu.

13

EXPLORING THE QUATTRO PRO DATABASE

Setting Up a Database

Sorting and Searching through a Database

Database Statistical Functions

So far you have learned much about Quattro Pro's considerable spreadsheet and graphing capabilities—and their interconnection. This chapter concerns a third powerful component: database management.

What Is a Database?

A database is an organized collection of information. Even without the aid of a computer, you work with databases quite often. For example, your noncomputerized database might be a stack of receipts or invoices; a checkbook; a list of employees, customers, or prospective clients; a Rolodex; a phone book; a file cabinet; or even a shoe box full of index cards.

Many tasks are involved in managing these databases. You may need to add, update, delete, and rearrange the information. You may also want to locate and perhaps extract specific information, such as all California residents with invoices that are past due. Quattro Pro's database capabilities let you perform all these tasks quickly and easily.

Structuring a Database

Most of your noncomputerized databases are composed of individual pieces of paper, each with the same kind of information on it.

For example, each Rolodex card might contain one person's name and address, as in Figure 13.1. A computerized database has a similar structure.

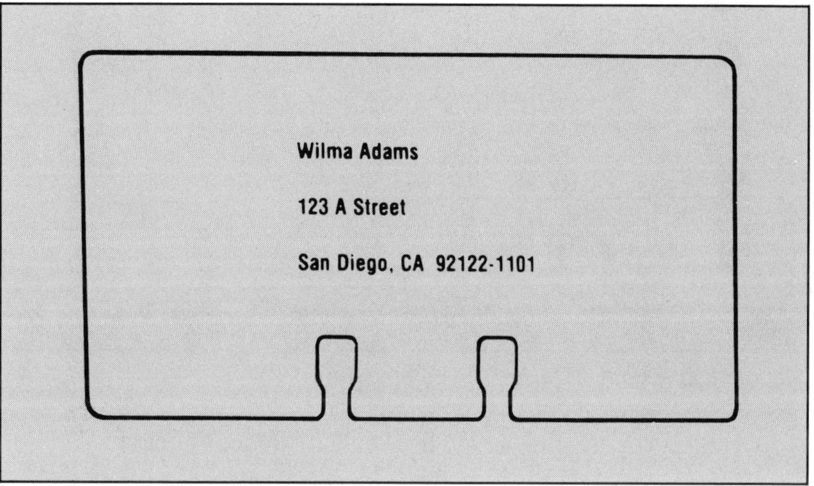

Figure 13.1: A sample Rolodex card

Setting Up Records and Fields

In a Quattro Pro database, the information on a Rolodex card is stored as one record (row) of information. The individual items on the card—the name, address, city, and so forth—are each stored in a field (column) of information. Figure 13.2 shows how information from several Rolodex cards might be stored in a Quattro Pro database. There are eight records in this database, each consisting of six fields. Row 3 contains column labels (field names) that Quattro Pro considers part of the database.

Because Quattro Pro can only perform sorts and searches on specific fields within a database, the manner in which you separate information into the individual fields is vitally important. The basic rule of thumb is to break down each record into as many meaningful fields as possible.

Notice that the names in the sample database are actually divided into two fields, FName and LName. Intuitively, you might want to

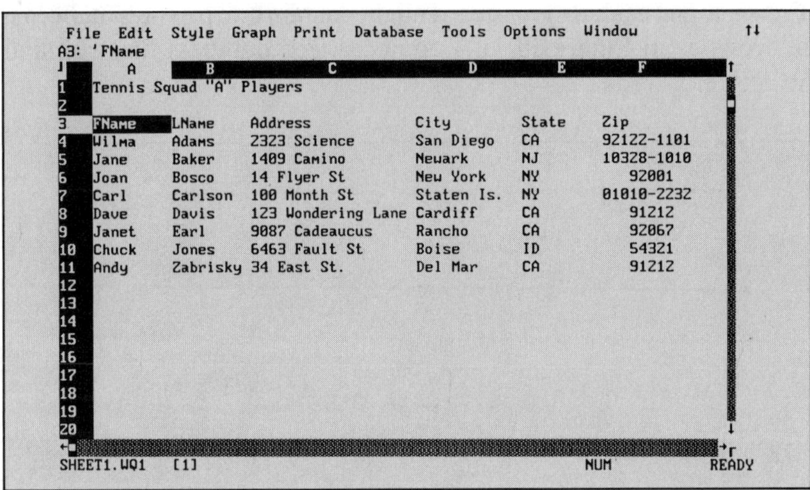

***Figure 13.2:** A sample Quattro Pro database*

store people's names in a single field called Name, as below:

Name

Chuck Jones

Andy Zabrisky

Jane Baker

Dave Davis

Joan Bosco

Wilma Adams

Carl Carlson

Janet Earl

However, if both the last name and first name were combined in a single field, Quattro Pro would not be able to sort the names into alphabetical order by last name; an alphabetical sort on the Name field above would place Andy Zabrisky above Wilma Adams. This is because Quattro Pro cannot operate upon information that is embedded within a field.

Notice also that the city, state, and zip codes are each stored in a separate field. Once again, you might be tempted to store this information in a single address field, as below:

City, State Zip

San Diego, CA 92122-1101

Newark, NJ 10328-1010

New York, NY 92001

Staten Is., NY 01010-2232

Cardiff, CA 91212

Rancho, CA 92067

Boise, ID 54321

Del Mar, CA 91212

If you combined these items into a single field, Quattro Pro would not be able to perform such tasks as sorting the database into zip-code order for bulk mailing or extracting all the records of people who live in the state of New York.

Guidelines for Creating a Database

When you store information in a Quattro Pro database, there are a few basic rules that you must follow, as summarized below:

- The database must be stored in an even, rectangular block of cells, and it cannot contain any blank rows or columns (a given record does not have to contain data in all fields, but at least one field must contain data)
- The first row must consist of field names (which are like spreadsheet column headings)
- An individual field name cannot be longer than 15 characters
- Field names cannot contain any of the operators +, −, *, /, or ^

- Avoid embedding blank spaces in field names. You can substitute an underline character (but not a hyphen!) for a blank space; for example, use *First_Name* rather than *First Name* as a field name
- A field cannot have the same name as another field or block on the spreadsheet
- All the data within a field must be of the same data type. For example, a field of zip codes cannot contain both numbers, such as 92122, and labels, such as '92J ZZL or '00112. If some of the zip codes need to be stored as labels, then all the zip codes must be stored as labels (e.g., '92122 rather than 92122)
- There can be no blank, or decorative, rows between field names and the first record (row) of data (for example, you cannot place underlines between the field names and the records)
- A field can contain a formula or function that refers to other fields in its own record. For example, a function that calculates an extended price based on the quantity and unit price in the same record as itself is okay. However, a function that calculates values based on information outside its own record will most likely lead to problems when you sort the database

The sample database shown in Figure 13.2 follows all these rules, and is indeed a valid Quattro Pro database.

Note that the size of your Quattro Pro database is limited by the amount of memory your computer has. In theory, the largest possible database consists of 256 fields and 8191 records.

Creating a Sample Database

Let's develop a sample database now to use in examples and exercises in this chapter. Rather than enter simple names and addresses, however, you'll set up one that includes some numbers so that you can experiment with techniques for performing calculations on a database. Open a clean spreadsheet and read on.

Suppose that, as the owner of a used-car lot, you want to set up a database that lets you help customers locate cars that suit their needs. You need to be able to find quickly all cars of a particular type, or within a particular price range, or with a specific number of doors. So you decide to divide the information about each car into the following distinct fields: year, make, model, number of doors, selling price, mileage, lot number, and date sold (leaving the date-sold field blank until the car is sold).

Figure 13.3 shows how you could set up the initial structure of the database. The field names are stored across row 3, and the Column Width command was used to set a reasonable width for each field. The main title above the field names is just a descriptive title; it is not an actual part of the database. Enter the title and field names for the sample database, and adjust the column widths as follows:

Column	Width (spaces)
A	5
B	11
C	9
D	6
E	8
F	6
G	7
H	10

Entering Records in a Database

You enter information into database records the same way that you type data into spreadsheet cells—by positioning the cell selector, typing in your entry, and pressing Enter. Just be sure to use the correct data type for the field. For example, enter all dates with either the Ctrl–D command or the @DATE function.

Figure 13.4 shows the used-cars database with some sample records. (The dates in the right-most column were entered with the Ctrl–D command.) Enter the records shown in the figure.

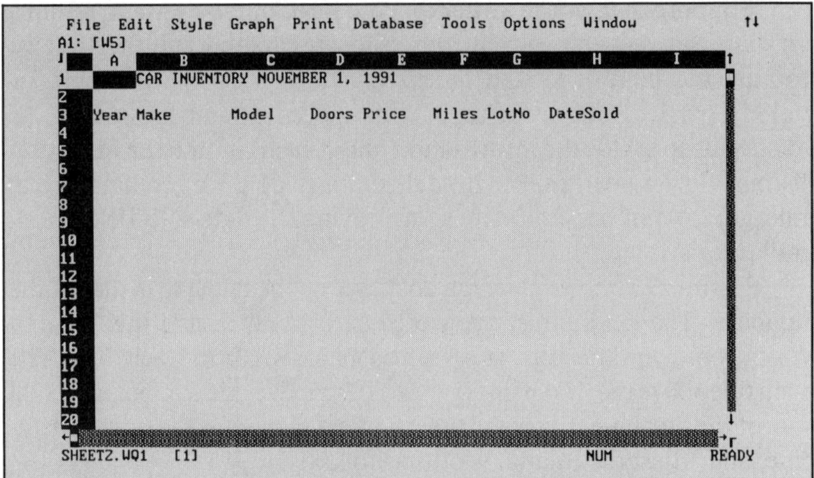

Figure 13.3: Sample database structure for information about used cars

File Edit Style Graph Print Database Tools Options Window
A1: [W5]

CAR INVENTORY NOVEMBER 1, 1991

Year	Make	Model	Doors	Price	Miles	LotNo	DateSold
87	Chevy	Corvair	2	2000	77	1842	
84	Chevy	Corvette	2	17000	33	9727	
69	Chrysler	Barracuda	2	1795	101	4602	
83	Ford	XLT Truck	2	3300	80	5384	
87	Honda	Civic	2	8890	55	3923	
81	Nissan	RX7	2	8966	84	2766	01/10/90
86	Chevy	Sprint	4	8996	22	2918	
85	Chrysler	Voyager	3	10500	64	1842	
87	Chevy	Capri	4	5900	22	9629	
74	Chrysler	Newport	4	500	150	2507	
87	Ford	Taurus	4	8800	35	2423	
85	Honda	Accord	4	9500	43	1779	
78	Chrysler	Omni	5	2200	71	9114	
84	Ford	Horizion	5	7300	41	3442	
84	Ford	Maverick	5	6500	55	5541	10/10/90
83	Nissan	Stanza	5	3800	66	6002	

SHEET2.WQ1 [1] NUM READY

Figure 13.4: Sample database with sample records

Sorting the Database

Typically, you enter information into a database as the information becomes available. But eventually you'll need to sort the information into some more useful order, such as alphabetical order by name, by zip-code order for bulk mailing, by part number, or perhaps by manufacturer. To sort a database, you would follow the steps below. (An example for you comes later.)

1. Type /**DS** to select the Sort option from the Database menu.
2. Select Block and specify the block containing all the fields and records, *excluding* the field names—i.e., just the data. (Be sure to include *all* the fields.)
3. Select 1st Key and specify the column on which you want to base the sorting order by moving the cell selector to that column and pressing Enter.
4. When prompted, select Ascending (smallest to largest) or Descending (largest to smallest) for the sorting order. With label fields, ascending order is *A* to *Z*, and descending order is *Z* to *A*. With dates and times, ascending order is earliest to latest, and descending order is latest to earliest.
5. If you want the sort based on more than one field (discussed later), select 2nd Key and specify the column for the secondary sort order. You can repeat this process for a maximum of five fields.
6. Select Go after specifying all the fields for the sort.

The records will be sorted immediately and the menu will disappear from the screen.

Sort the records in your sample database now into ascending order by price. Here are the steps:

1. Type /**DS** to select the Database menu and Sort option.
2. Select Block and specify the block of fields and records, A4..H19. (You can use the pointing method or just type in the coordinates and press Enter.)
3. Select 1st Key, move the cell selector to any cell in the Price field (say, cell E4), and press Enter.

4. Enter **A** for Ascending in the window that appears.
5. Select Go to perform the sort.

Immediately, the records are sorted by the used car's price, with the least expensive vehicle listed first and the most expensive vehicle listed last. This order makes it easy to locate vehicles within a customer's price range. Figure 13.5 shows the database after performing the sort.

```
File  Edit  Style  Graph  Print  Database  Tools  Options  Window
A1: [W5]
    A       B           C          D     E       F      G       H       I
1        CAR INVENTORY NOVEMBER 1, 1991
2
3   Year Make       Model      Doors Price   Miles LotNo  DateSold
4     74 Chrysler   Newport      4     500    150   2507
5     69 Chrysler   Barracuda    2    1795    101   4602
6     87 Chevy      Corvair      2    2000     77   1842
7     78 Chrysler   Omni         5    2200     71   9114
8     83 Ford       XLT Truck    2    3300     80   5384
9     83 Nissan     Stanza       5    3800     66   6002
10    87 Chevy      Capri        4    5900     22   9629
11    84 Ford       Maverick     5    6500     55   5541   10/10/90
12    84 Ford       Horizion     5    7300     41   3442
13    87 Ford       Taurus       4    8800     35   2423
14    87 Honda      Civic        2    8890     55   3923
15    81 Nissan     RX7          2    8966     84   2766   01/10/90
16    86 Chevy      Sprint       4    8996     22   2918
17    85 Honda      Accord       4    9500     43   1779
18    85 Chrysler   Voyager      3   10500     64   1842
19    84 Chevy      Corvette     2   17000     33   9727
20
SHEET2.WQ1    [1]                                         NUM       READY
```

Figure 13.5: Used-cars database sorted by the Price field

You may notice that although the location of the records changed, Quattro Pro still formatted the entries in the DateSold column as dates—i.e., it retained your formatting specifications after the sort.

Note that you must *never* include the field names (row 3 in this example) when specifying the block to sort, and always specify *all* the fields in the database. Failure to specify all the fields in a sort will cause the records to go out of alignment, rendering the database useless. However, if the Undo option on the Options menu is set to Yes before you make the sort, pressing Alt–F5 will revert the database back to where it was before the sort. (To play it safe, always save a database before performing a sort, so that you can call it back onscreen should you make a mistake.)

Sorting within a Sort

In some situations, sorting on a single field is simply not adequate. For example, if you had a database with 5000 names and sorted it by last name only, then all the Smiths would be clumped together—as expected—but they would be in random order by first name. Imagine if the telephone directory for a large city sorted names in this fashion, and you were looking for Joe Smith. You would have to read every Smith entry until you happened to come across Joe Smith.

To have Quattro Pro perform a sort within a sort, you use multiple sort keys. The first key you define is the primary sort order, which specifies the main order for the records. Then you define a second key to specify the secondary, or within-sort, order. For example, if you sort a database with *last* name as the first key and *first* name as the second key, the names will be sorted in alphabetical order by last name, then in alphabetical order by first name within a list of identical last names, as below:

Smidle	Zachary
Smith	Albert
Smith	Mille
Smith	Wilma
Smyth	Joan

You can specify up to five sort keys, each one arranged within the order specified by the previous key. For example, if you sorted a database of invoice records with date as the first key, customer number as the second key, and invoice amount as the third key, the database would be sorted overall by date; within each identical date, invoices would be sorted by customer number; and within each identical date and customer number, records would be sorted by the amount of the invoice.

Sort the used-car database by three keys: the number of doors, make, and model.

1. Type **/DS**, select Block, specify all the database fields and records (A4..H19), and press Enter. (Quattro Pro remembers the previous sort, so you will not have to make an entry.)

2. Select 1st Key, specify the Doors field (cell D4), and select Ascending order.

3. Select 2nd Key, specify the Make field (cell B4), and select Ascending order.

4. Select 3rd Key, specify Model as the field (cell C4), and select Ascending order.

5. Select Go to sort the database.

Figure 13.6 shows the database after it has been sorted. The records are sorted first by the number of doors, from two to five. Within each group of cars with the same number of doors, the records are sorted alphabetically by make (e.g., Chevy, Chrysler, Ford, Honda, Nissan). The records for cars of the same make with the same number of doors are sorted alphabetically by model (e.g., Ford Horizon comes before Ford Maverick among the five-door cars).

Each field was sorted in ascending order, but you can combine ascending and descending orders in any sort. For example, sorting a database of invoices into ascending order by date and descending order by charge would produce a file of records listed from earliest to latest date; within each identical date, records would be listed from the highest charge to the smallest.

```
 File  Edit  Style  Graph  Print  Database  Tools  Options  Window
A1: [W5]
     A         B          C        D      E       F      G         H        I
1         CAR INVENTORY NOVEMBER 1, 1991
2
3   Year Make        Model     Doors Price   Miles LotNo  DateSold
4     87 Chevy       Corvair       2   2000     77  1842
5     84 Chevy       Corvette      2  17000     33  9727
6     69 Chrysler    Barracuda     2   1795    101  4602
7     83 Ford        XLT Truck     2   3300     80  5384
8     87 Honda       Civic         2   8890     55  3923
9     81 Nissan      RX7           2   8966     84  2766  01/10/90
10    85 Chrysler    Voyager       3  10500     64  1842
11    87 Chevy       Capri         4   5900     22  9629
12    86 Chevy       Sprint        4   8996     22  2918
13    74 Chrysler    Newport       4    500    150  2507
14    87 Ford        Taurus        4   8800     35  2423
15    85 Honda       Accord        4   9500     43  1779
16    78 Chrysler    Omni          5   2200     71  9114
17    84 Ford        Horizion      5   7300     41  3442
18    84 Ford        Maverick      5   6500     55  5541  10/10/90
19    83 Nissan      Stanza        5   3800     66  6002
20
SHEET2.WQ1    [1]                                        NUM          READY
```

Figure 13.6: Used-cars database sorted by doors, make, and model

Note that if you sort a database that has a field containing a function or formula that makes reference to values outside its own record, the sort will wreak havoc on its result. However, a field in a database *can* refer to an unsorted value outside the database, as long as the reference is absolute. For example, if the sort block is A5..Z109 and a percentage figure is stored in cell A1, a formula that refers to $A$1 will still do so after the block is sorted.

Because the sort order will not pertain to any records entered *after* the database has been sorted, you must sort the entire database again to reorder the new records. (Be sure to include the new records in the block to sort.)

Searching a Database for Specific Data

Sorting a database can put records into a useful order, but it will not necessarily help you to locate a specific item of information, such as a person's address. Nor will it necessarily help you pull out all records that meet some criterion, such as accounts receivable that are over 90 days past due. To perform these kinds of tasks, you need to use Quattro Pro's searching, or querying, capabilities.

To perform a database query, you must first access the Query submenu from the Database menu. To do so, type **/DQ**. You'll be presented with several options, summarized below:

Block	Specifies the entire database, including all field names, before querying a database
Criteria Table	Specifies a block of cells on the spreadsheet that contains query criteria
Output Block	Determines where to store extracted records on the spreadsheet
Assign Names	Lets you use a field name, rather than a cell address, when entering a query formula
Locate	Locates the first record in the database that matches the specified query criteria
Extract	Extracts all records that meet a query criterion and places them in another part of the database

Unique	Extracts only unique values that match a query criterion—i.e., does not extract duplicate records
Delete	Deletes all records in a database that match a specified query criterion
Reset	Undoes all previous query criteria settings
Quit	Leaves the Query submenu and returns to the spreadsheet-ready mode

Defining a Query Block

Before performing a database query, you must select the Block option from the Query submenu and specify the entire database as the block to query. This time, the block you specify *must* include the field names at the top of the database. You can use the pointing method to specify the block to search or just enter the cell coordinates of the block (e.g., A3..H19). Press Enter after defining the block to return to the Query submenu.

Any time that you add new records to a database, be sure to select the Block option from the Query submenu and redefine the block so that it includes those new records.

Assigning Field Names

Before you enter the query criteria, you should select the Assign Names option from the Query submenu so that you can use field names in your query formula. It makes the formula easier to understand later on. For example, to search for all Fords in the used-cars database without first assigning field names, you would need to enter a formula like **+B4=Ford** (where B4 refers to the first cell under the Make field name). However, if you gave this field the name Make, you could enter the formula as **+Make=Ford**.

When you select Assign Names, you don't really have to do any assigning; you won't see any prompts on the screen. Quattro Pro assumes that the first row of the query block contains field names and automatically assigns these names to the fields. But watch out: problems may arise if any names have more than one word or are more than 15 characters long.

If you add new fields to a database structure or change any field names, you should remember to select the Assign Names option again to reassign the names to the fields.

Setting Up a Database-Criteria Table

A criteria table consists of field names in the top row and values to search for in the row(s) beneath. The field names in the table must match the field names in the database exactly. (You can use the Copy option from the Edit menu to copy the field names from the top of a database to a criteria table.)

After you set up your criteria table with field names, values to search for, and/or query formulas, select the Criteria Table option from the Query submenu. Quattro Pro will display the prompt

Block containing table of search criteria:

Use the pointing method to highlight the appropriate field names, search values, and formulas, and then press Enter. To actually perform the search, select Locate, Extract, or Unique from the Query submenu, as discussed later in this chapter. (Before choosing Extract or Unique, of course, you must select Output Block to tell Quattro Pro where to place the data found by the search.)

If you want to isolate records that meet one specific criterion, place the value to search for directly under the appropriate field name. For example, Figure 13.7 shows a criteria table that will search for records that have Ford in the field named Make.

If you wish to search for records that are less than or greater than some value, you must enter a formula that begins with a plus sign, followed by a field name, a logical operator, and a comparison value. For example, Figure 13.8 shows a highlighted criteria table that is set up to isolate records of cars with prices of $5,000 or less.

Note that you can only use field names in these formulas if you selected the Assign Names option from the Query submenu. When you enter such a formula, the cell will display either 1 or 0, for a true

```
 File  Edit  Style  Graph  Print  Database  Tools  Options  Window          ↑↓
A24: [W5]
     A         B            C         D     E       F      G        H       I
5   84 Chevy       Corvette        2   17000     33   9727
6   69 Chrysler    Barracuda       2    1795    101   4602
7   83 Ford        XLT Truck       2    3300     80   5384
8   87 Honda       Civic           2    8890     55   3923
9   81 Nissan      RX7             2    8966     84   2766  01/10/90
10  85 Chrysler    Voyager         3   10500     64   1842
11  87 Chevy       Capri           4    5900     22   9629
12  86 Chevy       Sprint          4    8996     22   2918
13  74 Chrysler    Newport         4     500    150   2507
14  87 Ford        Taurus          4    8800     35   2423
15  85 Honda       Accord          4    9500     43   1779
16  78 Chrysler    Omni            5    2200     71   9114
17  84 Ford        Horizion        5    7300     41   3442
18  84 Ford        Maverick        5    6500     55   5541  10/10/90
19  83 Nissan      Stanza          5    3800     66   6002
20
21  CRITERIA TABLE (A22..H23)
22  Year Make      Model      Doors Price     Miles LotNo  DateSold
23       Ford
24
SHEET2.WQ1    [1]                                        NUM          READY
```

Figure 13.7: Criteria table to search for Fords in the used-car database

```
 File  Edit  Style  Graph  Print  ||Database||  Tools  Options  Window      ↑↓
Enter criterion block: A22..H23
     A         B            C         D        E       F      G        H
6   69 Chrysler    Barracuda       2          1795    101   4602
7   83 Ford        XLT Truck       2          3300     80   5384
8   87 Honda       Civic           2          8890     55   3923
9   81 Nissan      RX7             2          8966     84   2766  01/10/90
10  85 Chrysler    Voyager         3         10500     64   1842
11  87 Chevy       Capri           4          5900     22   9629
12  86 Chevy       Sprint          4          8996     22   2918
13  74 Chrysler    Newport         4           500    150   2507
14  87 Ford        Taurus          4          8800     35   2423
15  85 Honda       Accord          4          9500     43   1779
16  78 Chrysler    Omni            5          2200     71   9114
17  84 Ford        Horizion        5          7300     41   3442
18  84 Ford        Maverick        5          6500     55   5541  10/10/90
19  83 Nissan      Stanza          5          3800     66   6002
20
21  CRITERIA TABLE (A22..H23)
22  Year Make      Model      Doors Price          Miles LotNo  DateSold
23                                  +PRICE<=5000
24
25
H23: [W10]                                                          POINT
```

Figure 13.8: Criteria table set up to isolate cars costing $5,000 or less

or false condition in the first record. To view the actual formula instead (as in Figure 13.8), format the cell(s) with keystrokes /**SNT**.

Locating and Changing Records

Regardless of whether you use a criteria table or enter a formula to specify your search criteria, the Locate option on the Query submenu will allow you to pinpoint and edit the records that meet those criteria.

When you select Locate, the cell selector highlights the first record in the database that matches your search criteria. For example, Figure 13.9 shows the result of selecting Locate after specifying the block A22..H23 to search in the criteria table. The cell selector is on the first (and only, in this example) record that includes lot number 9114.

```
 File  Edit  Style  Graph  Print ||Database|| Tools  Options  Window                  ↑↓
A16: [W5] 78
    A          B          C          D          E          F      G         H
6   69 Chrysler    Barracuda      2              1795   101   4602
7   83 Ford        XLT Truck      2              3300    80   5384
8   87 Honda       Civic          2              8890    55   3923
9   81 Nissan      RX7            2              8966    84   2766  01/10/90
10  85 Chrysler    Voyager        3             10500    64   1842
11  87 Chevy       Capri          4              5900    22   9629
12  86 Chevy       Sprint         4              8996    22   2918
13  74 Chrysler    Newport        4               500   150   2507
14  87 Ford        Taurus         4              8800    35   2423
15  85 Honda       Accord         4              9500    43   1779
16  78 Chrysler    Omni           5              2200    71   9114
17  84 Ford        Horizion       5              7300    41   3442
18  84 Ford        Maverick       5              6500    55   5541  10/10/90
19  83 Nissan      Stanza         5              3800    66   6002
20
21 CRITERIA TABLE (A22..H23)
22 Year Make       Model     Doors Price         Miles LotNo  DateSold
23                                                      9114
24
25
SHEET2.WQ1    [1]                                              NUM             FIND
```

Figure 13.9: Result of selecting Locate after setting up a criteria table

If you change some data in the database or information in the criteria table without adding or deleting rows from either, you can quickly repeat your database query by pressing the Query key (F7).

While the entire record is highlighted during a Locate operation, you can use any of the keys listed below to work with the database (e.g., type new values in a particular cell):

↓	Highlights the next record in the database that matches the search criteria (if none of the records below matches the search criteria, Quattro Pro beeps instead)
↑	Highlights the previous record in the database that matches the search criteria (if none of the records above matches the search criteria, Quattro Pro beeps instead)

→	Moves the reverse-video cell selector one field to the right in the current record
←	Moves the cell selector one field to the left in the current record
Home	Moves the cell selector to the first record in the database (whether it matches the search criteria or not)
End	Moves the cell selector to the last record in the database (whether it matches the search criteria or not)
F2	Lets you edit the currently selected cell (press Enter when done editing)
Escape	Quits the Locate operation and returns you to the Query submenu—or takes you back to the spreadsheet-ready mode if you did a search with the Query (F7) key

Extracting Database Records

You can also use criteria formulas and tables to extract (or "pull out") a copy of database records that meet some search criteria. The extracted records will be stored in an *output block* elsewhere on the database, which can contain all or some of the fields from the original database.

For example, suppose that you want to pull out from the sample database a copy of all records that have Ford in the Make field. To do so, follow these steps:

1. Create the criteria table shown in the block A22..H23 in Figure 13.10.
2. Create an output block that consists of field names from the database and has enough blank rows beneath the row of field names for the extracted records. (To play it safe, just put the field names for the output block below everything else in the spreadsheet.)

3. After entering the field names for the output block, select the Output Block option from the Query submenu. Highlight only the field names in the output block. In Figure 13.10 that block is A27..H37.

4. After assigning the criteria table and output block, select Extract from the Query submenu.

Copies of records that meet the search criteria will be copied into the output block, as shown in Figure 13.11.

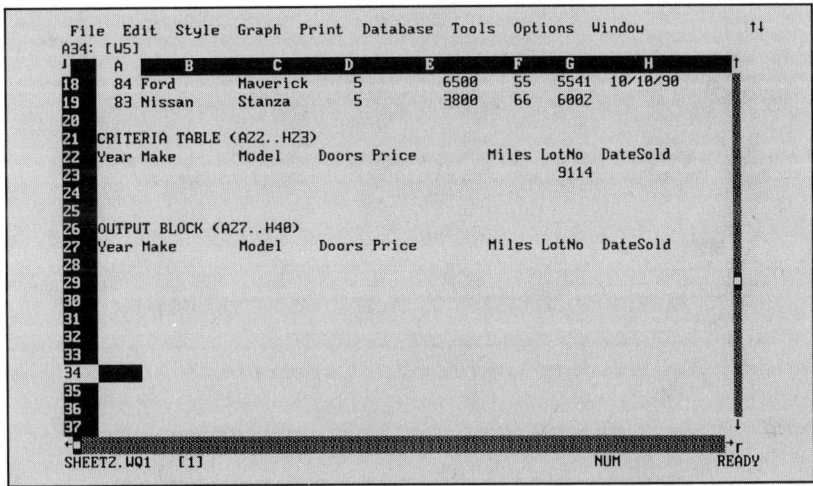

Figure 13.10: Criteria table and output block on the spreadsheet

Extracting Unique Values

In a very large database, you might want to extract certain entries from a database without having them repeated if they occur more than once. For example, suppose you want to see a list of all the car-makes in the used-car database. Follow these steps:

1. Set up a criterion formula that will not exclude any records in a given field. The simplest way to do this is to highlight a field name and the blank cell beneath it when you define the criteria block.

2. Create an output block that consists of only the field name you are interested in—i.e., the Make field. Figure 13.12 shows what you want: B27 is the output block and B22..B23 is the criteria block.

3. Select Unique from the Query submenu.

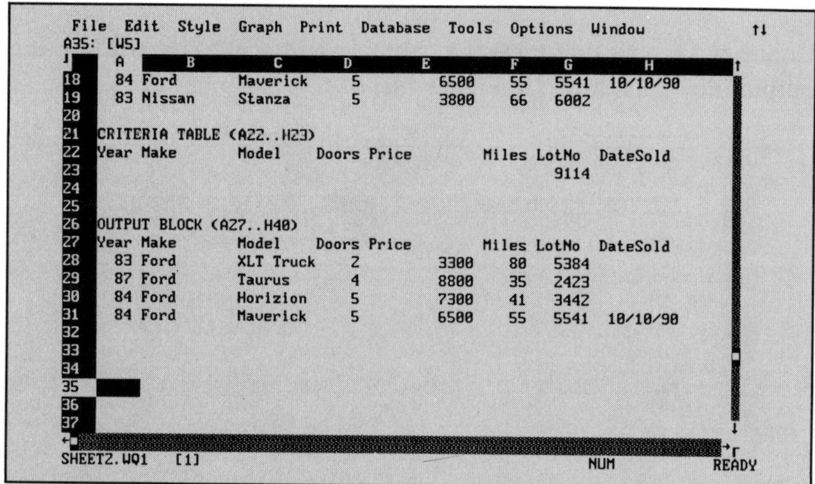

Figure 13.11: Copies of extracted records in the output block

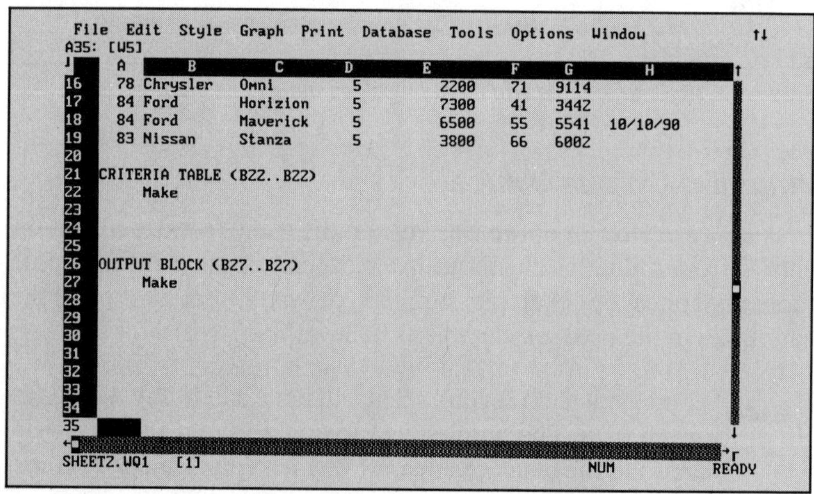

Figure 13.12: The truncated output block

A list of unique values in the Make field will appear in the output block, as shown in Figure 13.13.

Deleting Database Records

You can use the usual Delete and Rows options from the Edit menu to delete any single record from a database. But you can also use the Delete option on the Query submenu to delete all records that match a specific search criterion. To play it safe, always save your database before deleting any data, so that you can retrieve them if you make a mistake. You can also Undo a deletion (Alt–F5), providing Undo has been enabled.

Don't forget that the Delete option from the Edit menu deletes the *entire* row from a spreadsheet, all the way over to column IV. The Delete command on the database Query submenu, however, has no effect on cells outside the database block.

The technique for using Delete is basically the same as the one for using Locate: you call up the Query submenu, specify the entire database block, specify a query formula or criteria table, and then select Delete. For example, Figure 13.14 shows the results of a delete operation: because the criteria table specified records with DateSold values greater than zero, all cars that *had* been sold were erased.

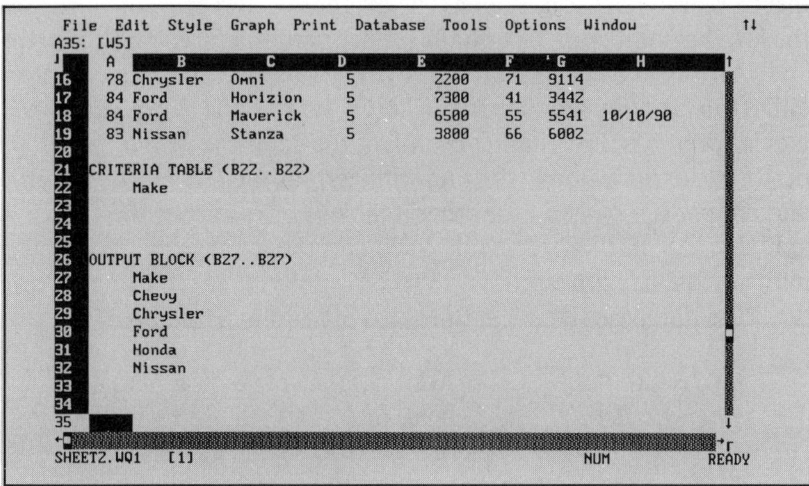

Figure 13.13: The unique output

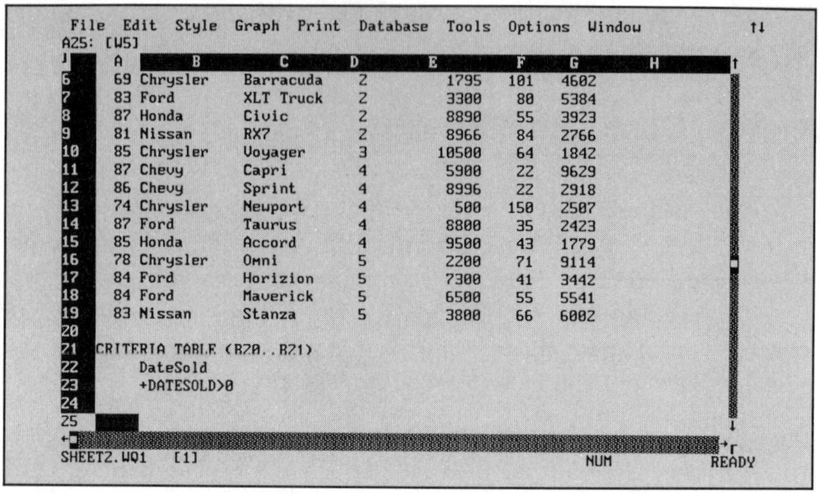

```
 File  Edit  Style  Graph  Print  Database  Tools  Options  Window
A25: [W5]
      A    B            C            D    E        F     G      H
6     69 Chrysler    Barracuda      2     1795   101   4602
7     83 Ford        XLT Truck      2     3300    80   5384
8     87 Honda       Civic          2     8890    55   3923
9     81 Nissan      RX7            2     8966    84   2766
10    85 Chrysler    Voyager        3    10500    64   1842
11    87 Chevy       Capri          4     5900    22   9629
12    86 Chevy       Sprint         4     8996    22   2918
13    74 Chrysler    Newport        4      500   150   2507
14    87 Ford        Taurus         4     8800    35   2423
15    85 Honda       Accord         4     9500    43   1779
16    78 Chrysler    Omni           5     2200    71   9114
17    84 Ford        Horizion       5     7300    41   3442
18    84 Ford        Maverick       5     6500    55   5541
19    83 Nissan      Stanza         5     3800    66   6002
20
21   CRITERIA TABLE (B20..B21)
22       DateSold
23       +DATESOLD>0
24
25
SHEET2.WQ1   [1]                                   NUM        READY
```

Figure 13.14: *Result of a database delete operation*

Database Statistical Functions

Quattro Pro's database statistical functions allow you to perform basic statistical operations, including sums and averages, on databases. Unlike Quattro Pro's regular statistical functions, these functions let you perform operations on only database records that meet a search criterion, such as the average selling price of Fords on the lot, the number of cars on the lot per manufacturer, and so forth.

All the database statistical functions use the basic syntax @D*X*(*block*,*column*,*criteria*), where *block* is the entire database block, *column* is the column position of the database field on which to perform the calculation (starting with zero as the left-most column), and *criteria* is a block in the criteria table. For example, the function @DAVG(A3..H17,4,B20..B21) calculates the average price of Fords in the used-cars database.

The database statistical functions are summarized below:

@DAVG(*block*, *column*,*criteria*)	Averages the entries in a numeric field, including only records that meet the specified search criteria

@DCOUNT(*block*, *column*,*criteria*)	Counts how many records in the database meet the specified search criteria
@DMAX(*block*, *column*,*criteria*)	Calculates the largest value (or latest date or time) in a numeric field, including only records that match the specified search criteria
@DMIN(*block*, *column*,*criteria*)	Calculates the smallest value (or earliest date or time) in a numeric field, including only records that match the specified search criteria
@DSTD(*block*, *column*,*criteria*)	Calculates the standard deviation of a numeric field, including only records that meet the specified search criteria
@DSUM(*block*, *column*,*criteria*)	Sums the entries in a numeric field, including only records that meet the specified search criteria
@DVAR(*block*, *column*,*criteria*)	Calculates the variance of a numeric field, including only records that meet the specified search criteria

Figure 13.15 shows the used-cars database set up with a criteria table in the block B20..B21 that limits calculations to Fords on the car lot. The database statistical functions calculate all statistics on prices of those cars, including a count of the number of Fords on the lot. Note that each formula specifies the entire database block (A3..H17), Price field (column 4), and criteria table (B20..B21). Changing the label in cell B21 from *Ford* to *Chevy* would instantly recalculate all the formulas to display the price statistics of Chevys on the lot.

The more you become familar with the workings of the Quattro Pro database, the more you'll realize that it provides an excellent means of recording and manipulating information, analyzing data, and discerning trends.

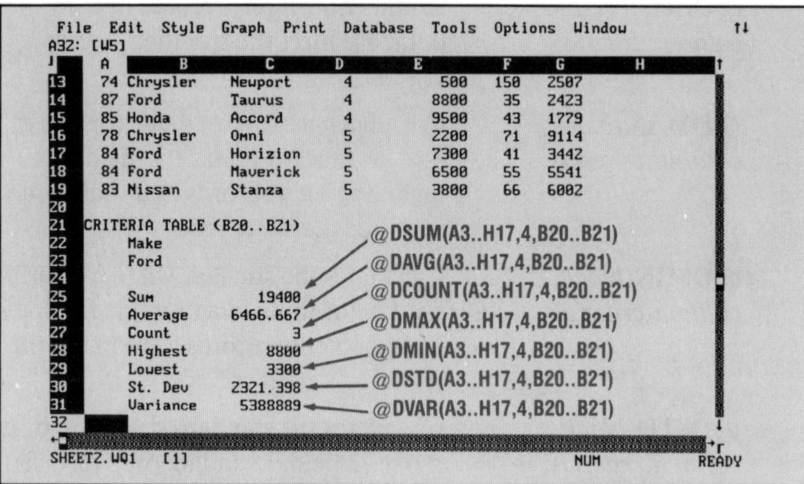

Figure 13.15: *Database statistical functions in the used-cars database*

CUSTOMIZING QUATTRO PRO

FEATURING

Modifying the Screen Colors

Changing how Currencies and Numbers are Displayed

Altering the Default Formats

Changing the Working Directory

Customizing Ctrl-Key Shortcuts

This chapter allows you to modify Quattro Pro to suit your particular needs and tastes. For instance, you might need (or prefer) to show dates in a non-American format—24/3/92 rather than 3/24/92. You might also like to change the color scheme on your monitor to something that seems a little more color-coordinated. Whatever your reasons, you need not feel stuck with the various default styles that came with the software. Customizing Quattro Pro is surprisingly easy—and fun.

Changing the Screen Colors

When you install Quattro Pro, it automatically checks the type of monitor and driver card you are using. On a color monitor, Quattro Pro displays the spreadsheet in colors that enhance readability. On a black-and-white monitor with a color graphics adapter, these colors appear in various shades of gray. If you have either of these monitors, selecting the Colors option on the Options menu (keystrokes /**OC**) allows you to change the colors or shades of gray. On a monochrome monitor, however, selecting Colors allows you to specify special screen attributes—boldface, underline, inverse-video, and empty (contents invisible)—for individual parts of the screen instead.

When you select Colors from the Options menu, a submenu appears with the following options:

Menu	Modifies colors for the various parts of the menus: frame, banner, text, key letter, etc.
Desktop	Modifies colors for the areas outside the windows: error messages, highlight status, background, etc.
Spreadsheet	Modifies colors for various parts of the spreadsheet: frame, banner, cells, borders, titles, graph frames, and the like
Conditional	Colors cells that do or do not meet some criterion (for example, you can choose to display negative numbers in red, positive values in green, and error conditions in yellow)
Help	Colors the Help screens
File Manager	Chooses colors for the File Manager windows
Palettes	Resets the colors to the original settings (Color, Monochrome, or Black & White)

Any changes you make will be immediately reflected on-screen, so you can see if the results are satisfactory. Note, however, that the changes you make affect only your current session with Quattro Pro. To apply a new color scheme for all future sessions, select Update from the Options menu. Doing so updates *all* current default settings, not just those on the Colors submenu.

Designing a Color Scheme

A good, general technique for designing a color scheme is to begin with a blank spreadsheet and then type /**OCP** to select Palettes. Select one of the appropriate options from the Palettes submenu:

Color	Select this if you have a color monitor
Monochrome	Select this if you have a monochrome monitor

Black & White	Select this if you have a black-and-white monitor with a color-graphics adapter

After you make a selection, Quattro Pro will revert to the default colors for that particular type of monitor. Later in the chapter, when you are specifying colors for specific parts of the screen, Quattro Pro will display the appropriate palette of options for your monitor. If you are using a color or black-and-white monitor, the palette will show a whirling star (or spinning propellor) on a dot of the foreground color against a band of the background color. Select a color combination by using thc ↑, ↓, ←, and → keys to move the whirling star to the color combination you like; then press Enter. Your selection will affect the appropriate part of the screen or spreadsheet immediately.

If you have a monochrome monitor (and select Monochrome from the Palettes submenu) you will see the following options instead:

Normal
Bold
Underline
Inverse
Empty

As with the color palette, select the option you want to use for the particular part of the screen or spreadsheet you are coloring. Your selection will affect it immediately.

Now let's look at the various parts of the screen that Quattro Pro allows you to color. When you select any of the options from the Colors submenu—Menu, Spreadsheet, Help, or File Manager—Quattro Pro displays a submenu of attributes: frame, banner, text, and so on. When you select the attribute you want to change, Quattro Pro will display the color palette.

Changing Menu Colors

To change the color of the menus, select the Menu option from the Colors submenu. Then choose the specific part of the menu that you want to color differently:

Frame	Colors the frame that surrounds the menu
Banner	Colors the titles at the top of the menu

Text	Colors the text within the menu
Key Letter	Colors the first letter of each menu option
Highlight	Colors the menu-highlight bar
Settings	Colors the current menu settings
Explanation	Colors the menu description on the status line
Drop Shadow	Colors the shadow under the menu frame
Mouse Palette	Colors the mouse buttons
Shadow	Shades in the menu drop "shadow" (the number is defined as an ASCII code number; the default is 177)

Changing Spreadsheet Colors

When you select the Spreadsheet option on the Colors submenu, you can change the colors of various parts of the spreadsheet:

Frame	Colors the box around the spreadsheet window
Banner	Colors the window banner on top of the spreadsheet when it is not zoomed
Cells	Colors the cells in the spreadsheet (see the discussion that follows on coloring cells according to their values)
Borders	Colors the row and column borders
Titles	Colors the rows and/or columns when they are locked
Highlight	Colors the cell selector
Graph Frames	Colors the frames around graphs that are inserted into the spreadsheet
Input Line	Colors the input line

Unprotected	Colors those cells that are defined as unprotected
Labels	Colors cells containing labels
Shading	Colors shaded cells
Drawn Lines	Colors lines drawn on the spreadsheet
WYSIWYG	Colors WYSIWYG mode (not in Version 2.0)

Coloring Cells According to Their Values

The Conditional option on the Colors submenu lets you specify colors of cells according to the values displayed in them. This is handy for pointing out values that fall above or below some predefined range of normal (or acceptable) numbers, and for highlighting erroneous values. For example, you could display all values less than 0 in red-on-blue, all values between 0 and 10,000 in black-on-cyan, and all values greater than 10,000 in yellow-on-black. On a monochrome screen, of course, you only have a choice of bold, underline, inverse-video, and empty. When you select the Conditional option, you'll have the following options:

On/Off	Determines whether or not conditional coloring is put into effect on the spreadsheet. The options are Enable (to use conditional coloring) and Disable (to turn conditional coloring off). The default setting is Disable because conditional coloring slows down Quattro Pro somewhat
ERR	Colors cells that contain the message **ERR**
Smallest Normal Value	Shows the lower limit of the normal numbers (unhighlighted) range. Press Enter to type a new lower limit. For example, if you enter **0**, all numbers *less than* zero will be displayed in the color you specify

Greatest Normal Value	Shows the upper limit of the normal numbers (unhighlighted) range. Press Enter to type a new upper limit. For example, if you enter **10000**, all numbers *greater than* 10,000 will be displayed in the color you specify
Below Normal Color	Colors those cells with numbers less than the value you specified with the Smallest Normal Value option
Normal Cell Color	Colors those cells with numbers between (and including) the values you specified with the Smallest Normal Value and Highest Normal Value options
Above Normal Color	Colors those cells with numbers greater than the value you specified with the Highest Normal Value option

Of course, the options you select for conditional colors will not take effect until the spreadsheet cells actually contain values that are less than, within, or greater than the ranges you have specified. Similarly, a cell that contains an error will not actually be displayed in your chosen color until that cell reads **ERR**. (You can easily test this by placing the @ERR function in any cell.)

To use conditional colors in all future spreadsheets, remember to select the Update option from the Options menu.

Changing Help-Screen Colors

The Help option on the Colors submenu lets you color the Help screens (those that appear when you press the Help key, F1). The options available when you select the Help option are as follows:

Frame	Colors the box around the Help screens
Banner	Colors the titles of the Help screen
Text	Colors the Help-screen text
Keywords	Colors the keywords in the Help text that you can select for additional help

Highlight	Colors the cell selector used on Help screens to highlight the keywords

Returning to the Default Colors

The Palettes submenu lets you select the type of palette (Color, Monochrome, or Black & White) for your spreadsheet. Whenever you select Palettes, all the original colors supplied with Quattro Pro will be reinstated. This can be a curse and a blessing.

Why? If you've gone to great lengths to develop the perfect color scheme, but not yet selected Update from the options menu, then reselecting a palette will instantly undo all of your previous changes. On the other hand, if your color scheme turns out to be a gaudy disaster, you can select Palettes again and return instantly to the original relatively simple color scheme.

How to Internationalize Quattro Pro

You can modify Quattro Pro to follow the formats used by other countries through the International option on the Options menu. This allows you to change the way you display numbers, dates, times, and currency signs.

The options on the International submenu do not globally affect all cell entries. Instead, they affect the way that certain Numeric Format options (available on the Style menu) are displayed. For example, if you specify a format of *mm.dd.yy* (e.g., 12.01.91) for dates, any serial dates that are entered will still be displayed in the General format (e.g., **33250**) until you specifically use the Numeric Format option to display dates in the Long International or Short International formats.

Changing the Currency Format

Normally, Quattro Pro displays currencies with a leading dollar sign, such as **$1,234.56**. Select other currency signs by selecting Currency from the International submenu. A box appears for you to replace the **$** with something else—such as **DM** for German marks, **Skr** for Swedish kronor, and the like.

If the currency symbol you want is not available on your keyboard, you'll need to hold down the Alt key and enter the appropriate ASCII code, using the numbers on the numeric keypad (not the numbers at the top of the keyboard) for that currency sign. These symbols and their ASCII codes are summarized below.

CURRENCY SIGN	KEYSTROKES
¢	Alt–155
£	Alt–156
¥	Alt–157
Pt	Alt–158
f	Alt–159

These ASCII codes may not work if you have loaded a memory-resident program such as SuperKey (Borland International, Inc.) into your computer.

After typing in the ASCII code and pressing Enter, you'll see the Prefix and Suffix options. Select Prefix to place the currency sign in front of the number; select Suffix to place it after the number. Any numbers currently displayed in the Currency format will be immediately updated to show the new currency sign. Remember that if you want to make the change permanent, you need to select Update from the Options menu.

Changing the Numeric Formats

To change the manner in which thousands are marked off in numbers, decimals displayed, or function arguments constructed, use the Punctuation option on the International submenu. When you do so, you'll be given a choice of eight different types of numeric formats and corresponding function-argument separators:

A. 1,234.56 (a1,a2)

B. 1.234,56 (a1.a2)

C. 1,234.56 (a1;a2)

D. 1.234,56 (a1;a2)

E. 1 234.56 (a1,a2)

F. 1 234,56 (a1.a2)

G. 1 234.56 (a1;a2)

H. 1 234,56 (a1;a2)

American punctuation is the default setting, as in **1,234.56**. A comma is also used to separate the arguments within a function, as in @PMT(1234.56,7%,30).

After selecting your preferred format, follow it! For example, option D uses the format 1.234,56 to display numbers. If you selected this option and entered a formula such as **@PMT(1.234,56,7%,30)**, the system would beep and return an error message—**Too many arguments**—because the formula contains three commas rather than the two required. Quattro Pro can't distinguish between the decimal separator (,) and argument separator (,). To avoid confusion, all formats employ different punctuation for each. The correct format for the formula, then, is **@PMT(1.234,56;7%;30)**.

Modifying the Date Format

The Date option on the International submenu lets you display dates in a Long International or Short International format other than the one available with the Numeric Format option on the Style menu.

When you select Date from the International submenu you'll see four options for displaying dates in Long International format. These options, along with each corresponding Short International format, are:

A. MM/DD/YY (MM/DD)

B. DD/MM/YY (DD/MM)

C. DD.MM.YY (DD.MM)

D. YY-MM-DD (MM-DD)

After you have selected a format, any dates already on the spreadsheet will be reformatted immediately.

Changing the Time Format

The Time option on the International submenu lets you select a format for serial times that have been formatted with /**SND** and either the Long International or Short International options. When you select Time you will see a list of four different time formats, each representing one of the long formats, as follows (the short version is shown alongside):

A. HH:MM:SS (HH:MM)

B. HH.MM.SS (HH.MM)

C. HH,MM,SS (HH,MM)

D. HHhMMmSSs (HHhMMm)

After you select a format, all serial times on the spreadsheet will be updated immediately.

Changing the Default Formats

The Formats option on the Options menu lets you select formats that affect the entire spreadsheet. When you choose it, Quattro Pro will display the following selections:

Numeric Format	Formats numbers. The default format is General. After selecting this, you can still use the Numeric Format option from the Style menu to format an individual cell or block of cells
Align Labels	Aligns labels. The default is left-align. Regardless of what you set here, you can override it for any cell or block by using the Alignment option from the Style menu
Hide Zeros	Normally, when you place a zero in a spreadsheet cell, Quattro Pro will display **0**. If you select the Hide Zeros option, then Yes, cells that contain zero will be displayed empty

Global Width	Defines a width for all columns on the spreadsheet, without affecting any previously set columns. The default is nine spaces. You can override any new setting for individual columns with the Style menu's Column Width option

How to Change the Working Directory

You can specify a different default directory for saving and retrieving spreadsheets and other files with the Startup option on the Options menu. The Startup submenu includes the Directory option. Here, you can enter a different directory for the Quattro Pro program and spreadsheet files. The current default is QPRO, as determined by the installation process (unless you chose otherwise when you installed Quattro Pro).

Under most circumstances, you should leave this setting unchanged, because Quattro Pro needs to access its program files often and processing will be much faster if you leave them in the QPRO directory.

You can temporarily designate a directory for spreadsheet files, however. To save files to somewhere other than the QPRO directory, type **/F** to access the File menu. Next to the Directory option is the current *path*, C:\QPRO\. Select the Directory option and a box will open, in which you can type the new pathname. For example, to save files in a directory named FILES on the C drive, type **C:\FILES** and press Enter. Now every time you save a spreadsheet file during the current session, it will be saved in the FILES directory. When you exit Quattro Pro, the default directory path will be reset to the C:\QPRO\ path.

Before designating a new directory, it must be created either with the MKDIR command in DOS before entering Quattro Pro, or by using the File Manager. To access the File Manager, select the Utilities option from the File menu. Choose the File Manager option and, when it is displayed, type **/F** to access the File menu. The Make Dir option will then be available for you to create a directory on your disk.

Creating Customized Shortcuts

You are already familiar with some of the Ctrl-key shortcuts that Quattro Pro offers, such as Ctrl–D for entering dates, Ctrl–G for implementing the Fast Graph feature, etc. Perhaps you've even discovered, as you work more with the software, that there are certain menu options that you frequently use. In that case, you can invent a Ctrl-key shortcut of your own.

Doing so is easy:

1. Simply enter the appropriate menu that contains the oft-used option and highlight its name. (For example highlight Save in the File menu.)

2. Press the Ctrl key down and hit Enter. Quattro Pro will display the prompt:

   Hold down the Ctrl key and press any Letter, or <DEL>

3. Do so—but do *not* choose a letter that Quattro Pro already uses; you'll get beeped at. (Consult the endpaper on the inside front cover that lists the default Ctrl-key shortcuts, so you know what's already been assigned.)

After you create the shortcut, it will appear next to the option name in the menu. If you want your shortcut to become a permanent part of the system, select Update from the Options menu.

You are not stuck with your creation. If you want to erase your shortcut, highlight the relevant option again, press Ctrl–Enter, and press Delete twice. Don't forget to select Update to make the change permanent.

SPECIAL FEATURES

Linking Data among Spreadsheets

This chapter discusses a feature that highlights Quattro Pro's effectiveness as a powerful spreadsheet and graphical software package. This feature allows you to link the data in several spreadsheets to a master file or graph, thus extending the scope of Quattro Pro's spreadsheet capability significantly.

Linking Spreadsheets

In Chapter 9 you learned about Quattro Pro's ability to load multiple spreadsheets onto the screen, allowing you to open up to 32 different spreadsheets simultaneously and move from one to the other by various means. You probably found this to be a helpful feature. But there is more. Quattro Pro can *link* several spreadsheets together.

Suppose you are responsible for developing sales forecasts for a corporation that has three different geographical regions, each with its own sales figures. With Quattro Pro's linking ability, you can first create a spreadsheet for each division: the West Coast, the Midwest, and the East Coast. Then you can display all three spreadsheets onscreen simultaneously and link them to a single operating statement (i.e., another spreadsheet), in which you display, say, the total sales of the three regions. The benefit of this is clear: if you revise one number in the West Coast part, the master spreadsheet will reflect that change immediately.

Creating a Spreadsheet Link

To link spreadsheets, you have to add a *link reference* to an entry in a cell. There are three ways to do this:

- Type in the reference and enclose it in square brackets
- Use the point method to establish the link
- Make a 3-D link, in which a link is established among the same cell addresses in every open spreadsheet

Once you establish a link reference, the spreadsheets to which a cell is linked do not have to be open to be active. Quattro Pro can "refresh" the links from the files on disk.

When you decide to create links, your work will be much easier if all the files are in the same directory. The master spreadsheet must be a Quattro Pro file, but the supporting files can be in any format that Quattro Pro can read, such as Quattro, Lotus 1-2-3, or Lotus Symphony.

Typing in a Link Reference

The format for entering a link reference is +[*filename*]*block*. For example, if the file you want to reference is in the same directory as the Quattro Pro software (probably the file Q on the C drive) and is named SALESW.WQ1, and the cell you wish to reference is cell B10, the entry would be **+[SALESW.WQ1]B10**. When you type this link reference in a cell, the cell will display whatever is in cell B10 in the SALESW.WQ1 spreadsheet.

Two spreadsheet files are open in Figure 15.1, both identical in design. The left one is concerned with the sales forecast for the entire company and is therefore the master spreadsheet, called MASTER. (Any name will work; MASTER is used for simplicity.) The spreadsheet on the right is a supporting spreadsheet named SALESW, which lists the sales forecast for the western region. (The files are displayed in the Tile format.)

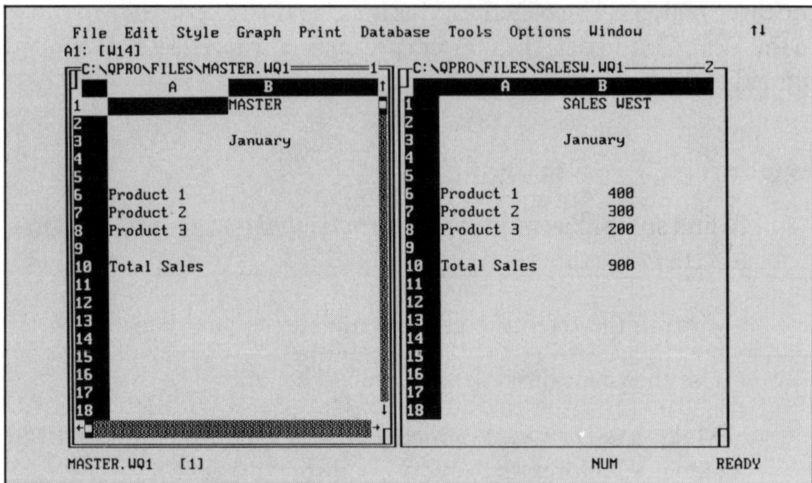

Figure 15.1: The MASTER and SALESW spreadsheets

To create the link reference, follow these steps:

1. Make MASTER the active spreadsheet, if it is not so already, by pressing Shift–F5 and selecting the name from the window.
2. Move the cell selector to cell B10 on the MASTER spreadsheet.
3. Type **+[SALESW.WQ1]B10**.
4. Press Enter.

The link will be established and the value 900 inserted in cell B10 on the MASTER spreadsheet. If the SALESW file had not been opened, the link would still have been created and the value inserted. In other words, you can create a link with *just* the master spreadsheet open, as long as you know the names of the supporting spreadsheet(s) and cell(s) you wish to reference.

Creating a Link Reference with the Point Method

Using the same two spreadsheets in the previous example, you can create a link reference with the pointing method:

1. Move the cell selector to cell B10 on the MASTER spreadsheet.

2. Press the Delete key to erase the existing spreadsheet link.

3. Type + to begin the formula.

4. Hold down the Alt key while you type the number of the spreadsheet that you want to reference. In this example, press Alt–2 to make SALESW active. (If it is in a differently numbered window, hit the appropriate number.)

5. Move the cell selector to cell B10. (You should be in the SALESW spreadsheet.) Notice on the entry line that the link reference is entered for you.

6. Press Enter to create the link reference and reposition the cell selector in the MASTER spreadsheet.

The pointing method is the most accurate way to create a link, since you can see the location of the cell(s) that you are referencing. However, unlike with the previously mentioned method, you must have *all* supporting spreadsheets open to make this method work.

Making a 3-D Link

If your master spreadsheet and supporting spreadsheets share the *same layout,* you can create a link reference with a single command:

1. Open the master spreadsheet and *all* the spreadsheets that support it.

2. Close any spreadsheets that do *not* support it.

3. In the master spreadsheet, move the cell selector to the cell in which you want the result to appear.

4. Begin your function (any will do). For example, if you want the total of all the supporting spreadsheet cells, begin the entry as you would any other function:

   @SUM(

   Next, type brackets and the *:

   @SUM([*]

The brackets indicate the use of other open spreadsheets, and the * indicates that every open spreadsheet should be linked. To finish the linked reference, add the cell or block of cells:

@SUM([*]B10)

This function will sum all the values in cell B10 of all the open spreadsheets and insert that value in the master spreadsheet.

Limiting the 3-D Link

In the previous example, the brackets contained the * symbol to indicate to Quattro Pro that *all* open spreadsheets should be linked to the master spreadsheet and included in the calculation. You can decide which open spreadsheets to link by substituting other codes for the *, as detailed in Table 15.1.

Table 15.1: *3-D Link Codes*

LINK CODE	EFFECT
[ ]	Quattro Pro looks first in the active spreadsheet for a value and then in all open spreadsheets
[*]	Links all open spreadsheets to the master
[AB*]	Links to all spreadsheets that have the letters *AB* (or any letters you choose) at the beginning of their names. For example, a spreadsheet named FIRSTQ would be linked to the master if the entry in the brackets were [FI*], while a spreadsheet named FQRTR would not be linked
[A*B]	Links the master to all open spreadsheets that have names that begin with the letter *A* and end with the letter *B* (or any letters you choose). For example, a spreadsheet named BREAD would be linked if the entry in the brackets were [B*D], while a spreadsheet named BROKE would not be linked
[A??]	Links the master to all open spreadsheets that have three-character names beginning with *A*. For example, a spreadsheet named ATE would be linked but a spreadsheet named ATED would not

Table 15.1: 3-D Link Codes (continued)

LINK CODE	EFFECT
[A?E]	Links the master to open spreadsheets that have three-character names that begin with the letter *A* and end with *E*. You can add question marks as needed. For example, [A???E] would link all open spreadsheets whose names begin with *A*, end in *E*, and have three characters in between

Moving and Copying Link Formulas

If you copy a cell in a master spreadsheet that contains a link reference, the cell addresses in the link will be adjusted in a relative fashion.

If you move a cell or block in a supporting spreadsheet to another location, any link references to it in an on-screen master spreadsheet will be adjusted accordingly. The supporting spreadsheet must be loaded in order for the adjustment to happen. If you want to create a link to unloaded spreadsheets, use block names in the link reference. Then, when you load a master spreadsheet, Quattro Pro will automatically update any block names that have been moved.

Updating Linked Spreadsheets

When you load a master spreadsheet that has links in it, Quattro Pro automatically verifies whether the supporting spreadsheets are loaded. If they are not, Quattro Pro displays the Link Update menu with the following choices:

Load Supporting	Directs Quattro Pro to load all referenced spreadsheets
Update Refs	Directs Quattro Pro to update the references without loading the supporting spreadsheets
None	Causes Quattro Pro to display **NA** temporarily in the link-referenced cells

If you choose not to open the supporting spreadsheets or update the references when prompted, you can open or update them at a later point. To do so, choose the Update Links option under the Tools menu by typing /**TU**. You'll have the following options:

Open	Opens one or more files linked to the master spreadsheet
Refresh	Updates the links to the reference spreadsheet files. Before the updating occurs, Quattro Pro presents a list of all the referenced files. Select the files from which you want the values by pressing Shift–F7 when the file name is highlighted. You can also press Alt–F7 after selecting this option to refresh all referenced spreadsheets
Change	Unlinks the master spreadsheet from a selected supporting spreadsheet and then creates the identical links to another spreadsheet of your choice
Delete	Removes the link references to one or more of the supporting spreadsheets. When you select this option, Quattro Pro presents a list of the supporting spreadsheets. Select which link(s) to delete by pressing Shift–F7

Adding a Graph to a Link

Just as you linked a cell from a supporting spreadsheet to a master spreadsheet, you can link a series of data to a master graph. For example, graph the total sales figures in the MASTER spreadsheet (choose a bar graph). If you tile the spreadsheet windows, you'll see how the bars in the graph move as you change the sales figures in any of the supporting, linked spreadsheets. (Make sure your screen is set to graphics mode [keystrokes /**ODB**].) Figure 15.2 shows an example of such a link.

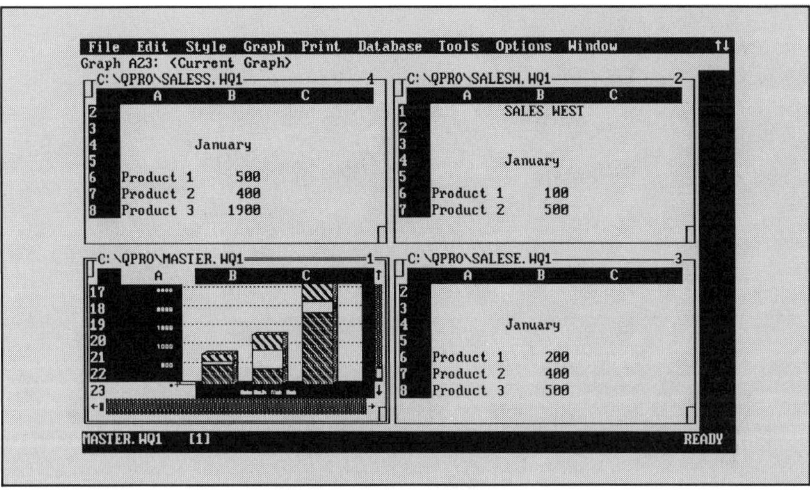

Figure 15.2: A graph linked to three spreadsheets

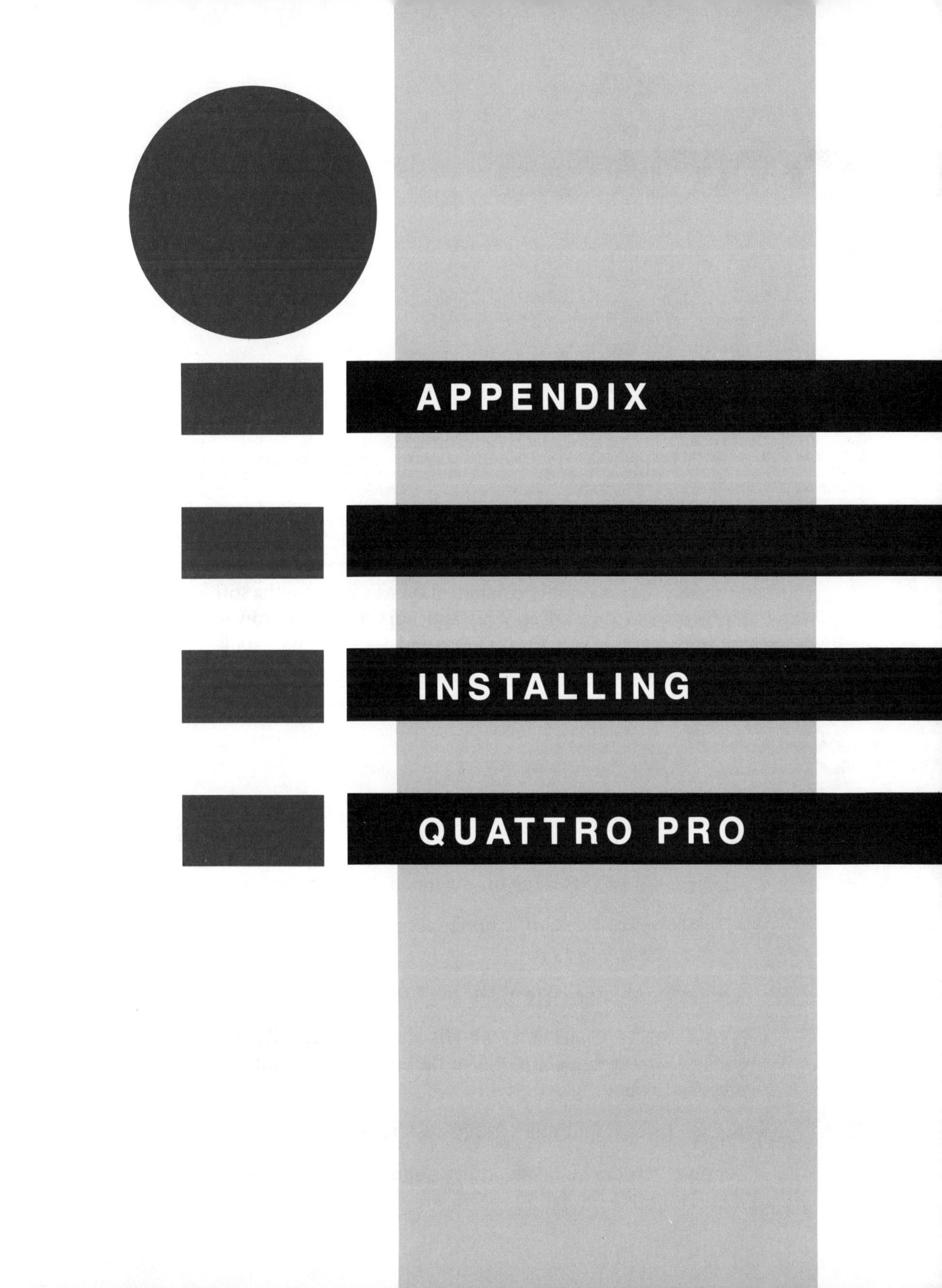

APPENDIX
INSTALLING
QUATTRO PRO

Before you can begin using Quattro Pro, you need to verify that you have the necessary computer equipment on which to run the software; then you need to install it. This appendix lists the hardware requirements for working with Quattro Pro and describes the installation procedure.

Computer Equipment

To use Quattro Pro you need, as a minimum, the following equipment:

- An IBM XT, AT, PS/2, or fully compatible computer
- A minimum of 512K of random-access memory or RAM (640K recommended)
- The DOS operating system, Version 2.0 or later
- A hard-disk drive with at least 5 MB of disk space available—check this by typing **CHKDSK** at the command prompt and pressing Enter
- A graphics card to display graphs on-screen
- A printer to print your spreadsheets and graphs

You may install a mouse; however, there is no particular advantage to doing so, and this book does not assume that you have one installed.

Installing Quattro Pro

To use Quattro Pro, you must install it on your hard-disk drive, most likely drive C. Turn on your computer and follow these steps:

1. Insert Disk 1 in one of your floppy-disk drives. (Disk 1 includes a serial number on the label.)
2. Make that disk drive active. If you inserted Disk 1 in drive A, switch to that drive by typing **A:** at the command prompt and pressing Enter. (If Disk 1 is in drive B, switch to it by typing **B:** and pressing Enter.)
3. When the screen prompt reads A: or B:, type **INSTALL** to start the installation program.

Several screen messages will be displayed. One asks for the directory to which you want to copy the program files. The suggested directory is C:\QPRO\. Unless you want the installation program to create a different directory, accept this as the place to install Quattro Pro.

During the installation process, you'll be asked several times to take out one disk and insert another. The copying of system files onto the hard disk is automatic. At the end of the disk-swapping part of the installation, the program will verify that one of the DOS startup files, CONFIG.SYS, is correctly set for running Quattro Pro.

Quattro Pro then checks the type of monitor you have: Color, Black and White, or LCD. If it cannot determine what type of monitor you have, it will guess. To change the monitor type, press F2 and select the correct type from the list displayed.

Next, Quattro Pro asks you to enter your company name and your personal name, and then it asks whether or not you are installing on a network.

The next question relates to the printer you have. You install a printer by pressing F2 and selecting the printer manufacturer, and then pressing F2 again to select the specific model. You may later install other printers if you need to without going through the entire installation process.

Version 3.0 can display screens in WYSIWYG mode. WYSIWYG is an acronym for "What You See Is What You Get." The concept is that it is easier to determine your printed output if your screen closely resembles what is printed. To run in WYSIWYG mode, you must have a system that has either an EGA or VGA monitor and has a resolution of 640 × 350 or greater. Quattro Pro asks if you want WYSIWYG to be the default display. The WYSIWYG display looks terrific but requires a good deal of processing power. You may wish to set the default as Text because you can switch to WYSIWYG at any time from within Quattro Pro.

Quattro Pro then asks if you are installing in a Windows environment.

The installation program will also ask you about font files. You have the option of installing no fonts, several fonts, or all the fonts. If you plan to use fonts frequently, you may as well take the time now to install them. You can still access the uninstalled fonts when you print a spreadsheet, but you will have to wait for them to be created.

When you are through with the installation, you will be asked to reboot or restart your computer from a cold start in order for it to recognize the new settings in the CONFIG.SYS file and properly run Quattro Pro. Empty the A (or B) drive and hold the Ctrl, Alt, and Delete keys down simultaneously to do this.

Before starting Quattro Pro, make sure you're in the C drive, then switch to the directory containing the program files by typing **CD\QPRO** and pressing Enter. Then type **Q** and press Enter to run the software.

Now that you have installed the software on your computer, you are ready to start reading Chapter 1.

Index

C

D

E

G

H

I

K

O

P

V

W

X

Y

Z

SYBEX®

FREE CATALOG!

Mail us this form today, and we'll send you a full-color catalog of Sybex books.

Name ____

Street ____

City/State/Zip ____

Phone ____

Please supply the name of the Sybex book purchased.

____

How would you rate it?

____ Excellent   ____ Very Good   ____ Average   ____ Poor

Why did you select this particular book?

____ Recommended to me by a friend
____ Recommended to me by store personnel
____ Saw an advertisement in ____________________
____ Author's reputation
____ Saw in Sybex catalog
____ Required textbook
____ Sybex reputation
____ Read book review in ____________________
____ In-store display
____ Other ____________________

Where did you buy it?

____ Bookstore
____ Computer Store or Software Store
____ Catalog (name: ____________________)
____ Direct from Sybex
____ Other: ____________________

Did you buy this book with your personal funds?

____Yes   ____No

About how many computer books do you buy each year?

____ 1-3   ____ 3-5   ____ 5-7   ____ 7-9   ____ 10+

About how many Sybex books do you own?

____ 1-3   ____ 3-5   ____ 5-7   ____ 7-9   ____ 10+

Please indicate your level of experience with the software covered in this book:

____ Beginner   ____ Intermediate   ____ Advanced

Which types of software packages do you use regularly?

____ Accounting
____ Amiga
____ Apple/Mac
____ CAD
____ Communications
____ Databases
____ Desktop Publishing
____ File Utilities
____ Money Management
____ Languages
____ Networks
____ Operating Systems
____ Spreadsheets
____ Word Processing
____ Other ____________________
(please specify)

Which of the following best describes your job title?

____ Administrative/Secretarial
____ Director
____ Engineer/Technician
____ President/CEO
____ Manager/Supervisor
____ Other ____________________
(please specify)

Comments on the weaknesses/strengths of this book: ____________________

PLEASE FOLD, SEAL, AND MAIL TO SYBEX

SYBEX, INC.
Department M
2021 CHALLENGER DR.
ALAMEDA, CALIFORNIA USA
94501

SEAL

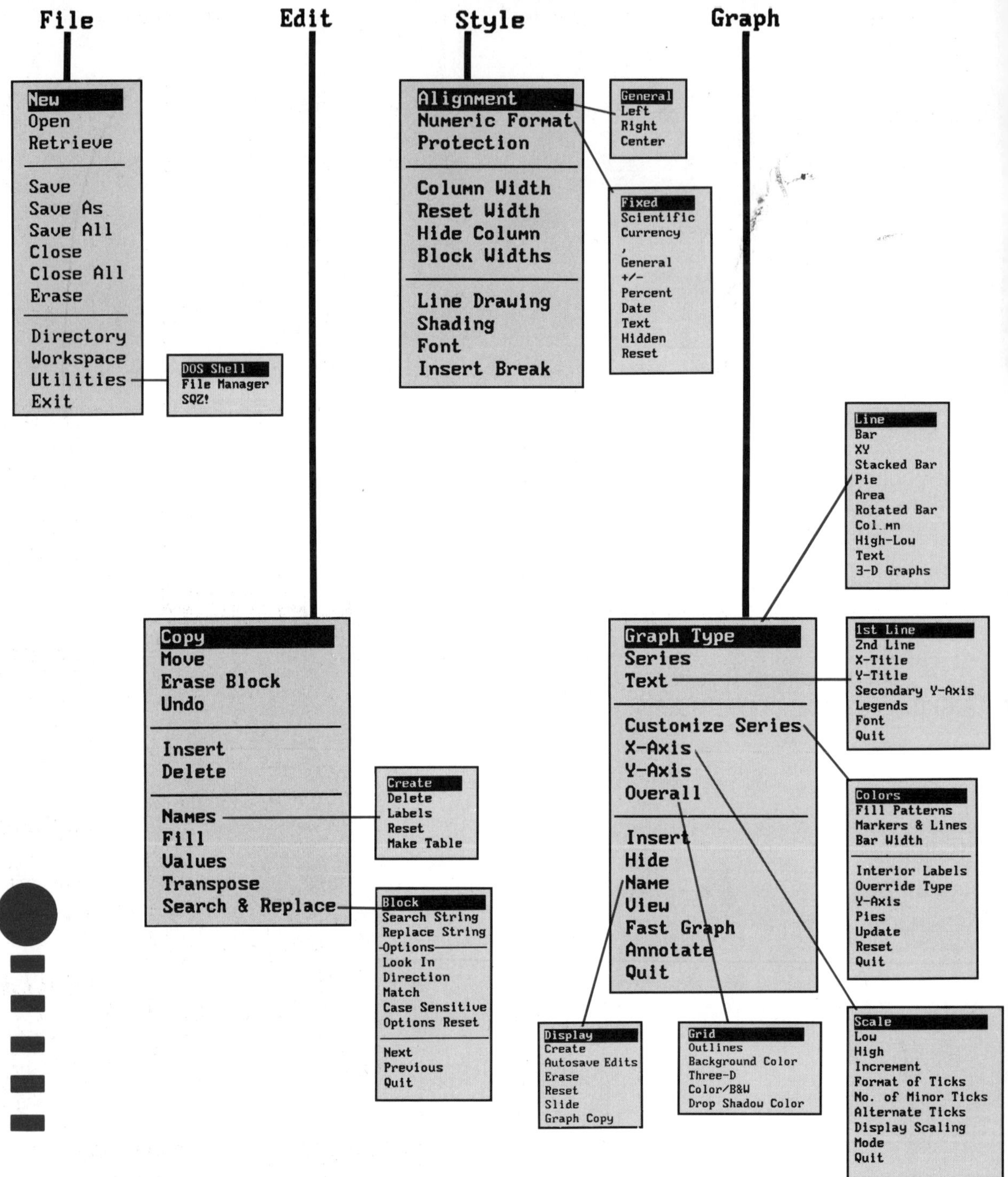

File
New
Open
Retrieve
Save
Save As
Save All
Close
Close All
Erase
Directory
Workspace
Utilities
Exit
DOS Shell
File Manager
SQZ!
Edit
Copy
Move
Erase Block
Undo
Insert
Delete
Names
Fill
Values
Transpose
Search & Replace
Create
Delete
Labels
Reset
Make Table
Block
Search String
Replace String
Options
Look In
Direction
Match
Case Sensitive
Options Reset
Next
Previous
Quit
Style
Alignment
Numeric Format
Protection
Column Width
Reset Width
Hide Column
Block Widths
Line Drawing
Shading
Font
Insert Break
General
Left
Right
Center
Fixed
Scientific
Currency
,
General
+/-
Percent
Date
Text
Hidden
Reset
Graph
Graph Type
Series
Text
Customize Series
X-Axis
Y-Axis
Overall
Insert
Hide
Name
View
Fast Graph
Annotate
Quit
Line
Bar
XY
Stacked Bar
Pie
Area
Rotated Bar
Column
High-Low
Text
3-D Graphs
1st Line
2nd Line
X-Title
Y-Title
Secondary Y-Axis
Legends
Font
Quit
Colors
Fill Patterns
Markers & Lines
Bar Width
Interior Labels
Override Type
Y-Axis
Pies
Update
Reset
Quit
Display
Create
Autosave Edits
Erase
Reset
Slide
Graph Copy
Grid
Outlines
Background Color
Three-D
Color/B&W
Drop Shadow Color
Scale
Low
High
Increment
Format of Ticks
No. of Minor Ticks
Alternate Ticks
Display Scaling
Mode
Quit